D1602629

COMMUNICATION AND HANDICAP

Aspects of Psychological Compensation and Technical Aids

ADVANCES
IN
PSYCHOLOGY
34

Editors

G. E. STELMACH

P. A. VROON

NORTH-HOLLAND
AMSTERDAM · NEW YORK · OXFORD · TOKYO

COMMUNICATION AND HANDICAP

Aspects of Psychological Compensation and Technical Aids

Edited by

Erland HJELMQUIST

Department of Psychology
University of Göteborg
Sweden

and

Lars-Göran NILSSON

Department of Psychology
University of Umeå
Sweden

1986

NORTH-HOLLAND
AMSTERDAM · NEW YORK · OXFORD · TOKYO

ISBN: 0 444 70034 x

Publishers:
ELSEVIER SCIENCE PUBLISHERS B.V.
P. O. Box 1991
1000 BZ Amsterdam
The Netherlands

Sole distributors for the U.S.A. and Canada:
ELSEVIER SCIENCE PUBLISHING COMPANY, INC.
52 Vanderbilt Avenue
New York, N.Y. 10017
U.S.A.

Library of Congress Cataloging-in-Publication Data

Communication and handicap.

   (Advances in psychology ; 34)
   Proceedings from a conference held in Stockholm,
Sweden, June 3-4, 1985, sponsored by the Swedish Council
for Planning and Coordination of Research.
   Includes indexes.
   1. Handicapped--Means of communication--Congresses.
2. Compensation (Psychology)--Congresses. 3. Communica-
tion devices for the handicapped--Congresses.
4. Communicative disorders--Congresses. I. Hjelmquist,
Erland, 1948-   . II. Nilsson, Lars-Göran, 1944-   .
III. Sweden. Forskningsrådsnämnden. IV. Series:
Advances in psychology (Amsterdam, Netherlands) ; 34.
HV1569.5.C66 1986   362.4'0483   86-11440
ISBN 0-444-70034-X (U.S.)

PRINTED IN THE NETHERLANDS

PREFACE

This book contains the proceedings from a conference on Communication and Handicap which was held in Stockholm, Sweden, June 3 - 4, 1985, and sponsored by The Swedish Council for Planning and Coordination of Research as part of a large-scale project on handicaps. The speakers presented theory and data on various aspects of cognition, communication and handicap. Although researchers in psychology were in majority at the conference, students of other disciplines also took part, and our ambition was to provide the basis for an exchange of ideas between researchers of various disciplines engaged in investigations of handicap problems. Research into problems related to various sorts of handicaps, usually requires a broad approach involving contributions from specialists in many fields.

The handicap problems discussed at the conference and in this book are problems related to communication. The concept of compensation constitutes a key vehicle for this enterprise.We distinguished between two types of compensation . On the one hand, basic principles of cognition are employed with the purpose of helping to overcome communicative difficulties among handicapped people. On the other hand, various sorts of technical aids are used for compensatory purposes.

A total of fourteen papers were presented at the conference, and a selection of them appear in this book in elaborated and extended form. In addition to the contributions from the conference, four papers have been added to the book afterwards.

The contributions have been grouped into four main sections. The first is Hearing aspects of handicaps, and contains chapter by Rönnberg and Lyxell, and House. The second section is Visual aspects of handicaps, and the contributors are Aitken, Ohlsson, Jansson, and Williamson, Muter and Kruk, and Drottz and Hjelmquist. The third section is devoted to Reading deficits, and chapters are written by Baddeley, Cohen, Lundberg and Leong. The fourth and final section is called Neurological aspects of handicaps, and contributing authors are Byng and Coltheart, Ahlsén, Muter, and Hunnicutt.

This grouping is only one possible way of organizing the material and some arbitrariness cannot be avoided. This is true in particular for Hunnicutt's contribution which presents a text- producing technique that is not necessarily tied to any particular handicap. It was placed under Neurological aspects since applications for people with such handicaps seem an obvious possibility. The same is also true, to some extent, for Muter's chapter on Bliss.

We hope this book will show that theoretical and practical progress is possible in the area of communicative handicaps through interdisciplinary research efforts, and that it will promote further discussion and research within this very challenging field of investigation.

The illustration on page 178 is reproduced with the permission of The Orton Dyslexia Society *(Annals of Dyslexia,* 1983, pp. 77, 78, 82, 83).

Finally, we thank Lillemor Östberg and Shirley Niklasson for typing the manuscript on the word processor, and Torbjörn Wikström for squeezing it out from the computer into the photoprinter.

Göteborg and Toronto, October, 1985

Erland Hjelmquist   Lars-Göran Nilsson

TABLE OF CONTENTS

Communication and Handicap: Aspects of
Psychological Compensation and Technical Aids
E. Hjelmquist and L.-G. Nilsson (editors)
© Elsevier Science Publishers B.V. (North-Holland), 1986

1

COMMUNICATION, COMPENSATION AND HANDICAP

LARS-GÖRAN NILSSON

Department of Psychology, University of Umeå
Umeå, Sweden

1   INTRODUCTION

In this chapter I will discuss the three cardinal concepts of this book: communication, compensation, and handicap. The primary aim of the chapter is to integrate these three concepts, and, to try to arrive at a general conceptual framework, on the basis of which, hopefully, one can approach various practical and theoretical problems about communication among handicapped people.

Few would probably disagree with a statement saying that communication constitutes a very important part of life in society today. Theorists in this area of research, for example, Cherry (1974), go as far as claiming that »society» could actually be defined as »people in communication» (p. 145). Without even going this far, it is probably fair to say that there is a consensus of opinion among practitioners who research in this field, as well as among people in general, about the important role communication plays in society today. In referring to such a definition, I, therefore, simply want to stress this important role of communication, and also to indicate that individuals who have difficulties in communicating may face problems, not only with respect to the communication per se, but also more generally in the sense that they may not feel as though they belong to the society of today.

People with various sorts of sensory handicaps do indeed fit the description of such a group; these people usually face considerable problems in communication with others and they commonly also report that, at times, they feel a great deal of alienation with the rest of society. In discussing the concepts of communication, compensation and handicap in this chapter, I will focus the conceptual framework to be proposed as applicable to this particular group of handicapped people.

Although many different approaches to communication already exist, I will not attempt to review or evaluate these here. Instead I will discuss one framework which has dominated research on communication for some time, and then I will outline another framework which, as hopefully will be apparent, will be particularly suitable for dealing with communication disorders in handicapped people. Moreover I will discuss how these difficulties can be overcome by means of various compensatory techniques. Or in other words, the conceptualization to be proposed will be used as a point of departure for applying the concept of compensation in the context of handicap.

2   COMMUNICATION

The particular conceptualization of communication to be discussed is derived from a general framework of memory and remembering. Actually, this is not a coincidence; many theories of communication share concepts with general memory theory. The concept of memory has a long standing reputation in communication research with respect to both theory and data. Hypothetical memory systems have been postulated as central components in many theories of communication. Also, as an example, experiments have been designed to demonstrate how communication may become exceedingly difficult or very inefficient because of, say, capacity limitations in memory.

At the end of the 1950's a new era began in psychology. The type of research which was initiated at that time has usually been referred to as the »information processing approach» (see e.g. Broadbent, 1958). I will not at this time go into any greater depth in describing the roots or the later development of this approach. However, a few basic facts should not pass without notice, since they will serve as a contrast to the overall framework which will be proposed here later. Moreover, some of these general aspects per se might be of general interest for students of communication and handicap.

One basic assumption in this early approach to communication was that information processing mental-activity should be regarded as a flow of information through various compartments of memory. The information reaching the individual first arrives at a very short-lived sensory memory. On the basis of selective attention, portions of this information is then transferred to another memory system -- short-term memory -- for a more thorough processing. (In general, short-term memory is also assumed to be the particular system from which all control processes originate, which are needed for communication, remembering and other cognitive activities.) Finally, the information processed is assumed to be stored permanently in a third memory system - longterm memory. At output, according to this framework, information moves in the reversed direction through the two latter systems; that is, information is retrieved from long-term memory back to short-term memory, and from this store the individual outputs it as a response. In its most general form this is a relatively simple and straightforward model. However, as the development of the model over the years has shown, the simplicity is somewhat deceptive. Commonly, several assumptions have to be added as successively more complicated situations are approached.

Important contributions in communication research have certainly been made on the basis of this type of theorizing and variants of this general framework will probably be around in communication research for many years to come. It should be made clear, though, that a framework of this sort (or the framework to be proposed, for that matter) cannot be applied to all forms of communication. Communication is a wide concept including many different forms of information transmission. At the one extreme, one can talk about communication when referring to electrochemical processes between cells in a biological system and at the other extreme, one can refer to communication as involving distribution of printed messages or other goods or materials in a countrywide or worldwide distribution system. The type of communication to be dealt with here will exclude these »micro» and »macro» forms of communication.

My main concern is to deal with human communication, involving at least one individual. More specifically, the framework to be proposed will primarily focus on situations which involve at least one sensory handicapped person. Situations involving only one person in a communication context are usually referred to as being concerned with one-way communication. We will deal with this form, but the aim is for the framework to be general enough to handle situations with two persons in interaction sequences as well, and such situations are referred to as two-way communication. In principle, a two-way communication may actually only involve one person. In that case the person interacts with a machine or some other sort of artificial device. In order to qualify as one unit in such a two-way communication, it is necessary that the device in question is able to receive and interpret information and, on the basis of what is received, produce a meaningful response to the interacting human being. This type of two-way communication is quite frequent in the case of communication involving sensory handicapped people.

In passing, I mentioned that information processing models have made important contributions to communication research. However, there are some shortcomings on these models that make them less suitable for the type of communication to be discussed here. Elsewhere I have described (Nilsson, 1980, 1981, 1983, 1984) some difficulties a memory theory encounters, if one, like Broadbent (1958, 1971) and many others (e.g. Atkinson & Shiffrin, 1968; Loftus, 1977; Murdock, 1974; Simon & Feigenbaum, 1964; Waugh & Norman, 1965), regards memory as a spatial entity into which information is encoded and from which this information can be retrieved after a search of long-term memory. Memory models of this sort have, to a large extent, focused on structural matters. A theory or a framework which is developed to encompass communication among handicapped people will have to focus more on functional matters.

The present framework states that cognitive processes, like remembering and communication, should be regarded as an interaction between available cognitive capabilities of the individual and the task demands at hand in the particular situation where the communication is taking place. Several cognitive capabilities are assumed to be involved and the demands of the task are assumed to determine which of these capabilities should be used in any given situation.

It is proposed that events, situations, objects, pictures, words etc., constituting the basis for the information to be communicated, and the context in which these events occur in the environment can be decomposed into a large number of physical *features*. These features are assumed to furnish the individual with the basis for various potential perspectives or *affordances* (cf. Gibson, 1979). For each particular event, object, word etc. the information about a given situation is there to be picked up by the individual and different combinations of features are assumed to set the stage for potential affordances. One example of an affordance (cf. Gibson, 1979) is a »sit-on-ability» for the object chair; another example of this concept discussed by Gibson at some great length is that a mail box affords that a letter can be dropped into such a box. Although this Gibsonian term is adequate for my present purpose, I may part company with Gibsonian terminology on other accounts and at a more general level.

Whereas features and affordances are concepts solely being contained in the environment, *gnostic units* and *functional dispositions* are the concepts used to describe the individual. These latter concepts are conceived of as being parallel to the former, i.e., gnostic unit is parallel to feature and functional disposition is parallel to affordance. Features of the environment are assumed to activate the gnostic units of the individual so that one gnostic unit is sensitive to each and every feature of the environment. In the same way as features combine to form affordances, it is assumed that the information from previous experiences contained in these gnostic units combine to form functional dispositions.

The functional dispositions express the readiness of an individual to react and to take specific action in a situation, whenever certain physical features and affordances are present in the current environment. The interaction between the environment and the individual, as expressed by means of these four concepts, is depicted schematically in Figure 1. As can be seen, this interaction is conceived of as both single sided and double sided. At the level of features and gnostic units, the interaction is one sided in the sense that the features activate the gnostic units, but there is no influence from the gnostic units on the physical features. At the level of affordances and functional dispositions, the communication is double-sided in the sense that there are certain functional dispositions ready to be utilized whenever a certain set of affordances is present in the environment. On the basis of the functional dispositions activated initially in a given situation, the individual can change the focus of attention on what the environment has to offer. That is, by means of selective attention and on the basis of previous experience and knowledge, the individual can re-orient his or her focus on the environment so that a given affordance, which was less important initially, may now be more important at the cost of other affordances, which were more important previously.

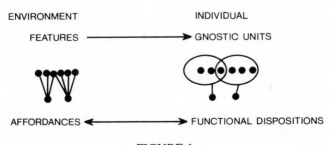

FIGURE 1

Schematic description of the interaction between the individual and the environment.

In a different context (Nilsson, 1980, 1983, 1984; Nilsson, Mäntylä, & Sandberg, 1985) I have also described how this conceptualization can be expressed in terms of a mathematical model. It would stray too far from the point here to go into this in detail. The interested reader may consult any of the papers referred to. However, a brief summary of the mathematical machinery is necessary before we can arrive at a conceptual framework for dealing with communication among handicapped people.

The mathematical model that has been developed uses matrix algebra to describe the environment, the individual, and the interaction between the two. More specifically, each object or event is described as a vector (called object vector) with the elements of the vector referring to the affordances of that object; a more important affordance is represented as an element with a higher value than a less important affordance. In a parallel way the perception of this object, in terms of functional dispositions of the individual, is described as another vector (subject vector). The elements of this vector represent the functional dispositions involved for perceiving this particular object. A more important functional disposition is represented as a higher element value.

These two vectors combine multiplicatively and the product is a matrix which describes the current experience of this object in light of the individual's previous knowledge and experience of the particular features composing this object. This matrix is temporary and cannot be retrieved or experienced again at a later occasion. Rather, the matrix is added to all other matrices formed in a similar way when experiencing other objects or events. The result of all these summations of instant, temporary matrices is an overall matrix representing the total experience and knowledge of this individual at each moment in time.

A very small number of features and gnostic units is depicted in Figure 1 and the reason for this is solely pedagogical. In reality, it is assumed that the environment consists of a very large number of features and affordances. Likewise, it is assumed that the storage system of the individual consists of a very large number of gnostic units and that the individual has the potential of using a large number of functional dispositions.

The model proposed so far has not yet been developed as a biological model, but on the basis of this latter assumption we may speculate about at least some of its biological implications. It is actually quite reasonable to assume that there is a large number of neuroanatomical entities in the human brain which may be the biological correlates to the gnostic units. One possibility is that the neurons in the brain constitutes the biological correspondence to the gnostic units. A conservative estimate is that there are at least 10^{10} neurons in the human brain. This number increases by 10^3 if instead we locate the gnostic units to the synapses. On average there are 10^3 synapses to each brain cell. If we were to assume that the gnostic units were located to the neurotransmittors at each synapse, this number would increase still further.

So far I have described the basic concepts of the framework without really saying too much about how communication per se is conceptualized. Although the concepts used in the model may seem complicated, the basic principles for communication are simple. At the time when a message of some sort is presented to an individual, a number of gnostic units are activated which, in turn, means that a number of functional dispositions are being formed. I will refer to the sum of all functional dispositions used to encode a certain message as a *code*. To be able to refer back to this message or to react to it in some other fashion on some later occasion, this code has to be a unique combination of the functional dispositions involved. Later, when the individual is going to produce a response to the message encountered, he or she has to reconstruct the code formed initially.

In mathematical terms this means that the subject vector formed initially (which is combined with the object vector representing the current message) has to be orthogonal to all other subject vectors used to encode other messages. When the individual needs to refer to the message in question or simply has to remember it again, the initial subject vector has to be reconstructed. Then, as a second step, this subject vector is combined multiplicatively with the overall matrix representing the total knowledge and experience of the individual at this moment.

In summing up, this model states (a) a continous interaction between the cognitive capabilities of the individual, and the particular task demands at hand in the communication situation and (b) that the functional essence of this interaction is the construction of the code at the time of perception and encoding, and the reconstruction of the same code at the time of reactivation or retrieval of an earlier message. It should be understood from this that the model presented so far is relatively simple. Elaboration on some accounts will be necessary as we approach practical, concrete situations involving sensory handicapped people. I will return to this shortly after having introduced the concept of compensation.

3   COMPENSATION AND HANDICAP

The concept of compensation has many different connotations and it is not always clear how it applies to psychology in general and, in this context, to handicap and research into handicap in particular. Maybe the most common way of using compensation is in relation to quite different matters (e.g. economy). People can be compensated for in a number of ways i.e., for a particular job they do, for being unemployed, for being poor, for the fact that they are handicapped, etc. This is, however, not the meaning of the term we intend to use here. Instead the aim is to discuss how and to what extent sensory handicapped people can adjust to the environment by means of technical aids or by means of their cognitive capabilities in a way which minimizes the influence of their handicap. In order to set the stage for a meaningful discussion the scope of handicaps has been limited to deal only with those aspects which concern communication and the difficulties involved in communication for people with sensory handicaps.

More specifically, I will try to tackle the problem of how sensory handicapped people communicate among themselves and with others by means of different sorts of compensation. A handicapped person may compensate for his or her difficulties in communication by utilizing those sensory channels which are intact. For example, a blind person may focus all or at least most of the information intake to the auditory modality, thereby seeking to compensate for the fact that no information intake can be made through the visual modality. A handicapped person can also compensate for his or her handicap by means of using various sorts of technical aids. For example a hard-of-hearing person can use hearing aids to make an auditory input possible. Combinations of the use of intact sensory channels and technical aids are of course also possible. For example, a blind person can use an optical-to-tactile converter -Optacon- for reading. Hence, in addition to this reading device this person would then use the tactual modality for input of visual information.

It would not seem to matter what kind of compensation the handicapped person attempts, communication of this sort supposedly means an extra load on the cognitive system as a whole. This extra load in itself makes the communication more tedious and difficult than it would need to be, if the individual could optimize the use of available cognitive capabilities, spare capacity etc., for the actual communication process. The communication process itself may, at times, require all the capacity and cognitive capabilities that the individual has available even in the normal case where no sensory handicaps are involved. Hence, a sensory handicapped person may, in fact, be seen as being handicapped in two ways. Firstly, he or she is handicapped in the sense that all sensory channels cannot be used for information input. Secondly, the handicapped person is also handicapped in the sense that he or she cannot use the remaining, intact sensory channels to full capacity, since some of this capacity has to be used for perceiving and interpreting a certain message which was actually not meant for any of the intact channels. For example, a lengthy description may be needed in order to describe a picture for a blind person. The processing of such a circumstantial input should, reasonably, detract a great deal of cognitive resources. Supposedly, these resources could be fully used for processing other information or for a more elaborate and deep processing, if this blind person could see the picture directly. Thus, the particular message presented to the handicapped person may not be ecological for the other sensory channels available. An important question would therefore seem to be whether this latter type of handicap could be compensated for as well. This question will be dealt with later (see also Ohlsson, this volume), before that, however, we will take a closer look at the concept of compensation per se.

In oral presentations at conferences and symposia and in discussions among researchers in psychology, one often hears the concept of compensation being used. For example, it may be said that a subject in an experiment can compensate for an impoverished stimulus situation by using other cognitive strategies than he or she would use if the stimulus was the most optimal one. Another example is an amnesic patient participating in a memory experiment; this patient would do very poorly when tested, say, in an non-guided free recall task, but he or she would be able to compensate for lacking memory functions by means of additional cues or stimulus support.

For some reason, however, the use of the concept of compensation in writing is much more sparse in psychological texts outside the domain of handicap research. When planning the conference that preceded this book, I checked a large number of subject indexes in psychology textbooks but could not find the concept of compensation in any of the more modern texts. Just about the only books in which compensation was included in any index was a book on Alfred Adler's contributions to psychology (Ansbacher & Ansbacher, 1956) and of course in Stevens' Handbook of Experimental Psychology (Stevens, 1951).

Since so little on compensation has been put into writing, we should consider it carefully in order to find out whether we can learn something essential which can be used for our present purposes. Although Adler's contributions to psychology were made a long time ago, it may contain insights that could be applied to the particular topic discussed here.

In order to explain the varied reaction to organic inferiorities, Adler proposed one of his most important early concepts, compensation, the process of which he initially described in organic terms. Soon, however, Adler shifted from organic to sociopsychological explanations. Since this development is not one of the main topics of the present book, I will not dwell too much on Adler's contributions at this time. However, I do think that it may be of some general interest to give some thought to Adler's original definition of compensation:

> »As soon as the equilibrium, which must be assumed to govern the economy of the individual organ or the whole organism, appears to be distributed due to inadequacy of form or function, a certain biological process is initiated in the inferior organs. The unsatisfied demands increase until the deficit is made up through growth of the inferior organ, or of some other organ which can serve as a substitute completely or in part» (Ansbacher & Ansbacher, 1956).

In Adler's thinking any kind of psychological response by the compensating person was stated as being due to organic changes taking place in the brain itself. Adler's suggestion was that the brain of a compensating person increases in size because of the effort to overcome the inferiority of a certain organ in much the same way as a muscle increases in size due to exercise. One more citation from Adler's writings express this very clearly

> »... compensation is due to overperformance and increased growth of the brain. This strengthening of the psychological superstructure is shown by the successful outcome; its relation to steady exercise is easily guessed ... The psychological manifestations of such an organ may be more plentiful and better developed as far as drive, sensitivity, attention, memory apperception, empathy, and consciousness are concerned» (Ansbacher & Ansbacher, 1956).

Since the brain has increased in size after such efforts, according to Adler, there is a higher probability than before that the individual will actually find some alternative, which can compensate for the weakness. Thus, the basic assumption was that the structural changes in the brain made the psychological or functional changes possible. Another possibility would have been that the psychological changes in strategy could be made by the same brain, without assuming any structural changes to begin with.

Apparently, such a view was not comme il faut at the beginning of this century. In present day psychology there is (probably) nobody who believes in a similarity between a muscle and the brain. However, the question of function versus structure is certainly still a valid one. With respect to sensory handicapped people, the most common cause that underlies the type of handicap we are dealing with here is structural damage . Our primary motivation is to see whether a functional compensation can be used to overcome such a handicap.

The second text mentioned on the topic of compensation, Stevens' Handbook of Experimental Psychology, is also primarily concerned with organic or structural matters. More precisely, in Stevens' book compensation is stated to be an effect of damage to the vestibular system. The immediate effects of bilateral labyrintectomy is, moreover, said to vary with phylogenetic status. These effects are quite striking, for example in the pigeon, which displays violent movements and is unable to hold itself upright after such damage. In mammals there is unsteadiness in standing, tremors of the head, and impaired running, jumping, etc. In the human being, Stevens reports, deaf persons often lack vestibular response and there is a correlation between the extent of hearing loss and of vestibular deficit. However, the effects are not as dramatic in the human being as in lower species of animals. Stevens uses the term 'compensation' to describe how human beings can learn to use visual, kinesthetic and other stimuli to gain dominance over the vestibular reflexes. Thus, Stevens' conceptualization of conpensation has much in common with the present view of this concept.

By learning how to use an intact sensory channel, a handicapped person can compensate for his or her handicap so that information intake is possible. This is one aspect of the present view of compensation and, apparently, it is in line with Stevens' view. However, there is also another aspect of compensation, which will be emphasized here, and which goes beyond the notion of sole substitution of sensory channels. This aspect, which I have already mentioned briefly, concerns how to overcome the influence of capacity limitation. The risk for such an influence arises when information intake is made through a substituting sensory channel. The functional framework for communication proposed in this chapter has been developed in an attempt to overcome this problem. Ohlsson (this volume) has elaborated on this functional view and presents a conceptualization of compensation as a skill. Ohlsson's view is interesting because it may provide a fruitful solution to the problem of capacity limitations in handicapped people.

According to this framework, the task demands are assumed to determine which cognitive capabilities are to be used in each situation and how much each of these should be used in relation to other cognitive capabilities. Viewed this way, sensory handicaps and other cognitive deficits can be considered and approached in a more »hopeful» way than from a strictly structural view. In the present context such a functional view seems to make sense, since it becomes possible to deal with handicaps in a reversible way. Handicapped people can compensate for their structural deficits by means of a broader functional use of intact sensory channels, technical aids or both. By such a compensation the handicapped person learns how to adjust or to adapt to his or her environment.

In this context another type of classificatory scheme for compensation should also be mentioned. This classification was suggested by Bäckman (1984) to conceptualize how elderly people can compensate functionally for a biological, structural deterioration as a consequence of age. While Bäckman (1984) focused on compensation in memory tasks only, it is possible that his scheme can be elaborated to hold for other cognitive functions as well, and also for other groups of subjects such as, for example, the group of sensory handicapped people we are dealing with here. According to Bäckman (1984) there are three main types of compensation to be considered in relation to age. First, there is compensation via experimenter - provided support (CEPS). In this type of compensation, the experimenter seeks to enrich the stimulus situation at the time of encoding or retrieval by instructing the subject, for example, how to organize the information to be remembered or by providing additional retrieval information. Secondly, Bäckman (1984) suggested compensation via inherent task properties (CITP). For this type of compensation the task per se informs the subject how the information should best be encoded or retrieved. Thirdly, compensation can also be made via cognitive support systems (CCSS).

The concept of cognitive support systems emanates from Bransford (1979) and was used primarily to conceptualize child development and mental retardation. While CEPS and CITP have not yet been applied to the area of sensory handicaps, the third form of compensation according to this scheme actually has. Rönnberg and Lyxell (1985) have employed this type of compensation when discussing linguistic comprehension abilities and visual memory capacity as potential support systems for efficient speech reading. It should also be noted that this type of compensation corresponds closely to the type of compensation emphasized in this chapter as the most optimal one in the case of cognitive compensation among sensory handicapped people. This type of compensation will be dealt with further in the chapter by Rönnberg and Lyxell (this volume).

The concepts adjustment and adaptation play major roles in any functional framework of psychology. Actually, one important way in which Darwin's theory of evolution (and its emphasis on these two concepts) was brought about through the concept of function. In biological terms, this concept suggested that anatomical structures, shaped as they were by natural selection, function in the way they do in order to further the survival of the organism. Statements of function are, in essence, descriptions of instrumental relations of the role a given structure plays in adaptation. Basically, a functional framework of psychology is concerned with success in living with the adaptation of the individual to its environment, and with the individual's adaptation of the environment to himself or herself. Any conception of the conscious or behavioral capacities of the individual as a means of achieving success is essential in all functional frameworks of psychology. More specifically, the framework proposed here is concerned with the coordination of the internal system and the external of one mental process with another, and of the single activity to the complex of activities. These forms of coordination or types of interaction constitute the proper units of analysis for the psychologist working with research on communication in handicapped people and they also set the stage for utilizing the concept of compensation. While a researcher oriented towards a structural framework of communication would analyze mental events into their elements, the functionalist investigates mental processes in terms of how they operate, what they accomplish, and the ecological and biological conditions under which they function. It is important to make this clear since the functional orientation of this framework has been emphasized. If no specific statement about this is made, someone might get the impression that the gnostic units and the affordances discussed earlier might indicate more of a structural than a functional view. This is not the case, however, although it is certainly believed that there has to be a structure underlying any function.

4 CONCLUSION

When presenting the model involving features, affordances, gnostic units and functional dispositions, it was stated that the basic requirements for a successful communication were that the individual could form a unique code at the time of perceiving and encoding, and that the same code could be reconstructed at the time of retrieval. The extent to which an individual is able to form a unique code for a given message in a certain communicative process depends partly on the richness of this message in terms of the number of features that activate gnostic units in the individual. Partly, the success in forming a unique code also depends upon the knowledge base of the individual. If there is a rich knowledge base, the probability is higher that the functional dispositions to be employed as a basis for the code will differ and vary more than if the knowledge base is less rich. It seems reasonable so assume then, everything else being equal, that the sensory input for a handicapped person should be more impoverished than that for a non-handicapped person. The reason for this assumption is that the input for at least one modality is lacking. If this is the case, it is also reasonable to assume that the amount of knowledge and experience that a handicapped person has accumulated during a given period of time is less than that of a non-handicapped person -- again, given that everything else has been equal. On the basis of these two prerequisites the model predicts that the communicative process involving a handicapped person should be less successful than a communicative process not involving a handicapped person.

The goal for any compensatory endeavours for handicapped people lacking the sensory input from at least one modality should therefore be to increase the uniqueness of any code used for perceiving and encoding communicative messages. However, this is not to say that each input should be richer in the sense that more information should be presented. As mentioned previously, the strategy to use many words to »display», for example, a picture to a blind person may have the effect of overloading the limited processing capacity of the individual. Instead one should try to present each piece of information so that it contains as many distinct features as possible. From there, the individual can engage in an encoding process which makes the code unique as opposed to other codes used to encode other messages. Assuming that the handicapped person manages to do this and assuming that the cues present at retrieval (for initiating the reconstruction of this code) are compatible with the general conditions present at encoding, the handicapped person may be able to utilize a strategy which compensates for his or her handicap. It is certainly not an easy task to acquire such a strategy. Many problems and pitfalls may arise along the way. However, it should be a challenge to researchers in this field to try to develop programs that could be used to make such learning smooth and efficient.

A final word of caution might be worthwhile mentioning before bringing this chapter to a close. It was mentioned initially that the framework proposed and discussed was derived from a model developed for research on memory and remembering in general. It may be a good strategy to start out by trying to understand the normal functioning of an individual in his or her interaction with the environment and then apply this knowledge to various other situations in which other groups of individuals or patients are involved. However, this need not always be the most optimal research strategy.

When dealing with research on communication among handicapped people it may not be sufficient to use our knowledge about the cognitive system as a point of departure for handicap research simply by assuming that the hypothetical effects of the lacking function can be subtracted from the known effects of the non-handicapped person. We can probably still make comparisons between the cognitive functions of handicapped and non-handicapped persons, but we should be aware of the fact that the handicap usually form the basis for a different interaction between the individual and the environment in the case of handicapped people. The compensation that the handicapped person accomplishes by using intact sensory channels or technical aids, or both, creates a new and unknown interaction with the environment as compared to the case of a non-handicapped person.

REFERENCES

Ansbacher, H.L., & Ansbacher, R.R. (1956). *The individual psychology of Alfred Adler*. New York: Basic Books, Inc.

Atkinson, R.C., & Shiffrin, R.M. (1968). Human memory: A proposed system and its control processes. In K.W. Spence & J.T. Spence (Eds.), *The psychology of learning and motivation: Advances in theory and research*. Vol. 2. New York: Academic Press.

Bransford, J. (1979). *Human cognition: Learning, understanding and remembering*. Belmont: Wadsworth

Broadbent, D.E. (1958). *Perception and communication*. New York: Pergamon Press.

Broadbent, D.E. (1971). *Decision and stress*. New York: Academic Press.

Bäckman, L. (1984). *Age differences in memory performance: Rules and exceptions*. Doctoral dissertation, University of Umeå, Sweden.

Cherry, C. (1974). Some values of communication technology for the future of the world order. In A. Silverstein (Ed.), *Human communication: Theoretical explorations*. Hillsdale, N.J.: Lawrence Erlbaum Associates.

Gibson, J.J. (1979). *The ecological approach to visual perception*. Boston: Houghton Mifflin.

Loftus, E.F. (1977). How to catch a zebra in semantic memory. In R. Shaw & J. Bransford (Eds.), *Perceiving acting and knowing*. Hillsdale, N.J.: Lawrence Erlbaum Associates.

Murdock, B.B., Jr. (1974). *Human memory: Theory and data*. Potomac Maryland: Lawrence Erlbaum Associates.

Nilsson, L.-G. (1980). Methodological and theoretical considerations as a basis for an integration of research on memory functions in epileptic patients. *Acta Neurologica Scandinavica, 62,* (Suppl. 80), 62-74.

Nilsson, L.-G. (1981). Minnet - överallt och ingenstans. (Memory - everywhere and nowhere). *Forskning och Framsteg, 16,* 1-6.

Nilsson, L.-G. (1983). Functionalism and distributed memory. *Umeå Psycholgical Reports,* No. 175.

Nilsson, L.-G. (1984). New functionalism in memory research. In K. Lagerspetz & P. Niemi (Eds.), *Psychology in the 1990's.* Amsterdam: North-Holland Publishing Company.

Nilsson, L.-G., Mäntylä, T., & Sandberg, K. (1985). A functionalistic approach to memory: Theory and data (manuscript).

Rönnberg, J., & Lyxell, B. (1985). On the identification of support systems for speech reading. *Umeå Psychological Reports* No. 183.

Simon, H., & Feigenbaum, E. A. (1964). An information-processing theory of some effects of similarity, familarization, and meaningfulness in verbal learning. *Journal of Verbal Learning and Verbal Behavior, 3,* 385-396.

Stevens, S.S. (1951). *Handbook of experimental psychology.* New York: Wiley.

Waugh, N.C., & Norman, D.A. (1965). Primary memory. Psychological *Psychological Review, 72,* 89-104.

Communication and Handicap: Aspects of
Psychological Compensation and Technical Aids
E. Hjelmquist and L.-G. Nilsson (editors)
© *Elsevier Science Publishers B.V. (North-Holland), 1986*

COMPENSATORY STRATEGIES IN SPEECHREADING

JERKER RÖNNBERG and BJÖRN LYXELL

Department of Education and Psychology, Linköping University and Department of Psychology, University of Umeå, Sweden

Speechreading is analyzed and empirical results from studies of normal hearing and hearing-impaired subjects are reported. Speechreading is discussed with reference to two aspects, coding and guessing. Among other things, it was concluded that excellent speechreaders must be able to shift between different coding strategies and also be able to apply different guessing strategies.

1 INTRODUCTION

In this chapter, we use the term speechreading instead of lipreading because it conveys that discrimination of lipmovements is not sufficient for communication. The term speechreading also indicates that residual hearing may be essential as well as gestural information.

The purpose of this chapter is to discuss two factors which are assumed to promote efficient speechreading. These factors, *coding* and *guessing* also seem to open up for compensatory strategy and training programmes (see Rönnberg & Risberg, 1985 for details). Coding strategy is defined here as the habitual mode of speech perception by which a person relies to a greater or lesser extent on either visual, auditory or audio-visual cues. Intelligent guessing is defined as the ability to utilize a wide range of cues (e.g., contextual, semantic, syntactic, and prosodic) for synthesizing the meaning of the message. It should perhaps be added that guess-work does not necessarliy depend on, or presuppose, coding into meaningful speech units. Very scanty perceptual evidence of the speechsounds may in some instances be sufficient to trigger conceptually driven guessing processes.

The notions of coding and guessing may be traced back to previous attempts to train speechreading ability (for a review, see Farwell, 1976; Jeffers & Barley, 1971). In essence, the *analytic* school has focused on how different speechsounds were revealed in the lipmovements of the talker. Consequently, drill exercises were designed to increase the trainee's perceptive awareness of phonemes and homophenes. The construction of visemic alphabets have also been reported. The *synthetic* school stressed a more holistic approach geared towards apprehension of intended meaning from more complex situations such as dialogues. The basic idea of the synthetic school was that the key to proficient speechreading is the ability to synthesize the multitude of auditory and visual, verbal as well as non-verbal and contextual cues. Thus, while the analytic school stresses the importance of »eye training» (i.e., coding) the synthetic school favours »mind training» (i.e., intelligent guessing).

A perusal of the factors found to correlate with speechreading (e.g., Jeffers & Barley, 1971) also leaves us with the impression that they may be grouped into two conceptually distinct categories. On the one hand, there are factors that seem to bear on the type of coding skills brought into play by the speechreader, viz. visual acuity, visual perception of speechsounds, and visual short-term memory. On the other hand, there are factors that seem to draw on, or may be summarized by a general guessing factor, viz. IQ, linguistic comprehension, rythmn sense, visual closure and conceptual closure (Barlow, 1983).

In the following, we will briefly review some recent and more precise attempts to delineate the coding compontent with respect to speechreading, and some pertinent data from our own laboratory will also be summarized. Thereafter, some studies relevant to guessing ability and speechreading will be reviewed as well as some of our own data. We will conclude the paper by discussing some general considerations with respect to compensation.

2   CODING STRATEGY

Conrad (1979) has reviewed a large volume of evidence with respect to the notion of *Internal Speech* (cf. the articulatory loop; Baddeley, this volume). One method for assessing internal speech is to present deaf or hearing-impaired subjects with homophone or non-homophone wordspan tests (cf. Conrad, 1964). From these data, the proportion of homophonic errors were computed in relation to the total number of errors (IS-ratio); if the ratio was larger than .5, the subject was considered to use internal speech for memorization. At least for printed words used as stimuli, an IS-ratio larger than .5 (dominant internal speech) was found to be correlated to degree of hearing loss in the sense that the probability of developing internal speech increases as a function of increased hearing loss. Conrad's baseline population, consisting of 119 normal hearing subjects, aged 15 - 16 1/2 years, used dominant internal speech in 94% of the cases.

It was shown that subjects who rely on internal speech, recall non-homophone words much better than subjects who do not use internal speech as the dominant code. The effect of hearing handicap (i.e., dB loss) was not as pronounced in this case. However, for homophone lists, the difference disappears with respect to these two variables (i.e., IS-ratio and dB loss). Most important in this context *is that the use of internal speech* (adjusted for Raven scores), *substantially influences the ability to speechread* when sentences are accompanied by sound (Donaldsson's lipreading test). Without the use of internal speech, a person with a rather moderate loss of hearing, say 70 dB, does not seem to extract more linguistic information than a person having, say a 120 dB loss, who codes the information by means of internal speech. Actually, Conrad's data seem to indicate that above a 65 dB loss there is a sharp drop in performance, unless the hearing-impaired use internal speech. It should also be noted that this effect was not due to impoverished language, since speechreading scores were corrected for this possibility.

However attractive Conrad's results may be, there are some recent data which cast doubt on the »true» representation of lipread stimuli. For example, Campbell and Dodd (1980) found that lipread stimuli (from silent faces) were interfered with by a lipread suffix *and* also by an auditory suffix; a result which is incompatible with the Crowder and Morton (1969) notion of precategorical acoustic storage (PAS), and with a phonetic inner speech representation of lipread items. As Spoer and Corin (1978) observed, it is also possible to obtain suffix effects with heard lists and lipread suffixes, i.e., the converse of Campbell and Dodd's (1980) results. Further, Greene and Crowder (1984) obtained evidence that silent mouthing may lead to modality effects and suffix effects in the same way as overt speech does, and there was also an interaction in the data suggesting that the compatible stimulus list-suffix combinations distracted performance the most; so for example, *adding* sound to a mouthed suffix will interfere *less* with a previously mouthed list. Again, this is clearly incompatible with the Crowder and Morton theory of PAS (see also Coltheart, 1984).

One resolution, according to Greene and Crowder (1984), may be to postulate that speech gestures represent the primary coding format. Specifically, visual information about a speech gesture may influence what is »heard» through the selection of auditory features. Pertinent to this hypothesis is the well-known experiment by McGurk and MacDonald (1967; see also, MacDonald & McGurk, 1978). The basic phenomenon found by McGurk and MacDonald is that there is a tendency for auditory speech perception to be influenced by conflicting visual lip movements. If, for example, the syllables <ba-ba> are spoken, however dubbed onto lip movements for <ga-ga>, then adult subjects in particular tend to perceive this mixture as *fused* <da-da> responses. That is, perception takes on a fused quality which is distinguishable from other combination responses such as <ga-ba> or <ba-ga>. The reason for this may be that in the absence of auditory input, visual <ga>:s are often misread as <da>:s. and in the absence of visual input, it may be argued that auditory <ba>:s display a waveform more similar to <da> (McGurk & MacDonald, 1976). Therefore, the unified percept is based on the shared denominator of both modalities, viz. <da>. When the reverse dubbing is made, combination responses predominate, and it may thus be the case that no common features exist for this case (sf. Dodd, 1977).

This is an important finding because it seems to testify to the possibility that suffix effects may be achieved on other grounds than purely auditory speech characteristics (cf. Gibson, 1979). Greene and Crowder's notion of speech gestures fits in with the findings of McGurk and MacDonald and those of Dodd (1977). McGurk and MacDonald's findings also suggest that the visual dominance may increase as a function of age.

However, Easton and Basalu (1982) obtained results that indicate an auditory dominance on speech perception, a result which opposes the McGurk and MacDonald findings. Arguing from an ecological perspective, Easton and Basalu used words as units to-be-perceived. and they did not bias the effect toward vision by any introduction of noise or the like (Dodd, 1977). Moreover, they did not bias the effect by only using a what-the-subjects-heard mode of reporting as did MacDonald and McGurk (1978).

Whatever the »true» state of affairs regarding dominance relations, the general implication seems to be that this relation in normal speech perception is not set at some optimal and fixed value once and for all. As has been suggested from the foregoing, dominance relations may be somewhat task dependent and when we introduce a hearing-impairment into the picture, the »normal» relation may be even more distorted.

In a pilot study from our own laboratory (Rönnberg & Lyxell, 1985a), hearing-impaired (x = 60 dB) and normal hearing subjects participated in a word-pair discrimination task. The procedure was as follows: A talker appeared on a TV screen saying the first word where half of the words were bimodally presented (visible lip movements + accompanying sound), and the other half was presented unimodally (visible lip movements only). Before the second word was spoken (visible lip movements only) a time interval of 0.5 (immediate) or 5 seconds (delayed) was allowed to elapse. All variables varied within subjects. The subject's task was simply to indicate whether the second word was the same as the first word. For the present purposes, we only present the data with respect to correct identifications, the analysis of lures is thus excluded. As may be observed in Table 1, it seems clear that the normal hearing subjects benefit from the presence of sound on the first word (bimodal presentation) for immediate identification of the second word, whereas the hearing-impaired display a reversed trend for the same immediate and delayed conditions. This crossover interaction suggests to us that normal hearing subjects use an internal speech code which is compatible with, and may be primed by, an auditory component for the immediate identification of the second unimodally presented word. However, in line with most estimates on echoic persistence (Crowder & Morton, 1969) and auditory recency in immediate free recall (e.g., Rönnberg & Nilsson, 1982; Rönnberg & Ohlsson, 1980; Rönnberg, Nilsson, & Ohlsson, 1982), the auditory superiority would not last for more than a few seconds (except in a certain mixed-mode condition). This is also what happens in the delayed identification condition; the normal hearing lose about 20% of their ability to identify the second word.

TABLE 1

Discrimination performance as a function of handicap group, presentation mode for the first word, and temporal interval between the first and the second word

	Hearing - impaired		Normal hearing	
	Bimodal	Unimodal	Bimodal	Unimodal
0.5 s	.42	.37	.57	.48
Temporal interval				
5.0 s	.48	.51	.38	.59

Apparently, the data suggest that the hearing-impaired deduct some other code (possibly dominated by vision) since they do not benefit from the auditory component on the first word (compared to the unimodal condition) and, if anything, they improve their performance as the delay increases. This improvement should be interpreted with due caution, though, since there is an overall tendency for subjects in both groups to improve in the unimodal conditions. This may be due to a general limitation of the task. The subjects have more time to »tune in» their decision criteria. A more elaborate account of the findings could be that a visually dominated coding strategy is compatible with the visual presentation of the second word and, hence, does not »distract» the adjustment of decision criteria.

At any rate, it is hard to escape the conclusion that the data suggest that the hearing-impaired deduct a code similar to the code used by the normal hearing when they *do not* rely on an explicit activation of internal speech. The same similarity holds true in the case when they themselves are not primed by the sound component of the first word.

This conclusion agrees with the Rönnberg och Nilsson (1985) interpretation of observed compensatory effects for the profoundly hearing-impaired with respect to free recall of visually presented word lists. The finding was that the profoundly hearing-impaired outperform normal hearing on recency items and the interpretation was that, due to the profoundly hearing-impaired's visual skills, they did not have to expend energy for recoding the visually presented material into an internal speech code (cf. Lundberg & Leong this volume, see also, Rönnberg, Öhngren, & Nilsson, 1981, 1982).

So the key point is that the hearing-impaired show a relative independence of mode of first-word presentation in the word-pair discrimination task, and that the memory data suggest a visual skill notion to be most parsimonious. In a broader sense, this might imply that they have developed a rather stable coding strategy. There is, however, another logical possibility: The hearing-impaired may »derive» some type of inner speech strategy *when task conditions so demand.*

In fact, we have obtained data from a levels-of-processing experiment (Rönnberg, Granlund, & Lyxell, 1985) which suggest that the coding capabilities, not only for the hearing-impaired but also for the deaf (when the handicap is acquired), *can* be stretched so as to encompass phonemic encoding conditions with the same efficiency as a control group of normal hearing subjects, matched for age.

Procedurally, phonemic encoding was manipulated by either letting the subjects answer rhyme questions (does the cue word x rhyme with the target word y?) and semantic encoding was manupulated by letting the subject answer the question, whether the cue word belonged to the same semantic category as the target word. Half of the target word-cue word combinations yielded yes- answers and the other half no-answers. This was an intentional learning paradigm and the variables varied within subjects. At cued recall, the target word was prompted by the cue used at encoding. Across subjects, one particular target word was employed for all encoding-response combinations.

As can be seen in Table 2, phonemic cues, given a phonemic encoding, result in a memory performance for the deaf (acquired) which is on a par with (or better than) the old adults' performance, and slightly worse than the young adults' performance. The same relation holds true for the semantic cues condition. The congenitally deaf, on the other hand, do not seem to be able to utilize phonemic cues at all. Only to a moderate extent can they take advantage of semantic cues. This result should not be surprising, since they suffer from insufficient linguistic skills. Perhaps even more interesting is the pattern of latency data for the phonemic and semantic orienting tasks. As the subjects answered the orienting questions, we collected latency data for their classification. As shown in Table 3, the deaf (acquired) are as fast as the old adults in deciding rhyme and semantic category status of a word, while the young adults are somewhat faster. Again, the congenitally deaf perform worse than the other groups. They use more time both for phonemic and semantic encoding questions. Thus, both at encoding and in memory storage, the subjects suffering from acquired deafness do have an ability to utilize acoustic properties of verbal items.

TABLE 2

Memory performance as a function of group, level of encoding and cue, for yes-answers to encoding questions

		Congenitally deaf	Acquired deafness	Old adults	Young adults
CUE	Phonemic	.08	.25	.19	.35
	Semantic	.36	.65	.58	.70

TABLE 3

Classification time as a function of group and level of encoding
question

	Congenitally deaf	Acquired deafness	Old adults	Young adults
Phonemic	5.11	3.72	3.86	2.61
Semantic	6.47	3.89	4.64	3.01

As a final aspect of coding strategy, we (Rönnberg, Öhngren, & Lyxell, 1985) employed Bransford and Franks' (1971, 1972) paradigm as a means of studying the degree to which profoundly hearing-impaired *abstract* linguistic materials. The data show no deficits and, if anything, they tend to show more signs of abstraction for some conditions than a control group matched for age (cf. Hoemann, Andrews, & DeRosa, 1974). Thus, the hearing- impaired gear their processing more directly towards the meaning of the message.

In summary, it appears from recent experiments on the representation of lipread stimuli in normal hearing that an audio-visual speech gesture code is the most plausible. However, the dominance relation between the auditory and visual components may be altered due to task demands. The hearing- impaired seem to use a code which is more independent of acoustic components of speech, but even they (the deaf) are able to use or »derive» an internal speech strategy when explicitly asked to do so (cf. Belmont & Karchmer, 1976, on instructed rehearsal strategies in the deaf). Finally, their ability to code linguistic material abstractly is not impaired. If anything, they tend to deduct and strive for meaning to a larger extent than the normal hearing.

3   GUESSING STRATEGY

The ability to make use of intelligent guesswork on the basis of imcomplete visual (and auditory) information constitutes one of the core problems for the hearing-impaired. In the introduction it was also suggested that IQ and linguistic capabilities may share an affinity with guessing ability. In fact, this is exactly what Barlow (1983) argues: *Intelligence is the capactiy to guess right by discovering new order.* In this vein, language represents a vehicle for redundancy reduction. On the premise that messages or information units are correlated with each other, the role of redundancies carried by language allows the speechreader to compensate for missing pieces of information by means of available cues.

For the deaf or hearing-impaired speechreader, the situation is rather drastic. Except for a general deterioration in the signal to noise ratio (cf. Erber, 1974), which at least on a logical basis would force the speechreader into a visual processing mode, there are at least two more basic difficulties which the speechreader has to deal with. First, estimates of phoneme visibility are disappointingly low (Berger, 1972; Jeffers & Barley, 1971). Second, it has been shown that speechreading performance is relatively independent of phoneme visibility and that this independence increases as sentence length is increased (Clouser, 1977). The above constraints seem to leave much room for guessing processes to operate.

In this respect, contextual factors seem to play an improtant role for the decoding process. For example, by providing topic (Sanders, 1971), situational cues (Garstecki & O'Neill, 1980) or additional gestures (Berger & Popelka, 1971), the same function is served: Speechreading performance improves since contextual support is increased and thus also the opportunities for intelligent guesswork.

Bode, Nerbonne, and Sahlstrom (1970) used a completion task to assess a subject's synthetic ability (i.e., a compontent of guessing ability). The subjects were to complete words (where letters were missing) in a sentence. Performance on this type of test and speechreading performance was significantly correlated (r = .36), but not impressively so. A rather low correlation (point biserial coeff = .27) was also obtained by Tatoul and Davidsson (1961) on a similar letter prediction task. However, in a study by Sanders and Coscarelli (1970) correlations ranged in the vicinity of r = .50 for three tests of synthetic ability: A visual closure test, a disemvowelled word test and a sentence completion test.

More interesting, perhaps, was that the better half of the lipreaders in Sanders and Coscarelli's study also exhibited a significant superior synthetic ability on all three tests; irrespective of hearing-impairment, duration of hearing loss and lipreading training. It is thus possible that the skill factor cuts across the boundaries of different handicap groups who depend on speechreading.

In a study from our own laboratory (Rönnberg & Lyxell, 1985b), we also obtained evidence suggesting that speechreading skill (defined as overall performance in the experiment) did *not* interact with a handicap group variable (congenitally deaf, hearing-impaired and normal hearing), or with any higher order interactions involving the group variable. However, there are some other interactions involving the skill variable which merits some attention ($p<.05$); one of the more important involves the familiarity of the sentence material employed. Presumably, sentences which are unfamiliar to a subject may also afford a lower redundancy (reliability was assessed by 10 independent judges, $r = 1.0$). For sentences of low familiarity, the skilled speechreader is able to pick up the »remaining» redundancies to a relatively larger extent than the unskilled speechreader. As can be observed in Table 4, the relative superiority for the superior group increased from 7% to 15% as familiarity decreased. Moreover, as message length was increased (from 6 to 12 word messages, thus pooled over the familiarity variable, see Table 5) the skilled group increased their superiority from 8% to 14%. Although it may be hard to argue that message length is intimately correlated to redundancy due to linguistic constraints, it certainly looks like the skilled speechreader can use these constraints to guess more efficiently. A third variable was included to assess the subjects' ability to make use of varying amounts of preexposed parts of the message (in print on the TV screen) immediately prior to the appearance of the talker on the same TV screen (no auditory component was used). Again, the superior group could use this extra information (e.g., increased redundancy) to a larger extent than the inferior group (see Table 6).

TABLE 4

Proportion correctly speechread words as a function of speechreading skill and familiarity of the material

		Familiarity	
		High	Low
	Superior	.64	.47
Speechreading skill			
	Inferior	.57	.32

In contrast to the skilled speechreaders, the hearing- impaired group as a whole (x = 60 dB) tended to show the opposite trend with respect to preexposed text aid. They performed relatively better than the other two groups for conditions of no

TABLE 5

Proportion correctly speechread words as a function of speechreading skill and message length

		Message length	
		Long	Short
	Superior	.50	.61
Speechreading skill			
	Inferior	.36	.53

TABLE 6

Proportion correctly speechread words as a function of speechreading skill and amount preexposed text

		Amount of preexposure		
		100%	50%	0%
	Superior	.86	.65	.15
Speechreading skill				
	Inferior	.66	.58	.09

preexposure. Compared to the normal hearing; they did *not* show any substantial relative improvement for the message length and familiarity variables.

Thus, the data with respect to skill and hearing-impairment suggest that *rather different guessing operations are invoked*. We have also obtained some data which suggest that for *some* variables, speechreading skill and hearing-impairment operate in the same direction. In a study by Rönnberg, Öhngren, and Nilsson (1983) speechreading was compared in conditions of TV- presentation and a real-life presentation of the same talker. For the hearing-impaired (x = 60 dB), performance was better in comparison to the normal hearing and the profoundly hearing-impaired groups for *long* word lists and a *real-life* presentation. Here, the *skilled hearing-impaired* performed at best. This result should be compared to the data of Rönnberg and Lyxell (1985b), where there was no difference between the skilled normal hearing and skilled hearing-impaired for long messages. Thus, for some special conditions, there may be an interactive effect between skill and hearing-impairment, but for conditions which demand more guessing skills (e.g., real sentences) the two seem to operate rather independently.

In order to assess guessing skills by independent means, we devised two types of guessing tests (Lyxell & Rönnberg, 1985). Further, to simulate the demands on guessing in a speechreading situation, we also introduced *time constraints.* Both tests were completion tasks, that is, word-completion and sentence completion where each word or sentence was allowed a maximum inspection time of 10 seconds per completion. Response interval was set to 15 seconds for word-completion and 45 seconds for sentence completion. By word-completion we mean measuring the ability to guess correctly without the aid of context, while sentence completion is assumed to measure the ability to guess correctly with the benefit of the sentence context. Put another way, word completion performance may be viewed as an index of the cognitive decoding process used for relatively context free linguistic units, while sentence completion presumably taps more synthetic aspects of language comprehension. According to the subjects' performance on these tests, they were ranked into either a superior or inferior subgroup. This skill variable was included in the ANOVA computed for the actual speechreading experiment. Care was taken so as to ensure that the sentences were simple declarative everyday-life sentences. They varied in length from 8 to 11 words. The words in the word completion task were also common everyday nouns. As will be observed in Table 7, the subjects who were skilled at sentence completion performed best for *long* sentences, while word completion procures significant effects for the case when *no text aid* was pre-exposed (see Table 8). Borth interactions were significant beyond the 5% level.

It is also important to note that a given individual who performs well on one of the two guessing tests does not necessarily perform well on the other. Correlations between the two tests (and some variations of the tests) did not suggest any significant association; this might indicate that different task demands are operating. Although not presented in table format, it should also be noted that one of the variations of the sentence completion test generated a sentence completion skill by text pre-exposure

TABLE 7

Speechreading performance as a function of sentence completion skill and message length

		Message Length		
		3-word	6-word	12-word
	Superior	.75	.58	.67
Sentence-completion skill				
	Inferior	.66	.54	.49

TABLE 8

Speechreading performance as a function of word completion skill and amount of preexposed text

		Amount of preexposure		
		0%	33%	66%
	Superior	.39	.69	.92
Word completion skill				
	Inferior	.17	.63	.91

interaction similar to the one procured by word completion skill. This variation included adding guessing support through a spoken filmed version of each sentence. This result further reinforces the task specificity of guessing and opens up the possibility that there is no straightforward guessing test - speechreading test compatibility, which otherwise might be considered trivial.

There is a general complication with respect to the data discussed so far: for example, the speechreading skill by familiarity interaction and the sentence length interaction may have been brought about due to a general underlying task difficulty variable (cf. Crowder, 1980, 1982). If we accept this possibility, it still seems unlikely that the completion data are based on a concomitant variation in task difficulty. It is hard to argue that a given word completion is either more difficult or less difficult than a given sentence completion. Therefore, the completion data seem to give credibility to the skill interactions discussed, since, for example, the speechreading skill by message length interaction and the sentence completion skill by message length converge on the same pattern. Moreover, the skill by text pre-exposure interaction was in a direction at variance with a task difficulty variable.

By way of summary, it may be stated that speechreading as related to a hypothetical guessing factor does not show any unitary pattern. Guessing skill is not an all or nothing affair in the sense that you either guess intelligently or you do not. It seems to be the case that a given individual is skilled at some task(s), but not all tasks. Further, a skilled speechreader, tested in conditions tapping various aspects of using redundancy for guessing, does not necessarily behave in the same way as a hearing-impaired person does. Skill per se is rather independent from the characteristics of the group as a whole.

Moreover, we have also obtained some correlational data (Rönnberg & Lyxell, 1985b), where we computed the associations between average hearing loss (i.e., dB loss for 500, 1000 and 2000 Hz) for the hearing-impaired group and speechreading in the conditions of familiarity, message length and pre-exposure of text (and their interactions). Data show unequivocally that there is *no* significant correlation whatsoever. This piece of evidence, in conjunction with Clouser's (1977) data on phoneme visibility, thus suggest that the process of speechreading, especially successful speechreading, *demands* skilled guessing operations. Skilled guessing constitutes a type of compensation which may be denoted *conceptually driven compensation,* and this compensation may be achieved in conditions where redundancy variations are large.

Finally, the results of the above studies agree with a recent study by Williams (1982) on the relation between reading and lipreading. Based on subtests such as eye-voice span, close ability, and a test on the ability to comprehend printed material presented one word at a time (300 words per minute; renders word by word reading impossible) in the absence of an opportunity to regress or scan ahead, it was concluded that skilled lipreaders do *not* engage in word-by-word reading, but rather that they synthesize visual and linguistic cues to arrive at the meaning of the message. On the basis of the correlational data, it was also concluded that a good reader may be both a good *or* poor lipreader; however, a poor reader is nearly always more likely to be a poor lipreader.

4   GENERAL CONSIDERATIONS WITH RESPECT TO COMPENSATION

We have mainly reviewed group data in this chapter. To use skill data is one of the means of approaching the problem of individual differences. Individual difference data is a necessary prerequisite for the construction of diagnostic and training programmes (see Rönnberg & Risberg, 1985 for applications to the interactive video system DAVE). On the other hand, individual difference data are not sufficient. What we have attempted to do in this chapter is to concentrate on the *general constraints* of information processing imposed by the handicap group factors, and we have also shown that the skill factor is dissociated from the group factor. Based on these two types of data we will make a few general statements with respect to compensation:

a.   In view of a general lack of correlation between phoneme visibility and hearing loss on the one hand and speechread ing performance on the other, there is a substantial possibility for conceptually driven compensation by means of training. The clinical observation that excellent speech readers outperform »normal» speechreaders many times over also testifies to this possibility. The situation is similar to chess players' many different levels of skill (Ohlsson, this volume).

b.   As suggested by the group data, the hearing-impaired code speech stimuli in a manner which is probably not dominated by auditory cues. Rather, what seems to be the case is that the hearing-impaired utilize the relative influence which vision has in the fusion of the percept. On a group basis, this may be viewed as their *habitual* way of coding. It is important, though, to make the distinction between a habitual way of coding and a *task demand induced* coding strategy. As we observed in the levels-of-processing experiment, it is possible even for the deaf (acquired) to answer rhyme questions effectively and to utilize a phonemic code for later retrieval in the same manner as a normal hearing subject. Thus, a given individual has a habitual way of applying a dominant coding strategy, and given the possibility of task induced strategies, here is where compensatory training should be set in. In other words, training of the non-dominant and non-habitual ways of coding may offer compensatory means for the hearing-impaired to deal with the variety of coding demands which (s)he inevitably meets in the »speechreading ecology».

c. Individual differences with respect to guessing skill and speechreading seem to suggest a large variation as well as a prominent skill factor. The interesting feature of the data is that the skill factor seems to obey its own laws irrespective of handicap type, and that intelligent guessing may be task specific. Training for compensatory purposes should focus on redundancy and allow the trainee to practise on tasks which afford various degrees of redundancy.

Obviously, for one and the same individual, the coding and guessing strategies will interact with task demands. How this interaction should be dealt with for both diagnostic and training purposes is discussed in Rönnberg and Risberg (1985). Nevertheless, we would as a final tentative thesis suggest that the following is a description of a skilled speechreader; an ideal towards which compensatory training should be designed: *An excellent speechreader must be flexible and adapt to the current task demands; (s)he must have the capacity to shift from the habitual coding strategy to other means of coding. The excellent speechreader must also be in possession of a broad repertoire of guessing subskills/strategies adapted to different types of task specific cues. Intelligent guesswork thus consists of rapid and flexible alternations between these subskills.*

REFERENCES

Barlow, H.B. (1983). Intelligence, guesswork, language. *Nature, 304,* July.

Belmont, J.M., & Karchmer, M.A. (1976). Instructed rehearsal strategies' influence on deaf memory processing. *Journal of Speech and Hearing Research, 19,* 36-47.

Berger, K.W. (1972). Visemes and homophonous words. *Teacher of the Deaf, 70,* 396-399.

Berger, K.W., & Popelka, G.R. (1971). Extra-facial gestures in relation to speechreading. *Journal of Communication Disorders, 3,* 302-308.

Bode, D.L., Nerbonne, G.P., & Sahlstrom, L.J. (1970). Speech reading and the synthesis of distorted printed sentences. *Journal of Speech and Hearing Research, 13,* 115-121.

Bransford, J.D., & Franks, J.J. (1971). The abstraction of linguistic ideas. *Cognitive Psychology, 2,* 331-350.

Bransford, J.D., & Franks, J.J. (1972). The abstraction of linguistic ideas: A review. *Cognition, 1,* 211-242.

Campbell, R., & Dodd, B. (1980). Hearing by eye. *Quarterly Journal of Experimental Psychology: Human Learning and Memory, 32,* 85-100.

Clouser, R.A. (1977). Relative phoneme visibility and lipreading performance. *Volto Review,* Jan., 27-34.

Coltheart, M. (1984). Sensory memory - A tutorial review. In H. Bouma & D.G. Bouwhuis (Eds.), *Attention and performance X. Control of language processes.* London: Lawrence Erlbaum.

Conrad, R. (1964). Acoustic confusion in immediate memory. *British Journal of Psychology, 55,* 429-432.

Conrad, R. (1979) *The deaf schoolchild.* London: Harper and Row.

Crowder, R.G. (1980). Echoic memory and the study of aging memory systems. In L.W. Poon, J.L. Fozard, L.S. Cermak, D. Arenberg & L.W. Thompson (Eds.), *New directions in memory and aging.* Hillsdale: Lawrence Erlbaum.

Crowder, R.G. (1982). General forgetting theory and the laws of amnesia. In L.S. Cermak (Ed.), *Human memory and amnesia.* Hillsdale: Lawrence Erlbaum.

Crowder, R.G., & Morton, J. (1969). Pre-categorical acoustic storage (PAS). *Perception & Psychophysics, 5,* 365-373.

Dodd, B. (1977). The role of vision in the perception of speech. *Perception, 6,* 31-40.

Easton, R.D., & Basalu, M. (1982). Perceptual dominance during lipreading. *Perception and Psychophysics, 32,* 562-570.

Erber, N.P. (1974). Effects of angle, distance, and illumination on visual reception of speech by profoundly deaf children. *Journal of Speech and Hearing Research, 17,* 99-112.

Farwell, R.M. (1976). Speech reading: A research review. *American Annals of the Deaf, February,* 19-30.

Garstecki, D.C., & O'Neill, J.J. (1980). Situational cue and strategy influence on speechreading. *Scandinavian Audiology, 9,* 147-151.

Gibson, J.J. (1979). *The ecological approach to visual perseption.* Boston: Houghton Mifflin.

Greene, R.L., & Crowder, R.G. (1984). Modality and suffix effects in the absence of auditory stimulation. *Journal of Verbal Learning and Verbal Behaviour, 23,* 371-382.

Hoemann, H.W., Andrews, C.E., & DeRosa, D.V. (1974). Categorical encoding in short-term memory by deaf and hearing children. *Journal of Speech and Hearing Research, 17,* 426-431.

Jeffers, J., & Barley, M. (1971). *Speechreading (lipreading).* Springfield, Illinois: Charles, C. Thomas Publisher.

Lyxell, B., & Rönnberg, J. (1985). *Guessing and speechreading performance.* Submitted manuscript.

MacDonald, J., & McGurk, H. (1978). Visual influence on speech perception. *Perception and Psychophysics, 24,* 253-257.

McGurk, H., & MacDonald, J. (1976). Hearing lips and seeing voices. *Nature, 264,* Dec., 23/30, 746-748.

Rönnberg, J., & Lyxell, B. (1985). *Word discrimination and coding strategy in the hearing-impaired.* Submitted manuscript (a).

Rönnberg, J., & Lyxell, B. (1985). On the identification of support systems for speechreading. *Umeå Psychological Reports,* No. 183. Department of Psychology, Umeå, Sweden (b).

Rönnberg, J., & Nilsson, L.-G. (1982). Representation of auditory information based on a functionalistic perspective. In R. Carlson & B. Granström (Eds.), *The representation of speech in the peripheral auditory system.* Elsevier Biomedical Press.

Rönnberg, J., & Nilsson, L.-G. (1985). *The modality effect, sensory handicap and compensatory functions.* Submitted manuscript.

Rönnberg, J., & Ohlsson, K. (1980). Channel capacity and processing of modality specific information. *Acta Psychologica, 44,* 253-267.

Rönnberg, J., & Risberg, A. (1985). On the implementation of computer-based diagnostic and training programs for speechreading. Paper presented at the symposium on »Communication and contacts between people in the computerized society». Göteborg 6-7 dec. 1984.

Rönnberg, J., Granlund, B.-M., & Lyxell, B. (1985). *Levels of processing as a function of hearing-handicap.* Manuscript.

Rönnberg, J., Nilsson, L.-G., & Ohlsson, K. (1982). Organization by modality, language and category compared. *Psychological Research, 44,* 369-379.

Rönnberg, J., Öhngren, G., & Lyxell, G. (1985). *Linguistic abstraction and hearing handicap.* Submitted manuscript.

Rönnberg, J., Öhngren, G., & Nilsson, L.-G. (1981). Memory and hearing deficiency. *Umeå Psychological Reports,* No. 157, Department of Psychology, University of Umeå. Sweden.

Rönnberg, J., Öhngren, G., & Nilsson, L.-G. (1982). Hearing deficiency, speechreading and memory functions. *Scandinavian Audiology, 11,* 261-268.

Rönnberg, J., Öhngren, G., & Nilsson, L.-G. (1983). Speechreading performance evaluated by means of TV and real-life presentation. A comparison between a normally hearing, moderately and profoundly hearing-impaired group. *Scandinavian Audiology, 12,* 71-77.

Sanders, D. (1971). *Aural rehabilitation.* Englewood Cliffs, N.J.: Prentice-Hall.

Sanders, J.W., & Coscarelli, J.E. (1970). The relationship of visual synthesis skill to lipreading performance. *American Annals of the Deaf,* January.

Smith, R.C., & Kitchen, D.W. (1972). Lipreading performance and contextual cues. *Journal of Communication Disorders, 5,* 86- 90.

Spoer, K.T., & Corin, W.J. (1978). The stimulus suffix effect as a memory coding phenomenon. *Memory and Cognition, 6,* 583- 589.

Tatoul, C.M., & Davidson, G.D. (1961). Lipreading and letter prediction. *Journal of Speech and Hearing Research, 4,* 178-181.

Williams, A. (1982). The relationship between two visual communication systems: Reading and lipreading. *Journal of Speech and Hearing Research, 25,* 500-503.

Communication and Handicap: Aspects of
Psychological Compensation and Technical Aids
E. Hjelmquist and L.-G. Nilsson (editors)
© Elsevier Science Publishers B.V. (North-Holland), 1986

COMPENSATORY USE OF ACOUSTIC SPEECH CUES AND LANGUAGE STRUCTURE BY HEARING-IMPAIRED LISTENERS

DAVID HOUSE

Lund University, Department of Linguistics and Phonetics, Lund, Sweden[*]

It is hypothesized that hearing-impaired listeners can develop and use perceptual strategies involving a combination of limited acoustic speech cues and language structure competence in a manner which differs from speech perception by normal listeners. We might even expect hearing-impaired listeners to perform better than normal listeners when confronted with identification tasks using filtered speech stimuli where the filter configuration conforms to the audiological configurations of the hearing- impaired listeners.

In a speech perception experiment, low-pass filtered speech stimuli consisting of a carrier sentence and target CVC words were presented to 25 normal listeners and 13 listeners with noise-induced hearing impairments. The target words comprised minimal triplets where the initial consonant was a voiced or voiceless stop. Results of the experiment indicated that the hearing-impaired lesteners were better able to identify both target stops and target words than were the normal listeners. Furthermore, a correlation was observed between filter frequency and hearing loss such that those listeners whose audiological configurations best matched the filter attained the best identification results. Finally, an error analysis indicated that those listeners who attained the best test results consistently chose the most frequent stop in Swedish, /t/ and the words having the highest frequency of use in Swedish thereby improving their results.

These results provide evidence that hearing-impaired listeners can develop perceptual strategies which enable them to compensate to a certain degree for frequency attenuation in the perceptual mechanism. Exactly how these strategies work is not yet clear but it seems reasonable to assume that use is made both of low- frequency acoustic cues and intuition about linguistic structure. Further work in this area is proposed involving relationships between linguistic structure and cues such as intonation and rhythm as well as the possibility of pedagogical applications of such compensatory strategies.

I would like to express my sincere thanks to Jarle Aursnes and the Department of Otorhinolaryngology, University Hospital, Lund, for making available both patients and equipment for the clinical part of the experiment. Thanks is also due to Bengt Mandersson for writing the pitch editing program, helping in constructing the stimuli and in interpreting the results of the experiment; and to Gösta Bruce and Eva Gårding for valuable discussion and comments.

1 INTRODUCTION

One of the goals of speech perception research is to determine how acoustic information is structured by the auditory periphery and how the central processor uses this information and codes it into meaningful linguistic units. When this information is altered or reduced by a change in the auditory periphery, for example through an acquired, noise-induced hearing loss, the central processor must then compensate for this loss either by restructuring the information or by using different acoustic cues or both.

The purpose of the experiments to be described was to find evidence of acoustic cues which can enable listeners with noise-induced hearing losses to compensate for missing cues, or evidence of a restructuring of the linguistic system to aid in speech perception. To this end listeners with normal hearing and hearing-impaired listeners were subjected to low-pass filtered speech so that a comparison could be made between the two groups and to test the relevance of simulating a hearing loss by means of low-pass filtered speech stimuli.

Since a noise-induced hearing loss often entails high-frequency loss, low-frequency cues such as fundamental frequency (Fo) might provide material which could help the central processor in its recoding task. Fundamental frequency is particularly interesting since it provides normal listeners with important cues concerning syllable stress, the most important syllable, (Fry, 1958) and sentence focus (Lehiste, 1970). Sentence focus is the »new» information not shared by the speaker and the listener (Jackendoff, 1972). Furthermore, it appears to be movement in the fundamental frequency which provides strong perceptual cues to the location of stress (Lehiste, 1970).

Fo movement then provides, from the point of view of dynamic perception (Johansson, 1975), a change in frequency over time which could be registered as an event by the perceptual mechanism. This event would in turn sharpen attention and aid in short-term memory retrieval of spectral cues. Since resolution of spectral cues can be seen as more crucial in the »bottom-up» processing of new information than in presuppositive »top-down» speech processing (Marslen-Wilson & Tyler, 1980), it would be interesting to investigate to what extent segmental resolution could be facilitated by varying degrees of fundamental frequency movement where semantic focus is constant in »bottom-up» process ing using semantically non-redundant speech stimuli.

A possible interaction between fundamental frequency movement and segmental resolution could be between pitch movement realized as frequency movement of harmonics of the fundamental in the vowel and vowel formant transition movement realized as resonance induced amplitude shifts between successive harmonics. Since formant transitions are important cues for stop identification, such interaction might facilitate perception of transitions and aid in stop identification. On the other hand, interaction might not necessarily result in an amplification of formant transitions and would therefore not facilitate stop identification.

Could Fo movement be used by hearing-impaired listeners as a correlate of stress to aid the central processor in restructuring the auditory input and thereby help in identifying stop consonants? It is well documented that individuals with moderate sloping sensorineural hearing losses have difficulty in identify ing place of articulation especially in voiceless stops. However, subjects having similar audiometric configurations can differ radically in their performance in both synthetic and natural speech tests (Van de Grift Turek, Dorman, Franks, & Summerfield, 1980; Picket, Revoile, & Danaher, 1983; Risberg & Agelfors, 1978). It could be that some listeners are successful at making use of certain cues whereas other listeners are not.

In attempting to answer these questions, word identification tasks were presented through a filter roughly corresponding in frequency to a typical noise-induced audiometric configuration for hearing-impaired listeners. By presenting the stimuli both to listeners with normal hearing and to hearing-impaired listeners, the experiment had two goals: 1) to test frequency movement interaction as an aid to stop consonant identification in filtered speech, and 2) to compare performance of normal hearing listeners with listeners whose audiometric configurations correspond to the filter frequencies used in the presentation. The latter goal might also help in exploring the relationships between perception of the speech wave filtered before reaching the auditory periphery and perception of the speech wave altered by an impairment of the auditory periphery.

2   METHOD

2.1   Linguistic Material and Stimuli

There is much debate concerning differences in perception of sense vs. non-sense speech utterances and utterances in and outside of a sentence frame in listening experiments (Johnson & Strange, 1982; Pastore, 1981). It seems, however, that when dealing with stimuli involving both sentence intonation and local segmental cues and their interaction, the closer the stimuli can be to real-life speech, provided of course that variables can be sufficiently controlled, the more we can learn about the communicative aspects of speech perception. (see also Gårding, 1967, for differences between juncture perception in sense and non-sense words.)

The carrier sentence »de′ va′, ja′ sa′» (It was, I said) was selected such that a vowel would immediately precede the target word. Twentysix single-syllable CVC words were chosen having an initial voiced or voiceless stop (Table 1). Target word initial stop was considered as the perceptual target phoneme and Fo movement in the preceding and following vowel was to be altered to test interaction between stop identification and frequency movement in the two adjoining vowels.

TABLE 1

Target words used in the stimulus sentences

	TAL	KAL	BAL	DAL	GAL
	(speech)	(bare)	(dance)	(valley)	(to crow)
PAR	TAR	KAR	BAR		
(pair)	(take)	(tub)	(bare)		
	TUR	KUR	BUR	DUR	
	(luck/turn)	(cure)	(cage)	(major key)	
	TÅR	KÅR	BÅR		GÅR
	(tear/toes)	(corps)	(stretcher)		(go/walk)
PÅG	TÅG		BÅG		
(boy)	(train)		(cheat)		
	TAM			DAM	GAM
	(tame)			(lady)	(vulture)
	TOK	KOK	BOK		
	(fool)	(potful)	(book)		

Five of the test sentences were recorded by a male speaker of Southern Swedish in two versions, first with emphatic high stress given to the target word, then with indifferent low stress. The 26 test sentences were then recorded by the same speaker using neutral intonation and stress.

The five low-stress and five high-stress tokens were digitized using a VAX computer at a sample rate of 10 000Hz. The tokens were then analyzed with a linear prediction analysis method (ILS program package). The five contours for the two intonation types were averaged to serve as a natural model for pitch editing of the sentences with neutral intonation. The 26 neutral intonation sentences were digitilized and analyzed in the same manner.

Two stimulus versions of each sentence were then synthesized from the linear prediction coefficients with the pitch contour select ed to conform to the low and high-stress intonation models respectively (Figure 1). The resulting 52 stimuli were randomized in the computer. A pilot test using four listeners was run to determine a satisfactory low-pass filter cut-off frequency which would allow correct initial stop identification of around 50% in the target word. An eight order Butterworth low-pass filter with the cut-off frequency set at 900Hz, -48dB/octave allowed the 50% correct identification in the pilot study.

The stimuli were recorded on tape through the filter in thirteen blocks each containing four stimuli with a 10-second interval between stimuli and a 20-second interval between blocks. An additional block was placed at the beginning as a practice buffer.

D. House

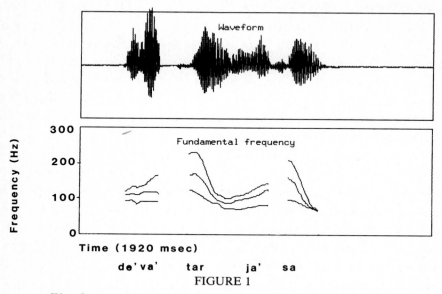

Time (1920 msec)

de'va'   tar   ja'   sa

FIGURE 1

Waveform and fundamental frequency contours of one stimulus
sentence. The middle contour represents the original neutral stress,
the upper contour is the high-stress edited version and the lower
contour is the low-stress edited version. The wave-form represents
the neutral version. Only the two edited versions were used in the
test.

2.2   Subjects

Twenty-five beginning speech pathology students at Lund University with normal
hearing and unfamiliar with the test material participated in the experiment as part of a
course requirement. Thirteen patients at the Department of Otorhinolaryngology,
University Hospital, Lund, with noise-induced hearing losses of roughly similar
audimetric configuration (beginning of slope at around 1000Hz, approximately -40dB
at 2000Hz and -60dB at 3000Hz) voluntarily participated in the experiment as an
extended part of routine audiological examinations. Patients were selected on the basis
of previous pure-tone audiograms where relative symmetry of hearing loss was a
criterion as well as break frequency and degree of slope.

2.3   Procedure

The normal-hearing subjects were tested in three groups on three different occasions.
Written instructions and answer sheets were handed out and the instructions were read

aloud by the experimenter. The subjects were informed that they would hear the carrier sentence »Det var - jag sa» presented through a filter and that they should try to write the word following »var» in each sentence. If they were unsure they were requested to guess the word closest to the sound they heard. After the practice block was run subjects were allowed to ask questions. Testing took place binaurally in a sound-treated perception laboratory using a Revox A77 tape recorder and Burwen PMB6 Orthodynamic headphones. Sound level was checked as comfortable during the practice block. The test took 15 minutes.

The hearing-impaired persons were tested individually while sitting in a sound-insulated room. Routine pure-tone and speech audiograms were first made after which Békésy sweep-audiograms with pulsed stimuli were performed for each ear. This was done to more closely define the steepness and frequency location of the hearing loss. The same instructions were presented to the listeners except that they were asked to repeat the words orally instead of in writing. The responses were monitored outside the sound-insulated room over a loudspeaker and recorded on tape.

The stimuli were presented monaurally through a Revox A77 tape recorder, via the speech channel of a Madsen Clinical Audiometer Model OB70 and matched TDH-39 headphones with MX-41/AR cushions. The stimuli were presented at most comfortable level established during the practice block and generally corresponding to 30dB over speech threshold and to the level for maximum speech discrimination established during speech audiometry.

Monaural presentation was deemed advisable since hearing loss was not completely symmetrical. A second randomized version of the tape was made, and learning effects were minimized by presenting half the first version to the left ear, the entire second version to the right ear and then the remaining half of the first version to the left ear. After hearing the filtered stimuli the subjects were given a break and then the test was repeated using non- filtered stimuli. The test, including the Békésy audiograms but excluding the routine audiograms, took approximately an hour and a half. The patients were extremely cooperative especially considering the length of the test.

3 RESULTS

3.1 Normal-hearing Listeners

All three groups showed similar patterns of initial stop identification for the filtered stimuli. Roughly one-half of the stops were correctly identified, and a general bias toward labials was observed. The voiced-voiceless distinction was perceived by all subjects in nearly all target words with place- of-articulation for voiced stops being somewhat easier to identify than for voiceless stops. The mean number of correct stop identifications for the normal-hearing subjects as a group (Group 1, Figure 2) was higher (14.5 of 26) when the sentence and target word carried the indifferent, low-stress intonation contour than when the sentence and word carried emphatic, high stress (12.7 of 26). The difference was significant, $p < 0.05$, running contrary to the hypothesis. Correct word identification, however, did not reveal a significant difference between low and high stress, although more low-stress words were correctly identified. Labials /p,b/ and the voiced velar /g/ were favored by the normal-hearing listeners (Figure 3). In only one phoneme /d/ were substantial differences observed relating to stress contours. The low-stress versions received more than twice as many correct responses compared to their high-stress counterparts. The vowels were nearly always correctly identified.

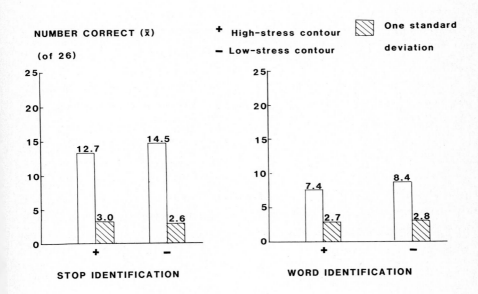

FIGURE 2

Mean number of correct identifications for stops and words in low-pass filtered sentences with high and low-stress fundamental frequency contours. (Group 1, listeners with normal hearing).

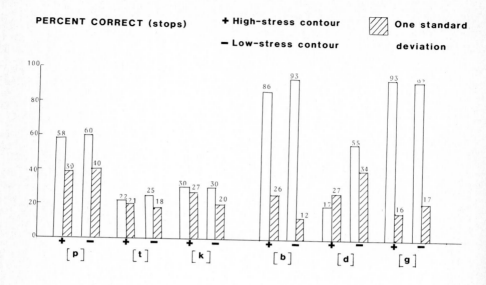

FIGURE 3

Correct initial phoneme identification in percent for
Group 1 (Normal hearing).

3.2　Hearing-impaired Listeners

The number of stops and words correctly identified by the hearing-impaired listeners as a group was about the same as for the normal group: about one in two for stops and one in three for words (Figure 4). Again, for both words and stops, identification was slightly better for sentences having the low-stress Fo contour, although here this difference was not significant, p>0.05. Labials and velars were again favored in the voiced stimuli results, but the dental phoneme /t/ was favored in the voiceless results (Figure 5). Standard deviation for both stops and words in both stress categories was greater for the hearing- impaired group than for normals. As with the normal group, the vowels were nearly always correctly identified.

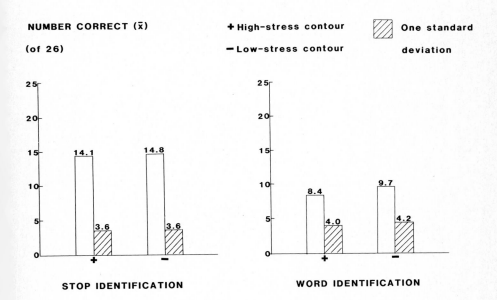

FIGURE 4

Mean number of correct identifications for stops and words in low-pass filtered sentences with high and low-stress fundamental frequency contours. (Group 2, hearing-impaired listeners).

PERCENT CORRECT (stops)

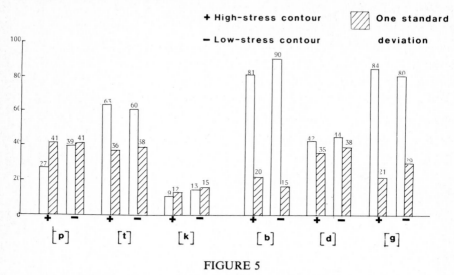

FIGURE 5

Correct initial phoneme identification in percent
for Group 2 (Hearing-impaired).

3.3   Differences Between The Two Groups

As previously mentioned, the hearing-impaired group as a whole did better on
both stop and word identification in the filtered speech, although the difference was
not significant, p>0.05. There was, however, a striking difference between the two
groups manifested by the preference for the voiceless dental /t/ among the hearing-
impaired group which contrasted to the labial preference /p/ among the normal
group.

Reactions to the test by subjects of the two groups also differ ed. Members of the
normal-hearing group felt that the test was extremely difficult and frustrating. There
were, however, substantial differences among members of the hearing-impaired group
in both performance and reactions to the test. These listeners basically fell into two
categories. Either they reacted much like the normal group complaining about the
difficulty of the task and obtaining results similar to the normal group or they made
many correct responses from the very beginning of the test, performed better
throughout the test than the other groups, and did not feel that the presentation was
particularly difficult or unusual.

In order to interpret these differences, subcategories of the normal-hearing group (Group 1) and the hearing-impaired group (Group 2) were made. The results were combined for low vs. high stress since those differences were generally not significant. The two groups were then divided up on the basis of best results (28 or more correct identifications for stops, Groups 1A and 2A) and worst results (Groups 1B and 2B). Figure 6 shows correct identification for these subcategories. The difference in stop responses between the best hearing-impaired group (2A) and the normal group as a whole (1) was highly significant p<0.003. The difference in word identification was also significant, p<0.05. This difference is, however, less convincing when the best hearing-impaired group is compared to the best normal group. The hearing-impaired group still performed better (34 correct vs. 30 correct for stops, 24 vs. 18 for words), but the differences were not significant, p>0.05.

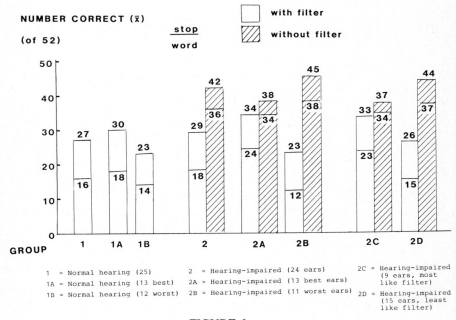

FIGURE 6

Mean number of correct identifications for stops and words for various group subcategories. (See text for subcategory criteria).

Since any group can be subcategorized using a best-results criterion, the hearing-impaired group was divided into two new categories using pure-tone audiogram configuration criteria. The categories were (Group 2C) those ears most closely resembling the filter function used in the test, i.e. severity of hearing loss increasing sharply at a drop-off frequency lower than 1500Hz and at least a -35dB threshold drop between 1000Hz and 2000Hz and a threshold of less than -50dB (HL) at 2000Hz; and (Group 2D) those ears which least resembled the filter function, i.e. either the slope was too flat or the drop-off frequency was greater than 1000Hz (see Figures 7 and 8 for example audiograms). Correlation between the best-ear group (2A) and the most-like-filter group (2C) was high with all the ears occuring in 2C also being represented in 2A. Identification results for these two groups, for both stops and words, were also very similar, as can be seen in Figure 6. Differences in identification for both stops and words between Group 2C (most-like-filter) and Group 1 (normals) were significant, $p<0.05$.

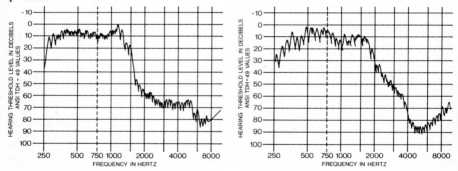

FIGURES 7 and 8

Example audiograms of a »most-like-filter» ear (left) and a »least-like-filter» ear (right).

A final point of interest when comparing the hearing-impaired subgroups concerns listener reactions to the non-filtered test version. In general, those listeners who performed best on the filtered version noted little or no difference between the filtered and non-filtered versions, while those listeners who performed worst on the filtered version performed best on the non-filtered version (Figure 6) and noted a considerable improvement in »clarity». There were, however, no significant differences which could be attributed to low or high stress. The normal listeners were not tested on the non-filtered version as an informal test indicated 100% correct identification.

4   DISCUSSION

4.1   Fo Movement and Stop Identification

The results of these tests provide a negative answer to the question of whether or not increased movement of Fo in the vowels adjoining a stop can aid hearing-impaired listeners in identifying stops. The same results apply to normal listeners using filtered speech. In fact, in all groups and on all tests, identification of both stops and words was slightly better when the vowels carried low-stress pitch movement, i.e. lower Fo and little absolute movement. An explanation for this could lie in the fact that a lower fundamental produces a tighter series of harmonics which could in turn supply more energy to the critical formant amplitude shifts in the transitions thereby enabling better identification. The improvement, however, can only be seen as highly marginal as the differences were not statistically significant.

It seems then that at least regarding filtered speech in Swedish and for hearing-impaired listeners, heightened Fo movement related to focus and sentence stress serves as a marker to direct the attention of the listener to the focussed word but does not intrinsically aid the perceptual mechanism in segmental resolution. It could be that the perception of Fo movement is integrated over a longer time interval than the perception of segments and, at least where global Fo movement is concerned, Fo movement perception is related to the pragmatic intentions of the speaker rather than to the phonemic content of the word in focus. If this is the case, then the perceptual mechanism could rely on increased intensity in the vowel and increased vowel duration during stress to aid in segmental resolution. During an informal listening session it was felt by several listeners that the high-stress stimuli sounded »thinner and weaker» than their low-stress counterparts. This could be due to the fact that the increased intensity normally associated with high stress was missing.

An aspect of production which could also contribute to a separation in perception of the two kinds of frequency movement dealt with here, i.e. Fo and formant frequency, is that of source. If perception of movement in the speech wave can be coupled to articulator movements as described by Fowler, Rubin, Reméz, & Turvey, (1980), then the separate nature of the sources, i.e. tongue and jaw movement to alter resonance and laryngeal movement to alter fundamental frequency, could be perceived as relating to these separate sources from a production standpoint and therefore be processed separately. Clearly, these kinds of production-perception inter actions and the processing of different kinds of movement need to be investigated further.

4.2   Compensation and Hearing Impaired Listeners

Perhaps the most interesting result of the experiment pertains to the difference in performance between the normal-hearing listeners and the hearing-impaired listeners, especially those whose audiograms best matched the filter. The greatest difference in performance can be attributed to the tendency for hearing- impaired listeners to choose /t/ instead of /p/ or /k/ while the normal listeners tended to choose /p/. As the frequency of /t/- words dominated in the test material, the hearing-impaired group naturally came out ahead. A possible explanation for this could lie in the fact that listeners with a hearing loss, being accustomed to hearing speech resembling the filtered stimuli, were able to distinguish between the presence or absence of /p/ (low-frequency burst and low-frequency F2 transitions) while the low frequency nature of the filtered stimuli sounded labial to those unaccustomed to speech sounding similar to the stimuli. This would also account for the difference among members of the hearing-impaired group. Basically, the closer the correspondence between filter and hearing, the better able the listener is to comprehend the sentence.

While a hearing loss cannot be described as a filter function in absolute terms, the correlation in this experiment between performance results, filter frequency and audiometric configura tion seems to indicate a certain performance predictability. Thus, if audiometric similarity is narrowly defined in terms of break frequency and slope, listeners tend to perform similarly when the filter function resembles the audiometric configuration. They even tend to perform better than listeners with normal hearing.

If we assume that those listeners with a hearing loss corresponding to the filter were able to discriminate between presence vs. absence of /p/, why then did they nearly always pick /t/ where the actual stimulus contained either /t/ or /k/? Were the better results simply a matter of chance, there being more /t/-words than /k/ or /p/-words in the test material? In a computer analysis of word frequency in Swedish newspaper material (Allén, 1972) the frequency of /t/-initial words used in the test was greater than /p,k/ in all but one case (Table 2). In the same material, t was also the most frequent letter of the six representing stops (Table 3). On the basis of this material, it could be tentatively conjectured that certain hearing-impaired listeners, when presented with semantically non-redundant speech, choose the most frequent or probable word from the lexicon which matches the incomplete phonetic signal. This could be done on the basis of the presence vs. absence of a low frequency burst and

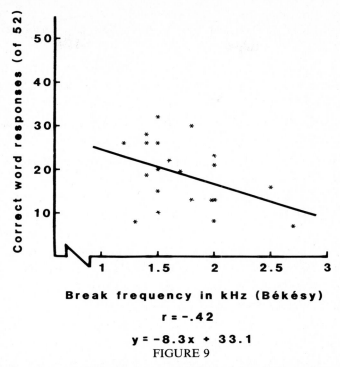

Break frequency in kHz (Békésy)

r = -.42

y = -8.3x + 33.1

FIGURE 9

Negative correlation between audiological break frequency and correct word response for the hearing-impaired group as a whole.

low frequency formant transitions which could then be restructured by the central processor as information concerning /p/ vs. /t/ or /k/. To separate /t/ from /k/, the listeners could make use of a frequency or probability strategy built up during the long period of time often associated with the progression of a noise- induced hearing loss. All listeners but one in the »most-like-filter» group were over 58 years of age, had very similar audiograms and performance, and had long histories of working in noisy environments. The one exception, 39 years of age, had of course a similar audiogram but did not perform nearly as well as the older listeners on the test.

An additional point of interest was that one listener with an asymmetrical loss performed better on the filtered stimuli test with his worse ear. This was noticed by the listener himself who expressed considerable surprise over it. His worse ear audiogram, however, fit the filter function almost exactly. His better ear loss began at around

TABLE 2

Frequency of target words in a study of newspaper material (Allén, 1972)

	T-	K-	B-	D-	G-
	TAL 200	KAL	BAL	DAL 15	GAL
PAR 427	TAR 1964	KAR	BAR		
	TUR 137	KUR	BUR	DUR	
	TÅR 10	KÅR 12	BÅR		GÅR
PÅG	TÅG 55		BÅG		
	TAM			DAM 137	GAM
	TOK 8	KOK	BOK 876		

2200Hz. This seems to indicate that he was processing auditory inputs from different ears in different ways. He had learned to compensate for the auditory periphery of his worse ear, but not for his better ear.

Finally the fact that persons with impaired hearing tended to choose words beginning with /t/ could have certain clinical implications. A greater awareness of compensation strategies both on the part of those using the stragegies and those who are often in contact with persons suffering from a hearing loss could be instrumental in improving the communication ability of a relatively large group of people.

Further work with perception, hearing loss, and compensation strategies could also provide us with interesting insights into speech perception as a whole. One area of interest involves the relationships between linguistic structure and speech cues such as intonation and rhythm. If mechanisms of compensation can be isolated among certain individuals, it might be possible to train others to use these mechanisms. Even normal listeners might be able to make use of such compensation when engaged in everyday speech in non-optimal, noisy environments.

TABLE 3

Frequency of letters representing target-word initial stops used in the test. (From Allén, 1972)

	ABSOLUTE	RELATIVE
t	456035	8.238
d	225548	4.084
k	170580	3.089
g	166999	3.024
p	86131	1.560
b	64902	1.175

5 CONCLUSIONS

The results of this study demonstrate that some hearing-impaired listeners can make use of intuition about linguistic structure combined whith a restructuring of auditory speech cues to enable them to compensate to a certain degree for a loss of important acoustic information. Normal listeners did not show this tendency when confronted with stimuli comprising a similar loss of acoustic information. The compensation meschanism used by the listeners seems to be a complex one probably developed over a period of several years involving a combination of stored linguistic knowledge and a restructured acoustic speech cue paradigm.

REFERENCES

Allén, S. (1972). *Tiotusen i topp*. Stockholm: Almqvist & Wiksell.

Cutler, A. (1976). Phoneme-monitoring reaction time as a function of preceding intonation contour. *Perception & Psychophysics, 20,* 55-60.

Fowler, C.A., Rubin, P., Remez, R., & Turvey, M. (1980). Implications for speech production of a general theory of action. In B. Butterworth (Ed.), *Language Production*. (pp. 373-420). London: Academic Press.

Fry, D.B.(1958). Experiments in the perception of stress. *Language and Speech, 1,* 126-152.

Gårding, E. (1967). *Internal juncture in Swedish*. Lund: C.W.K. Gleerup.

House, D. (1983). Perceptual interaction between Fo excursions and spectral cues. (Working papers 25:67-74). Department of Linguistics and Phonetics, Lund University.

Jackendoff, R.S. (1972). *Semantic interpretation in generative grammar*. Cambridge, Ma.: MIT Press.

Johansson, G. (1975). Visual motion perception. *Scientific American, 232* 6, 76-88.

Johnson, T.L., & Strange, W. (1982). Perceptual constancy of vowels in rapid speech. *Journal of the Acoustical Society of America, 72,* 1761-1770.

Lehiste, I. (1970). *Suprasegmentals*. Cambridge, Ma.: MIT Press.

Marslen-Wilson, W., & Tyler, L.K. (1980). The temporal structure of spoken language understanding. *Cognition, 8,* 1-71.

Pastore, R.E. (1981). Possible psychoacoustic factors in speech perception. In Eimas & Miller (Eds.), *Perspectives in the study of speech.* Hillsdale, N.J.: Erlbaum.

Picket, Revoile, & Danaher (1983). Speech-cue measures of impaired hearing. In Tobias & Schubert (Eds.), *Hearing research and theory 2.* New York: Academic Press.

Risberg, A., & Agelfors, E. (1978). On the identification of intonation contours by hearing impaired listeners. Quarterly Progress and Status Report of the Speech Transmission Laboratory (2/3: 51-61). Royal Institute of Technology, Stockholm.

Van de Grift Turek, S., Dorman, M.F., Franks, J.R., & Summerfield, Q. (1980). Identification of synthetic /bdg/ by hearing- impaired listeners under monotic and dichotic formant presentation. *Journal of the Acoustical Society of America, 67,* 1031-1039.

Communication and Handicap: Aspects of
Psychological Compensation and Technical Aids
E. Hjelmquist and L.-G. Nilsson (editors)
© Elsevier Science Publishers B.V. (North-Holland), 1986

IT MAKE SENSE: FORM, CONTENT AND USE OF INFORMATION

STUART AITKEN

Royal Blind School, Craigmillar Park, Edinburgh, Scotland and Department of Psychology, University of Edinburgh, Edinburgh, Scotland[*]

This paper considers the issues which could usefully be addressed in investigating communication. The problem space is set apart from the phenomenononological stance of an hypothetical child who is 'handicapped'. From her position, a number of fundamental questions are raised which, it is argued, should be our criteria for any research and intervention. These questions are distinguished arbitrarily within a division into the form, content and use of information. In the analysis presented, language or conventional communication in this child serves as a focus for examination of these issues. The clarification of these issues further raises serious implications for how Information Technology might be harnessed in the interests of the communicationally disabled.

1   INTRODUCTION

The history of Psychology has, with noticeable exceptions, been one in which a gulf existed between its theory and application. A sceptic might say that this gap has in recent years been narrowed artificially due to a demand at government level (that is,

---

[*]   I gratefully acknowledge the valuable discussion and criticism offered by Duncan H C Robb, Queen Margaret College, Edinburgh.

where the money comes from) for a greater congruence between the two. Therefore, researchers have responded by looking for their wallet under the streetlamp and channelled their energies into the applied field, mainly in the hope that by studying processes in an abnormal population, implications might thereby be offered for processes in the normal population. The ethics of this line of approach have been questioned by many, such as McGurk (1983). So too should the conceptual rationale be questioned. Otherwise we will remain in the area of the Psychology *of* handicap, rather than demonstrating what Psychology has to offer to disabled and impaired persons, leading in turn to the study of handicap which is more legitimately defined as incorporating society's attitudes to disablement. Some have pursued a middle ground in this in offering an evaluation of intervention strategies with a population defined narrowly by themselves. To carry this out, requests are typically made to people working with, for example, a sample of infants who are totally and congenitally blind aged up to about 12 months and who have no additional impairments. An additional bonus would be if they lived within travelling distance of the research centre. In my own case, somehow subjects were obtained and the research carried out while at the same time the persons providing the subjects pool would say »But what about X, who also has cerebral palsy, we are not sure if she is blind and will never have speech?« Implicit assumptions are that developing technologies (whether at the 'information' or at the hardware end) will come to the rescue of practice. This begs the question of *how* it will come to the rescue - necessitating an exposition of theory in its application. It is in this field that Psychology may have much to offer, as this paper hopes to demonstrate. In particular, it addresses issues raised in the area of communication, where it will be argued that communication might be usefully considered in a much wider sense to that which is normally generally investigated.

As a starting point, instead of beginning with technical aids or stimulus definitions or any other definitions offered by various specialisations, it may be worthwhile to adopt a phenomenonological account. Consider the issues raised for us today if we are 'Carol'. Assessed at 5 months as totally blind, a 9 months as partially-sighted, at 12 months as having no hearing loss, and at 30 months as hearing-impaired by conventional testing and with no speech. Additionally, mental handicap has been diagnosed. How does Carol find out about the world?

In trying to tackle this problem, there are many possible ways in which the questions which arise might be discussed. For the purpose of this presentation, a distinction has been made among the form, content and use of information. Although this distinction is made, it should not be seen as other than an arbitrary, although timeous, division, set up to allow the study of how material becomes meaningful to the organism. This particular distinction already exists in one form in a great deal of the more recent literature on language, wherein the pragmatic level at which analysis of types of utterances is represented by »use', syntactic level at which analysis of grammatical structure is represented by »form; and the semantic level where the 'meaning' of the utterance is represented by »content». In discussions on language development, such a trichotomy has been offered by Bloom (1978), for arguing that these different aspects of language interlock in the integration of form, content and use. In our present discussion, this distinction is to be seen as no more than a useful metaphor, a conceptual tool onto which arguments might be attached. It is not intended that focus should be placed upon the literal level. Nor should emphasis be placed upon any particular level. With this proviso in mind, we may turn to such an analysis.

2   FORM

For Carol, information picked up through one modality, that of vision, will be missing. How therefore can information about objects, events and the what goes with what in the world be realised? The variety of responses to this question is an illustration of how differing professional skills will have widely differing implications for intervention, not simply differing in practice but also in what could even be countenanced within their individual conceptual frameworks as being possible within an intervention setting. For Carol, information about the world will have to be obtained through modalities other than vision. Perception of objects, events and what goes with what can be observed in natural sensory substitution. In this case, free play is still given to the 'uncanny facial vision of the blind, obstacle sense and blind man's sense', wherein the implicit assumption (centering around the doctrine of specific nerve energies) is that if pressure is felt on the skin as a primary projection area, then that must be the locus of proximal stimulation. And yet, Dallenbach and his co-workers (Supa, Cotzin, & Dallenbach, 1944) showed several years ago that the basis of the percept of pressure was sound, with the ear acting as the modality detecting this information. There was no special 'skin sense' in the blind people, with obstacles being detected by patterns of sound changes by the ears. Greater problems are posed when we turn to artificial sensory substitute, wherein technical aids are provided, not as an extension to the specific modality by which information is normally detected (such as would be the case with telephone or radio for sound), but offering as an alternative to the normal modality.

The proposition of sensory substitution will be seen as widely different by, for instance, a neurophysiologist, an engineer, a neuroanatomist, a psychologist interested in development and a psychologist interested in sensory-specific correlates of perception. Let us take two of these, beginning with what a neuroanatomist would say. Recently, the impossibility of sensory substitution was brought to my attention when discussing with an anatomist the use of a vibrotactile stimulator for the deaf (Saunders, 1983). When informed that the locus of stimulation was the abdomen of the subject, our anatomist observed that, as there were no auditory nerves in the abdomen, such a device could not possibly transmit sound information. Such is the prognosis if one is to accept the tenets of a doctrine of specific nerve energies. The sensory-specific psychologist mentioned is no better off. De Valois and Marrocco (1973) work on cells in the visual cortex responding to angles, corners, etc., refutes the notion that information about angles and corners need not be transmitted through light and therefore have to be specific to the visual cortex, but could be provided through an alternative modality and have the same informational value for the organism. The analysis given by Morgan is useful here. He asks whether, given the same information about an object - say its distance, size, direction and texture - but where the information is provided through an alternative modality, and given the same responses to that information, would the organism be said to be able to see. Morgan would argue in the affirmative, or else »Psychology as a science is impossible» (Morgan, 1977).

It was perhaps fortunate that engineers, beginning with Alexander Graham Bell (Bell, 1900), did not consult with anatomists prior to designing substitution aids. Many sensory-impaired persons have been shown to be capable of using these substitution aids. In consideration of how Information Technology (IT) might make sense, it is argued in this paper that not only engineering, acoustics and physiology (to name but a few) but also psychology has much to offer in defining what form information should take in sensory substitution. The question may be formulated as to whether the organism has a 'perceptual emphasis or a learning emphasis', to borrow from Sherrick's terminology (Sherrick, 1982). The former would suggest that sensory prostheses should focus on the problem of reorganisation of encoding of information at the receptor site. The learning emphasis rests on the »adaptability of the nervous system» (Sherrick, 1982) so that any display of the information would eventually be usable through a process of learning. Provided the information bore a consistent relationship to events over time, the manner of provision of the information would be irrelevant. Through frequency and duration of exposure to a set of arbitrary events over time, the organism would come to detect a meaning in the stimulus material. Before turning to the evidence, it is worth considering what the learning emphasis would require to be already specified in the genetic code of the organism.

As Spelke (1979) has indicated, a detection of contingency relations among sensations to explain learning about events begs the question of how the event is perceived as stable in the first place. For this initial perception of an event, there must be present structures which allow; (1) an ability to discriminate which stimulus is which (invariants from other sets); (2) an ability to respond and discriminate this response from other possible responses; (3) an ability to detect relationships; (4) the presence of some sort of selection mechanism to discriminate within short intervals (Bower, 1982). In short, there has to be an array of perceptual structures and perceptual constraints on learning allowing detection of these invariant relationships in order that associations might be made between response and event. These would appear to be a logical requirement for a perceptual ground to be present against which associations might then be made.

An experiment was initiated in order to test directly the relative merits of the perceptual ground versus associationist accounts of what constitutes the form of information. The experiment, described in detail elsewhere (Aitken, 1983), used the perception of approach as a paradigm. Approach was specified in an evolutionarily-novel way using a particular sensory substitution device - the Sonicguide™ On a perceptual ground account, the stimulus material should have more informational value when presented in a form similar to that which is detected through the usual modality of transmission - in this case the form of the sound to the ears registering for the invariants of distance and size of the approaching object, invariants that are usually presented through vision. On the perceptual ground explanation, any tampering with that form should inhibit rapidity of use. If, however, learning is all that is involved, then the form of stimulation should be irrelevant, provided the stimulus array bears some consistent relationship over time with events in the world.

Due to ethical constraints, sighted infants tested in total darkness formed the sample, with 20 experimentally naive subjects aged 4 to 20 weeks being presented with sonar information about approach and withdrawal of an object. In the approach phase, object movement was specified by the distance cue - as the object approached the sonar aids, the pitch index lowered. This pitch change over time conforms to the change function over time of a visibly-specified object's expansion pattern on the retina of the eye. The form of the information on approach/withdrawal was therefore specified through sound in the same way as it would have been specified through light. Object withdrawal was given by the inverse of this higher-order time-change function. Two conditions were employed. Firstly, where the sonar aid, mounted at a distance from the subject but providing information through extension leads, signalled approach/withdrawal of an object sliding along a track and, simultaneously, a second object sliding along a separate track ended in gentle contact with the subject's face (see Figure 1).

This is the CONGRUENT condition, that is where echoic spatial information was consonant with the real world. The second, NON- CONGRUENT, condition was where sonic information on approach/ withdrawal of the object on Track 1 was the inverse of the object's movement along Track 2. In this case then, sonar information would signal withdrawal/approach while the event on the second track would specify approach/withdrawal. If, therefore, learning is all-important then there should be no difference between the two conditions. Association between the two events - sonar signalling approach then withdrawal (and vice- versa) - could be linked equally well with either withdrawal then approach or approach then withdrawal, of the object on the track which ends in contact with the infant. If, however, form of information is of importance then there should be a difference between conditions with the CONGRUENT condition eliciting greater discrimination than the NON- CONGRUENT condition. The response measure was head retraction as measured by a pressure pad attached through a tape adaptor to an oscilloscope.

Specific predictions were:

a. CONGRUENT - contact/contact greater than non-contact/non- contact (i.e. object coming to contact infant and sonar specifying approach gives greater response than object with drawal and sonar signalling withdrawal). This is the *control condition.*

b. NON-CONGRUENT - *form hypothesis* is that response greatest in non-contact/contact series (object receding, but sonar signalling approach). Learning hypothesis is that response greatest in C/NC series (object approach, but sonar

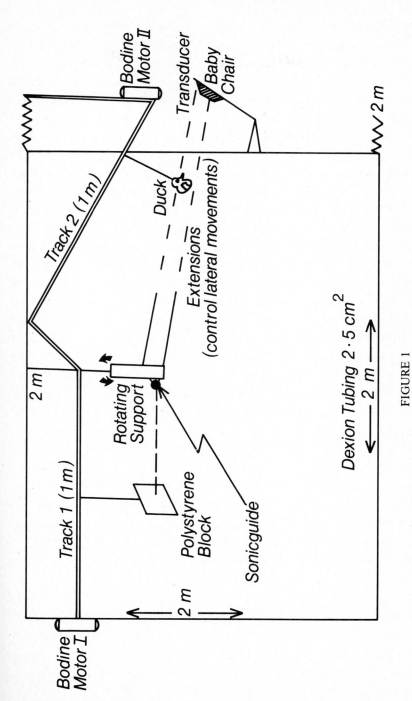

FIGURE 1

The experimental apparatus for the Study of the perception of approach.

specifying withdrawal). This is because the infant would have associated arbitrarily the signal over time as an object coming to him/her, it being irrelevant that signal form specified the opposite.

Results showed that in the three time intervals studied, covering the final 2 seconds of movement along the tracks, there was a continuous rise in pressure in the contact/contact presentations while as the object withdraw (NC/NC) the pressure reduced. Correlated t-tests performed on the Difference (or D) scores (Guilford, 1956) found $p<0.05$ for the Congruent, and $p<0.1$ for the Non-Congruent conditions. Although not reaching a level of statistical significance, the pattern of the non-congruent condition was in the direction of the pick-up of form, that is greatest head retraction was shown when the object *receded* from the infant but was signalled by the sonar aid as being in the *approach* phase. On further analysis of the data, there appeared to be an age difference in subject's responses where, in the Congruent condition, younger infants demonstrated head withdrawal more clearly than older infants. In the non-Congruent condition, however, the major contributors to form pick-up appears to be the older age-group, the younger infants showing little differences across the two types of presentation.

This apparent discrepancy was resolved when the change-over from one condition to the other was looked at in more detail. In the case of the older infants, it appeared that they continued to respond at the same level to the form change ignoring any change in the contingency of the signal with the event in the environment. With the younger infants, it appeared that they, too, at first picked-up the form of the stimulation but this could be altered by overlaying discrepant information. They continued to show head withdrawal more to the sonar specified approach than to actual approach but it appeared that the change in signal was a source of confusion. Because the young infant was exposed to this 'discrepant' information only briefly it served as a source of confusion. With the older infants, there was no confusing factor as this information was ignored and treated as a discrepant. These results are discussed in more detail elsewhere, particularly in their relevance to ontogenetic arguments (Aitken, 1981, 1983). For the purposes of the present discussion, it would appear that evolution has acted to provide us with perceptual structures which detect some form of stimulation more easily than others.

These results would suggest that close attention should be paid to the form of information presented to the organism. That form should retain the highest-order invariants of information presented to the modality usually transmitting the information. In a similar vein, Dodd (1983) has suggested that a phonological code might usefully be considered as being non-modality specific, a view supported by evidence showing that the deaf can pick up a phonological code from lip-read information (identifying rhymes, matching homophones, developing a spoken phonological system and converting lip-read words to graphemes). Lechelt (1983) too, has recently taken anisotropy out of the visual system and demonstrated a similar effect cutaneously in using the Optacon, device which translates print into tactile patterns (Bliss, Katcher, Rogers, & Shepard 1970). In Lechelt's experiment, subjects were poorer in reporting the orientation of a 'bar' when it was oriented obliquely than when oriented in either a vertical or horizontal position (Lechelt, 1983). Sherrick's cutaneous rabbit (Sherrick, 1982) is similar to the amodal nature of perception suggested by Michotte Tunnel and Compression Effects (Michotte, 1963).

For the stimulus to have the potential to become a maximal informational value to Carol, it must retain the highest-order properties of the stimulus array. By returning to the question of how Carol would use information, we hope to re-emphasise the consideration of a particular technical aid is not the issue. Similar arguments about form of information might equally have been made about the physical characteristics of the speech signal.

For IT to make sense, investigation should be made of the form information should take.

3   CONTENT

Recognising that content is inextricably linked with form, we can nevertheless, for present purposes, give consideration to issues which may fall within the domain of content. For Carol we must determine what information should be presented, through which modality it might be presented (this could also have been subsumed under 'form'), and how much information should be presented. (Furthermore, these three issues may be sensitive to the consequences of developmental change). Here focus is made on the issue of how much information should be presented. In this respect, there is again a noticeable division dependent upon the particular background of the researcher and/or interventionist.

3.1   How Much Information

Consideration of this is regarded almost universally as an information processing notion of quantity of information with the organism being more likely to be capable of coping with fewer bytes of information. In a developmental context, the view is generally taken that the younger the organism, the less bytes of information that can be processed. Therefore if one wishes to work with younger children, simpler stimuli are utilised thereafter working up to more complex stimuli. Naturally, simplicity and complexity are as defined by the researcher/interventionist. One researcher has stated explicitly that if it is too complex for the mature organism (the programmer) then it must be beyond the abilities of the young organism (Prazdy, 1980). However, it may well be that the provision of the correct form of information, that is a form which is constrained by the appropriate perceptual ground parameters as defined above, necessarily entails presentation of a greater *quantity* of information, where quantity is expressed in information processing terms. A associationist account is much more comfortable with an information processing approach, where frequency and duration of exposure allows for greater processing facility and capacity - through processes such as »chunking» for example. The results reported above should, however, caution against an account based solely upon association of events.

Again, two examples, which may help to illustrate the need to consider quantity of information in terms wider than simplicity of stimulus. One is taken from the artificial world of perception offered by technical aids, and the other from the natural world of language acquisition. In the field of language acquisition, several authors have shown how difficult it is, if not impossible, to attach any meaning to a paragraph spoken in an unfamiliar foreign language. And yet, when the same paragraph is embedded with meaning being additionally provided by context, then the meaning of the piece becomes clear. In doing so, however, the complexity of the stimulus was greater, there was additional information which should have had to have been processed within the same time frame. There was a greater quantity of information. This problem is not confined exclusively to that evolutionarily-familiar world of the non-sensorily-impaired. In the artificial perceptual world provided through sensory substitution aids (where novelty of information is defined in sensory- specific terms), the same problem is generated. The argument would be that if it is found that the organism does not show use of the information (or at the point of introduction when it is least familiar), then the engineering parameters of the signal mix should be modified in order to simplify the signal. The result is that an expensive piece of technology goes through an even more expensive filtering mechanism of buffers to produce a less complex signal.

With at least one device known to the author which underwent this process for these reasons, the net result was that of a set of information which could have been supplied by a device costing a few cents, and with virtually no running costs and no servicing costs.

It has become widely accepted as a lay-view that most information comes through the visual modality. People then feel they have to somehow quantify these amounts, arriving at the conclusion that 85%, or figures of that order, of information comes through the visual modality. The implication would then be that Carol only has available to her 15% of information about the world (that is, if we ignore her possible hearing loss). Such figures have then been used to justify numerous diverse positions - such as demands for early stimulation, inaccessibility to the acquisition of language and so on. By themselves, such figures are, however, meaningless.

It is quite likely that in the figure of 85% loss of information to the blind person, that a substantial proportion was in any case redundant. Redundancy in this view is where it is defined by the user of information. The organism may use different information at different ages, that is there are developmental issues which will dictate how much information can be meaningfully used at different ages. Just as information contents, in addressing how elements might be combined by the organism, cannot be isolated from informational structure, so too must content be closely interrelated with its use. In this we would concur with Bloom (1978). Having indicated that content must be considered from the standpoint of the organism for IT to make sense, we can turn now to the use of information.

4 USE

So far, there has been little stated explicitly about communication. It is in its use of information that an organism can be said to communicate. Consider firstly the contention by Watzlawick, Beavin, and Jackson (1983) that there is no such thing as a non- behavior and that therefore to not-communicate is a metalinguistic impossibility. For Carol, however, this is not a particularly helpful statement. Communication entails both information detected and information imparted. One-sided versions of this definition are to be found in many instances current in psychology, much of it based upon statement such as Stevens' (1950) definition of the »discriminating response of an organism to a stimulus«, ignoring as it does the parting of information.

There is a clear contribution to be made by Psychology in clarification of the issues centering on use of material. To reiterate, use cannot be considered separately from the form and content of information. Bottom-up approaches to design of sophisticated hardware/software of machinery/technology should not be divorced from how it will be used. Success under these circumstances will be achieved solely by trial-and-error or by chance. Consideration of use must take into account: (1) the definition of the population with whom work might be initiated; (2) the investigation of learning parameters necessary for uptake; (3) development of a program of evaluation; (4) indexing of the class of behaviors which would signify use.

4.1   Population

Ascription of the population with whom intervention/remediation would be carried out often differs depending upon whether it is the researcher or the interventionist who is carrying out the work. Most often there is an interesting split here between those who are oriented to research and those oriented to intervention. In the first case, emphasis is placed upon tight constraints upon the sample population. In the latter case, adoption of the particular intervention as a generic form applicable to too wide a group is the usual format. There are many case which could be cited but, as before, one will be taken from the technical aid world and another from that of the study of more conventionalised view of what constitutes communication. In the particular sensory substitute described earlier, results had suggested that some subject might be able to use the information optimally if worked with early in life (Aitken & Bower, 1982, 1983). In follow-up studies by others, these results were not entirely supported (e.g. Ferrell, 1981). Yet in several of the children reported in these studies, it would have been surprising had the subjects shown any use of the aid. This came down to a definition of blindness. As Goldstein (1980) has suggested, the biggest cause of blindness in the world is in its definition. There is a large range of functional information which can be available in the range between total blindness (such as would be with anophthalmia) and that of measurable acuity. That is subjects for whom a definition of total blindness is given, may well have a range of functionally useful vision. It is worth noting that neonates are, by most definitions, legally blind. However, they have vision sufficient to sustain reaching (directed in both distance and direction); to allow following of a moving object; to index the approach of an object and whether that approach is on a hit-path or a miss-path; and to allow imitation of certain facial gestures (Meltzhoff & Borton, 1980), and something requiring a degree of pattern vision. The sensory aid described earlier would not provide as much information (in terms of resolving power) as this. Yet subjects were discussed, in the later studies, in whom there was measurable visual acuity, that is they already had more informational content through vision than was being provided through the sensory aid. It is not surprising that the evolutionarily-familiar modality would be preferred to its use, since it was capable of a greater resolution of information in any case. The consequence would then be that the technical aid provided no additional information - instead providing a comparative skeleton of the visual world. Without ascertainment of the sub-groups which might benefit from intervention, the pitfall is present of taking on board the most recent piece of technological hardware/software.

The same criticism may be made of many infant stimulation programs of remediation, such as those offered by Portage, EDY systems. The assumption is that they are applicable generically to any population, disabled or delayed in a developmental sense. But consider a child who does not reach to an object. Is it because of a perceptual, a motor-execution problem, or a perceptual-motor problem? The basis of the deficit should have widely different consequences for intervention. Therefore generic approaches concentrating at the level of the overt behavior may be failing with many children. This is not a remote problem, examples of cerebral-palsied visually-impaired children are becoming more common in many industrialised countries. Good diagnostics in psychological terms is of the utmost importance. For IT to make sense, it must be known *for whom* it is to make sense.

4.2   Assessment of Carol

Assessment of Carol was representative of the problems attendant with most methods of assessment of vision in young children who are visually-impaired, as well as being representative of the problems in working with a wider age-range of children who are visually-impaired and have additional disabilities. In a current survey of visually-impaired pre-school and school-age children in Scotland, it was found that 40% of those under 12 months were referred for eye tests by their parents, in other words paediatric examination had failed to indicate a visual impairment. One major reason for this finding may be that young infants show a high degree of intersensory co-ordination - they orient visually to auditorily presented stimuli. This behavior later drops out (Bower, 1979), only to be re-instated in the sighted infant, but not with the blind child - they later gain nothing from centralising a stimulus visually. The blind child loses out both ways in assessment, firstly in being diagnosed wrongly as sighted (a false positive), and subsequently as being diagnosed as deaf (a false negative) as well as blind. It is of further interest that this child's deafness was diagnosed at around a 60dB loss. In the child's home, conversations generally took place at up to 60dB, the television was on constantly, a source of irrelevant material. Conversations went on around her - they were not communicational, that is they may not have had informational relevance for Carol. In short, it is quite possible that this child had learned not to »listen» to sounds in that loudness range. This will be returned to later in consideration of learning issues, for the present it is noteworthy in a further context. It concerns selection criteria for populations.

The literature is abundant with examples of how this approach underlies a circularity of argument on definition of impairment. Elstner (1983) has indicated that children in one kindergarten (KG I) demonstrated different types of errors in language, articulatory, from those in KG II, wherein children demonstrated structural errors. He accounted for this difference by the fact that there were many more multiply-handicapped children in KG II. It would appear however, to be unsurprising that there was a great deal of delay/impairment in the multiply-impaired. This is because language is so wrapped up in the assessment measures employed. The argument goes something like »Look only at the blind singly handicapped child, the multiple-impaired requires a different categorisation. How do we know that the presence of additional impairments did not have as an underlying causation the disability of blindness concomitant with poor/no intervention? We know this because there are blind children who are singly handicapped and who do not have language difficulties». There are, however, equally plausible interpretations, not predicated upon this circular argument. There may be many cases (it is not argued that this would be so in all cases) of multiply-impaired blind children who have as the primary cause of these impairments (delayed speech, motor control, socialisation and so on) the presence of a severe visual impairment. Placing these children on such a dimension would then reflect a continuity of disability as opposed to a categorically different group. In essence, this may help to undercut the ethical dilemma suggested by McGurk (1983) and referred to in the introduction to this paper.

A hesitation is apparent in adoption of the term »assessment», since it is all too often separated from any consideration of intervention. Weddell (1985) among others, has argued that assessment and intervention should be more closely linked. To form an assessment, a further level of abstraction from the specific one under investigation is here suggested. In our example, perhaps Carol has impaired speech production as opposed to being language-impaired. This distinction, if valid, would have important consequences for intervention. How this inter- vention might be carried out requires a familiarity first with the learning parameters involved in an analysis of communication.

4.3   Learning

If we look to Steven's definition of communication given earlier as the »discriminating response of an organism to a stimulus», then this indeed is the intuitive (but with a powerful implicit theoretical premise) view of learning adopted by many working within the intervention/remediation of communication. It is the domain of learning theory adopted by speech therapists, physiotherapists, by most of those involved with application of intervention »programs», by engineers in designing technology, by the manufacturers of machines which are designed to »stimulate the child».

It was also for long at the root of much of the work on infancy which attempted to determine whether, and at which point in development, infants could be said to be capable of learning.

It might, therefore, be useful to consider briefly what such studies found. In these studies, experimenters would typically present coloured lights, ringing bells, loud music and other interesting stimulus events as reinforcement to subjects (interesting, that is, as defined by the experimenter) (e.g. Watson, 1966). What was ignored was that it seemed that the infant was not particularly interested in the event, she was much more interested in the control she could have over the stimulus event. That is, the infant was attempting to detect and influence the relationship between a response and its outcome. Here, form and content of the event are seen to be inextricably linked with the organism's use of its detection, awareness and utilisation of contingencies between response and outcome.

The implication drawn is that communication occurs when organisms detect and utilise contingencies in information about their world. It is the solving of these contingencies which serves as motivator. For such as the blind, one modality is not available for detection of contingencies. But there would be no reason why this could not be offered where it is predicated upon an alternative, but equally valid, system to that of the visual modality.

For the sighted, learning language, information (that is, material that is meaningful as defined by the user) on contingency detected is represented widely through vision - objects causing others to move; facial expressions congruent with sounds and others are all available. Many of these sources of information are not available to the sensorily-impaired. Crucially, however, on a contingency analysis there is no necessity for the contingency to be specified by vision. Contingencies about the world are still available. For Carol, how might we optimise the affordance of contingencies?

4.4   From Contingency to Conventional Communication

A first language might be seen as conveying intentionality between communicants. For example, McShane (1980) has offered such an analysis where communication is defined within a sphere of intentionality, with intentionality leading to conventional language. In his account, he shows how a Gricean theory of meaning (Grice, 1957), formulated in terms of utterances (statements and imperatives) might lead to intentional communication, this in turn leading to conventional communication. This paper argues, however, that such an approach to intentionality can be extended beyond the realm of speech-acts (Searle, 1969). Instead it is operating as an antecedent at a more abstract level than this, in which intentionality is dependent upon the detection, awareness and utilisation of contingencies between events. In this view then, there is nothing special about conventional communication, i.e. language. Instead, it is simply a specified or differentiated form of use of information. Intentionality of shared meaning would be but one specification of contingency control.

If this account is adopted, then there follows a radically different set of questions to consider in work on research/intervention. It is proposed to consider a few of these. Lest it be thought that a sledgehammer is being used to crack a nut, it may be worthwhile to re-focus by returning to Carol. What does this reformulation have to offer her? If a shared meaning system develops from intentionality deriving from material gaining the status of information from its meaning for the organism, then a shared meaning system might be obtained through an alternative modality. In current accounts of language acquisition, communication is deemed to exist in the sighted infant prior to conventionalised communication. These are variously termed linguistic precursors, antecedents or prerequisites (see Sugarman, 1983, for a distinction of these terms). A great deal has been cited by authors of the essentials for language acquisition of deictic gaze, pointing, eye contact, shared reference, and turn-taking (Bruner, 1975). Consideration is then given as to how these develop and how children come to use these pre-linguistic skills. The arguments then proceeds that because of the inaccessibility of these precursors to the blind, then study of them as a sub-population will give information on the processes of language acquisition in the normal child. But if these so-called »precursors of language« in the sighted are, as this paper would argue, but one specific mode of a more abstract intentionality - via the contingency detection and utilisation discussed above - then that particular mode of communication could be regarded as only one of other possible modes within a core of intentionality in communication. If so, then it would follow that the use of one of these other possible avenues could be explored in intervention. Language, by this analysis, assumed that status of being merely a more specific form of communication added on to that core.

On this view, not only would it be possible for Carol to be 'given' a signing system as a set of precursors, onto which language as conventional communication would be added as a more differentiated system. This view would go beyond this and assume in the first place that a blind child (the argument could be extended to other disabilities) should be afforded the opportunity of an alternative set of precursors through the tactile modality. 'Sign' language could be offered as that set of precursors. Communication at a more abstract level would not be altered, communication as to shared meaning would be possible. The avenue of manual 'signing' would be an alternative means of production of a set of precursors.

It may be argued that this arbitrary system would be too private, existing as it would between mother/father/close family and infant/child. To this it might be countered (as McShane, 1980 pointed out) that the set of gestures so often referred to as being essential to normal language acquisition is itself no more than a set of private gestures which has become culturally conventionalised, where culture is regarded in the sense of cultural evolution, as opposed to cross-cultural considerations. Others may argue that it would not work as the set of gestures - pointing etc - is biologically determined. If so, one could counter why then should the blind child never use them. Such considerations of biological determinism are widely held in the notion of a sensory impairment being a biological handicap, e.g. Elstner espouses this view (Elstner, 1983). But this is only true at the surface level, that is, for the aetiology of the disability. In a sensory impairment, however, we are encountering what is in fact an environmental disability - that which is lost being one or more modalities of input of information about the world. As has been seen earlier, this »form» need not be regarded as qualitatively different from other information detected through other modalities, and would therefore potentially be available.

A second area that would have to be reconsidered in this formulation is exemplified by study of the so-called 'empty verbalisms' of the blind. On the present analysis, this term itself would be devoid of meaning. When see/look terms are functional referents within an intentional framework they have no sensory-specific correlate of necessity. Instead they are used in the functionally relevant sense of 'orient to', 'attend to' (or, in colloquial Scots, 'goodbye'). On this basis, one would hypothesise that it is only once the informational content of that particular modality has been superseded, that the sensory- specific nature of the meaning would be lost. It is not an absence of information due to categorical discontinuities, but an absence of more specific information within a continuity of information. There might then be some interesting experiments that might be conducted in an attempt to determine whether the same word is being represented but at a greater level of specificity of meaning. As our analysis began with observation of one child with whom intervention was being conducted, it is perhaps not surprising that the reformulation offered here should have most implications for her.

If one considers that efforts should concentrate on contingency detection and awareness, then communication intervention has to concentrate on a wholly different set of tasks and questions to consider. Before discussing future priorities within such a framework, consideration should be given to one major caveat. If one is to encourage a pre-verbal communicational system, will this in any way militate against the later acquisition of speech? It would seem from the results of Kiernan, Jordan, and Saunders (1978) and Walker (1982) that such a possibility is not supported. Against such a view, we would also argue that, if it were true, there would be no evolutionary reason for the natural pre-verbal communication skills, referred to by many, to have developed as precursors of language acquisition, if they would have in some way interfered with true language (that is, conventional views of what constitutes language). To take an example, there is no prior reason why, in a pointing gesture, it should be taken to refer to an »out-there» as opposed to »attend to my finger». If one adopts a biologically deterministic view that it arose to serve the purpose of shared meaning, then this assumes that shared meaning was something which existed prior to the arrival of this gesture; one might well ask therefore what the first gesture was predicated upon if it involved shared meaning. Teleological arguments of this nature serve no useful purpose.

In any case, aside from this conceptual argument, some empirical support for the notion that signing would not lead to militate against later acquisition of speech may be marshalled. It comes from the results of a signing program used in the Royal Blind School of Edinburgh currently being conducted with a group of multiply-impaired blind children (recalling that such a definition is problematic and worthy of reconsideration). For some of these children and for Carol herself, with whom work has only just been initiated, expressive speech was found to emerge as a side effect of a signing program. This speech-freeing of signing has been noted in the adult literature on dyspraxia in remediation of stroke victims (Dean, 1985). Taken together, these three strands of evidence - from previous though sparse literature, theoretical rationale and empirical results of present work - would suggest that the possibility, of gestures adversely affecting later speech acquisition, is remote.

Given that in communicational exchanges, the child's repertoire includes a range of behaviours - for examples, gestural - then it would be possible to offer an alternative, but equally valid, medium for detection and awareness of contingencies. Having stated that the context of information is as defined by the organism in its use, it would then be possible through signing to present a shared meaning which would allow the sensory-impaired child to understand that it can communicate.

In understanding that it can communicate, it would also begin to afford the understanding of what it is not communicating. Perhaps this would be a motivation to further specification of routines for communication - the best example of a more specific mode of communication being conventional language.

5   CONCLUSION

If importance is attached not just to the stimulus, but to how the subject effects control over contingencies in the world, then we are forced to adopt a different set of criteria to investigate in our intervention/remediation protocols. In this light consideration would have to be given to latency of onset of stimulus, duration, level of activity required, response-event contingencies. In short, we have to return to form and content of information. If learning occurs within the constraints of a perceptual-ground, then criteria for investigation and intervention must be couched within an enquiry of all three of these interlinked criteria - form, content and use.

On this view technical aids may have a very different role to play in the work on communicationally-disabled or delayed. This would be reflected in their mode of intervention, in training strategies adopted, form of information presented, the learning parameters manipulated. Consider the emphasis, for instance, placed in this paper upon the importance afforded to control of information. If control is of importance in obtaining information about events that is meaningful (recalling that on our analysis »information» that is not meaningful to the *organisms* is not information), then it may well be that affordance of the opportunity to control information is more important than the fact that this affordance would have the adverse effect (in an information processing sense) of providing more bytes of information per unit of time. In other words, a straightforward information processing view might well suggest that this affordance of an opportunity to control should not be provided. A clear example of this would be in the case of Carol - the material impinging on her sense modalities does not offer the same degree of control afforded to the sighted child who has available the options of gaze aversion, eye movements, head movements. In provision of an aid working by sensory substitution, one provides extra material to be detected by an alternative modality, in other words it might be considered to pose an extra load on the cognitive system in one view of what constitutes information. One option open to use in order to reduce that cognitive load would be to cut down on the information, but in doing so this may well obviate the possibility of the subject's exercising control over information. Therefore, one's view of the meaning of information will have profound influence on the presentation of the stimulus array to the organism.

Statements such as one made that progress in Information Technology is happening so quickly that there is simply no time to evaluate new technology, techniques and methodologies abound. In their framework, attention is paid to Input/Output devices, compatible hardware; evaluation of software packages for spatial deficits; introduction to alternative learning environments. In attempts to use the computer as a window on to the capacities of the communicationally-disabled, it is not surprising that a great deal of the extant software and hardware available within an intervention/remediation is universally castigated by those trying to use it. It is hoped that this paper will encourage an optimism for the future, in consideration of communication for Carol.

FOOTNOTE

The term Sonicguide™ refers to the Sonicguide, manufactured under trademark by Wormald Vigilant.

REFERENCES

Aitken, S. (1981). Differentiation theory: intersensory substitution and the use of the Sonicguide. Unpub PhD Thesis, Univ. of Edinburgh, Scotland.

Aitken, S. (1983). Infant response to amodal information on approach. Proceedings of Society for Research in Child Development, April, 1983.

Aitken, S., & Bower, T.G.R. (1982). Intersensory substitution in the blind. *Journal of Experimental Child Psychology, 33,* 309-323.

Aitken.;, S., & Bower, T.G.R. (1983). Developmental aspects of sensory substitution. *International Journal of Neurosciences, 19,* 13-20

Bell, A.G. (1900). Giving eyes to the ears of the blind. Dictated at Washington DC, April 11, 1900. Reported in Beinn Bhreagh Recorder April 26, 1910.

Bliss, J.C., Katcher, M.H., Rogers, C.H., & Shepard R.P. (1970). Optical-to-tactile image conversion for the blind. In IEEE Trans Man-Machine Syst. MMS-11, 58-64.

Bloom, L. (1978). Form, content and use in language development. In J.F. Kavanagh & W. Strange (Eds.), *Speech and language in the laboratory, school and clinic.* Cambridge: MIT.

Bower, T.G.R. (1979). *Human development.* San Francisco: Freeman.

Bower, T.G.R. (1982). *Development in infancy* (Second Edition). San Francisco: Freeman.

Bruner, J. (1975). The ontogenesis of speech acts. *Journal of Child Language, 2,* 1-19.

Dean,. E. (1985). Personal communication.

De Valois, R.L. & Marrocco, R.T. (1973). Single cell analysis of sativation discrimination in the macaque. *Vision Research, 13,* 701-11.

Dodd, B. (1983). The visual and auditory modalities in phonological acquisition. In A. E. Mills (Ed.), *Language acquisition in the blind child.* London: Croomhelm.

Elstner, (1983). Abnormalities in the verbal communication of blind children. In A.E. Mills (Ed.), *Language acquisition in the blind child.* London: Croomhelm.

Ferrell, K.A. (1980). Can infants use the Sonicguide? Two years experience of Project VIEW! *Journal of Visual impairment and Blindness, 74,* 209-220.

Goldstein, H. (1980). *The demography of blindness throughout the world*. American Foundation for the Blind: New York.

Grice, P. (1957). Meaning. *Philosophical Review, 66,* 377-388

Guilford, J.P. (1956). *Fundamental statistics in psychology and education*. New York: McGraw-Hill.

Kiernan, C., Jordan, R., & Saunders, C. (1978). *Starting off*. London: Souvenir Press.

Lechelt. G. (1983). Anisotropy with the Optacon. Paper read at University of Alberta, Edmonton.

McGurk, H. (1983). Effectance motivation and the development of communicative competence in blind and sighted children. In A.E. Mills (Ed.), *Language acquisition in the blind child*. London: Croomhelm.

McShane, J. (1980). *Learning to talk*. London: Cambridge University Press.

Meltzoff, A.N., & Borton, R.W. (1980). Intermodal matching of human neonates. *Nature 282* (5737), 403-404.

Michotte, A. (1963). *The perception of causality*. New York: Basic Books.

Morgan, M. (1977). *The Molyneaux question*. London: Cambridge University Press.

Prazdny, S. (1980). A computational study of a period of infant object-concept development. *Perception, 9,* 125-150.

Searle, J. (1969). *Speech acts*. London: Cambridge University Press.

Spelke, E. S. (1979). Exploring audible and visible events in infancy. In A.D. Pick (Ed.), *Tribute to E.J. Gibson*. Hillsdale, N.J.: Lawrence Erlbaum.

Stevens, S. S. (1950). *Handbook of experimental psychology*. New York: Wiley.

Sugarman, S. (1983). Empirical v logical issues in transition from pre-linguistic to linguistic communication. In R.M. Golinkoff (Ed.), *The transition from prelinguistic to linguistic communication.* Hillsdale, N.J.: Erlbaum.

Supa, M., Cotzin, M., & Dallenbach, K.M. (1944). Facial vision: the perception of obstacles by the blind. *American Journal of Psychology, 57,* 133-138.

Walker, M. (1982). What is the Makaton Vocabulary. In M. Peter & R. Barnes (Eds.), *Signs, symbols and schools,* Chester: NCSE.

Watson, J. C.(1966). Perception of object orientation in infants. *Merrill-Palmer Quarterly, 12,* 73-94.

Watzlawick, P., Beavin, J., & Jackson, D.(1980). The impossibility of not communicating. In J. Korner & J. Hawthorn (Eds.), *Communication studies.* London: Arnold.

Weddell, K. (1985). Future research directions for children with special educational needs. *British Journal of Special Education, 12,* Research Supplement 2.

Communication and Handicap: Aspects of
Psychological Compensation and Technical Aids
E. Hjelmquist and L.-G. Nilsson (editors)
© Elsevier Science Publishers B.V. (North-Holland), 1986

85

COMPENSATION AS SKILL

KJELL OHLSSON

Department of Technical Psychology, Luleå University of Technology, Luleå, Sweden[*]

In this chapter, the concept of compensation of sensory loss will be briefly discussed. Different types of compensation resulting in a cognitive restructuring of information will be examplified. A compensatory matrix will be introduced as an analytical tool for different compensatory phenomena. Furthermore, it is argued that compensation in a deeper psychological sense should be regarded as a skill, rather than an extended utilization of intact modalities. Data from an experiment on blind chessplayers is presented as support for this view. Half of the subjects were novices. In total 24 subjects participated, assigned to six subgroups. Congenitally blind subjects performed very well on a tactile matching task in comparison with adventitiously blind or blindfolded sighted subjects, provided that they possessed a substantial knowledge of chess. In the case of naive subjects, almost contradictory results were obtained, implying that blindfolded subjects outperformed blind subjects.

The accomplishment of the present study was supported by a grant (No. F 507/85 from The Swedish Council for Research in the Humanities and Social Sciences and a grant (No. 85/145:3) from The Swedish Council for Planning and Coordination of Research. The author is much indebted to research assistant Jan Skog for his enthusiastic work with the recruiting of blind subjects.

1   INTRODUCTION

1.1   Theoretical Underpinnings

A review of the literature on visually and auditory handicaps revealed that the concept of compensation is used in a rather sloppy way. Considering the miscellaneous research approaches and a plethora of laboratory tasks at different functional levels, it is not surprising to foresee the difficulties to reach a consensus about compensation. One conclusion drawn from the literature is that there is no simple explanation of compensation. For instance, compensation may be analysed in terms of discriminative learning, focused attention, functional substitution, communicative facilities and so forth. Despite all the pros and cons, the concept of compensation seems to survive all paradigm shifts in psychology (cf. Warren, 1978).

A broad approach to compensation is proposed in the present chapter. Frequently, the extended utilization of intact modalities is considered as compensation for sensory loss. In my opinion, this is hardly a case of true compensation, which is also indicated by ambiguous and contradictory results of experimental handicap research. The fact that a visually or auditorily handicapped person depends on one modality more than ever before, or more than normally hearing or sighted persons, does not unequivocally imply that a reliable compensation has taken place. In this chapter, I will argue that compensation should be regarded as a special *skill* rather than a frequent use of »unharmed» modalities. I commence this exposition of the central topic of this paper by introducing a matrix demonstrating two basic forms of information processing and a few instances of compensation in Figure 1.

Firstly, I maintain the distinction between *modality specific processing and a more central processing*. There are several reasons for preserving this distinction within handicap research. For instance, Posner (1967) demonstrated that retention of visual information is aided more by the presence of central processing capacity, while kinesthetic information is less so. From our own laboratory we also know that the modality specific processing of auditorily and visually presented verbal information is at great variance during different experimental conditions (Nilsson, Ohlsson, & Rönnberg, 1977, 1980; Rönnberg & Ohlsson, 1980; Rönnberg, Nilsson, & Ohlsson, 1982). One long-term aim of handicap research would be a systematic investigation of processing of modality-specific information as a function of kind and degree of the

BASIC FORMS OF INFORMATION PROCESSING

	Modality specific	Central
Automatized compensation		
Didactic compensation		
Technical compensation		
Intact mod. more used		
Intact mod. less used		

(TYPES OF COMPENSATION)

FIGURE 1

Compensatory Matrix as a tool for analyzing the relationship between two basic forms of information processing and types of compensation for a given sensory handicap.

sensory handicap. Secondly, there is a number of types of compensation which might be more or less relevant or dominating in functional communication situations.

For instance, in many cases a sensory loss implies that an *automatic* improvement of information processing has taken place without any prior practising or external support. This kind of compensation may involve primarily a qualitatively different information processing. Of course, this could reflect biological and adaptive mechanisms in general, and certainly developmental effects in infants, but a more plausible and vital explanation is that behind these »spontaneous» forms of compensation there are probably thousands of hours of arduous practising in colloquial situations. At first glance, this is a harmless, albeit a non- trivial explanation in a broader context. For instance, a commonly presumed superior music ability of the blind falls into this category of compensation (cf. Pitman, 1965).

Another form of compensation takes place when formal education is applied to rehabilitation of a sensory handicap. This could be called *didactic compensation* which may involve a general sharpening of the senses, an efficient utilization of residual capacities, a systematic exploration of new strategies based on both scientific and practical knowledge and so forth.

A third form of compensation is *technological compensation,* whereby perceptual and cognitive functions are manipulated by means of various technological aids. Many new possibilities for information pick-up, transmission, and generation, have emerged with the growing computer technology, which has benefitted various groups of handicapped. However, our standpoint is that before the manufacturing of hardware components of handicap devices takes place, it is urgent to examine other forms of »self-determined» compensation and of course individual's interaction with or via a particular device. This is especially important nowadays, as the vast majority of technical aids for sensory handicapped is considered as spin-off effects from space research programmes and other high-tech industries. Another aspect of technological compensation of great importance encompasses the development of guidelines, manuals and appropriate training programmes, which is usually a neglected field among technicians. Hardly any progress has been made, irrespective of technical standard, if a proper introduction to a new device is missing. Empirically, this has been the case in the development of too many devices during the last decade. For instance, two recently conducted surveys concerning blind subjects' interaction with a computer-attached text-to-speech converter and a radio-transmitted »speaking newspaper» respectively, confirms this statement. In both surveys the subjects who were thoroughly acquainted with, and allowed ample time for guided testing of possible facilities, were more frequent users and gave more favourable ratings of the new device than the subjects who were less well acquainted.

As I stated initially, the fourth type of compensation is not really a matter of true compensation. This is the case when intact modalities are more frequently used, without any substantial improvement of either modality specific or central processing. However, the possibilities of qualitatively different patterns of information processing makes this type of compensation potentially interesting from a communicative point of view. Pertinent to this issue is a reminder of the controversy between Vygotsky and Piaget about a general intellectual handicap as a consequence of a sensory loss (see, Furth, 1966).

The remaining type of compensation, when intact modalities are less frequently used, is in many respects a peculiar way of compensation that is occasionally described in the literature. In some cases, a partially handicapped person may be stuck with a handicap to the extent whereby all compensatory behaviours are directed to the damaged modality,. This reliance on a less functional communication channel is sometimes regarded as an obstacle for an efficient utilization of intact modalities (e.g. Eaves & Klonoff, 1970).

A good portion of overlap between different types of compensation seems inevitable. The »compensatory matrix» presented here is not exhaustive in any sense, but I consider it as a promising point of departure for research on compensatory behaviour and its effect on information processing. The multiplicity of scientific approaches to communication and handicap increases the need for an integration of ordinary results as well as more conspicuous ones. One research strategy from the large volume of existing research is to take different types of compensation as a starting point for research focused on human information processing. A second research strategy with its offspring in the information processing tradition, is to take the information processing per se or disturbances in postulated processes and mechanisms as a starting point for research into different compensatory behaviours. A third strategy which originated from communication research may be focused on different handicap groups and their ability to compensate for information loss. A fourth strategy is to hold onto adaptive mechanisms in a broader context in various handicap populations. Finally, a more ecological approach, constituting a synthesis between the strategies presented above, is proposed here. The emphasis would be on interactive aspects of communication and handicap, with special attention given to cognitive components of this interaction. To pursue this proposal as well as to strive for the accumulation of strict arguments for the compensatory matrix would stray too far from the main topic of the present chapter. Nevertheless, I still find it convenient to use the compensatory matrix as a general framework, and the proposed research strategy as support for arguments in favour of the notion of compensation as skill.

From the literature it can be concluded that the acquisition of a skill for any communicative behaviour usually takes hundreds or even thousands of hours. For instance, Marmolin, Nilsson and Smedshammar (1979) demonstrated that this holds true for the mastering of the Optacon. Certainly this holds true also for chess-communication, whereby the number of possible moves and patterns probably exceeds the number of words that could be said. On the other hand, we also know from our own laboratory that listening to synthesized speech demands a minimum of training.

Evidently the compatibility between natural and synthesized speech is fairly good. With few exceptions, people are rather skilful in the decoding of natural speech. It may be argued that the mastering of a speech synthesizer will certainly change the information processing of a blind person interacting with the environment and, accordingly, the use of the concept of skill seems appropriate. This leads unequivocally to my next point. Irrespective of the type of compensation, the result will be a cognitive restructuring of information. In that sense it might be appropriate to use *cognitive compensation* as a master term for a large number of compensatory phenomena. As previously indicated, there are both situational demands and types of handicaps influencing the opportunity for compensation. Thus, training does not always imply compensation. For instance, Berlá (1981) demonstrated that older blind subjects, when training scanning of a tactile display, failed in comparison with younger blind subjects. Bartley (1953) also demonstrated that blindness may result in a poor tactile discriminability. It has been known for a long time that early auditory deprivation might negatively affect visual information processing (e.g., Sterritt, Camp, & Lipman, 1966).

This seems to be especially true when complex motor activities are required. The list of examples might be sufficient for a demonstration of the phenomenon. The purpose of the compensatory matrix was to use it as an incentive for a discussion of potential outcomes related to various degrees of handicap and to specific situational demands. However, this is the objective of a more ambitious long-term project. I am now satisfied with the presentation of *one* example of cognitive compensation via systematic training.

The experiment to be presented below was conducted on semi-professional chessplayers or classplayers, including the world champion in chess for the blind. The experimental set-up is shown in Figure 2.

The subjects' task was to search for colours, values and positions of pieces on a chessboard (the search-board) for periods of two or four minutes. From a second board (the piece-board), the subjects had to pick up pieces selectively, which they matched on a third board (the matching-board) according to their memories of the initial configuration. They were instructed to work as fast and accurately as possible. The whole session was videotaped. Eight trials were randomized and varied with respect to information load. Thus, four of the configurations were chosen from the end of classical games and characterized accordingly as possessing a low degree of information load. Four configurations representing a high degree of information load were chosen from the middle parts of classical games. In fact, in the first case there

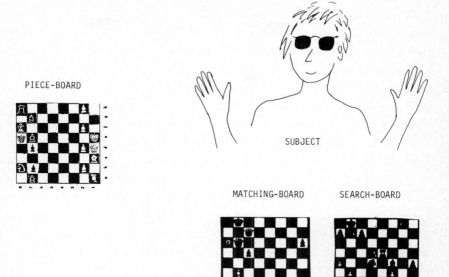

PIECE-BOARD

SUBJECT

MATCHING-BOARD   SEARCH-BOARD

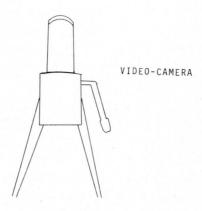

VIDEO-CAMERA

FIGURE 2

Experimental set-up.

were nine pieces and in the second, 17 pieces. Prior to the experiment, the subjects were told to study board No. 1 for a certain configuration and, simultaneously, match this on a matching board, as fast as possible, although the inspection time was not limited. After the experiment, they were given a compatible task. For this task also, they were not supposed to rely on memory but rather on tactile sensitivity. Six subgroups participated in this experiment. The dark symbols represent skilled chessplayers which matched according to their points on the national ranking lists. The mean ranks was about 1600. The signs used in the figures below were as follows: The black triangle represents skilled sighted subjects who were blindfolded. The black circle represents skilled subjects with an acquired blindness, whereas the black cube represents skilled congenitally blind subjects. In order to fulfil our ambition to draft the latter subjects, we had to travel all over the country and even to Denmark. Great efforts were also made to compose appropriate control groups consisting of completely naive subjects who had no knowledge whatsoever of chess, denotations of pieces, possible moves and so forth. Unfilled symbols are used analogously for the novices. Thus, the unfilled triangle stands for naive blindfolded subjects, whereas the unfilled circle stands for naive accidentally blinded subjects and the unfilled cube for naive congenitally blind subjects.

2   RESULTS AND DISCUSSION

Some of the results from the present study elucidate nicely cognitive compensation. Figure 3 demonstrates the number of spatial mistakes or mislocations for skilled chessplayers. Here, the number of squares from the correct position was counted. T1 and T2 are the pre and post-tests where the information load is considered to be very low, although the number of pieces was seventeen.

By inspection of Figure 3, it can be stated that there is a large difference between congenitally blind chessplayers and the other two groups. This superiority for the former group is especially true for a situation with a high degree of information load. These data are in line with several investigations of the importance of vision for the detection of spatial relationships. For instance, Jones (1975) argued in a paper that vision is *not* a necessary condition for spatial awareness. Data comparable to those of Figure 3 are depicted in Figure 4 for the novices.

Despite more mistakes in general, the unskilled groups demonstrate some interesting effects. The sighted subjects were significantly better than the blind subjects. We also obtained an interaction showing that the performance of the

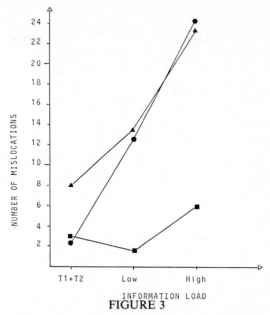

FIGURE 3

Number of spatial mistakes for three groups of skilled chessplayers over different degrees of information load.

congenitally blind declines with increasing information load, contrary to their skilled counterparts. My interpretation of these data suggests that a severe visual handicap does not automatically imply a general compensation in the tactile modality. On the contrary, tactile information might be relatively worse for blind than for sighted persons, with respect also to proximal information. If so, this suggestion is in line with Bartley's findings. On the other hand, congenitally blind subjects might be able to develop a unique chess competence and, simultaneously, an extraordinary skill for tactile information processing. This could not be explained by their skill in chess, since they were approximately as good as their counterparts in the other skilled subgroups. As Luria (1980) has pointed out, the onset of an injury might be critical to the development of compensatory skills (see also Hoemann, 1978). It might be that visually-based images for the adventitiously blind are too competitive with tactile information. A »unique memory» explanation could certainly be ruled out on the basis of a large volume of contra evidence. DeGroot (1965) and numerous followers have demonstrated that both grandmasters and classplayers perform equally well or

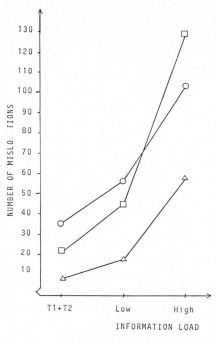

FIGURE 4

Number of spatial mistakes for three groups of »naive chessplayers» over different degrees of information load.

sometimes even worse than casual players on random configurations. It has been stated elsewhere that chessplayers are usually neither richly endowed nor in possession of excellent memories, but rather supported by extraordinary perceptual skills. Simon and Chase (1973) suggest that chess- specific knowledge is a matter of practise. This seems also to be the most plausible and straightforward explanation of our data. There are always methodological difficulties in the assessment of hours of practise in retrospect, but in our case it seems plausible that congenitally blind subjects are more experienced, although this is not reflected in their ranks. The discrepancy between sighted and blind subjects at T1 and T2 may indicate the impact of practise. This relationship is even more pronounced if the comparison is made between Figures 3 and 4, i.e., between skilled chessplayers and novices.

In figure 5 we have plotted the total number of mistakes for the six subgroups. We decided to pool the mistakes about values and colours of pieces together with the spatial mistakes, since the former were so few.

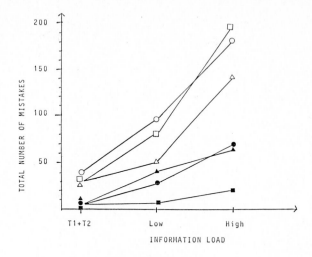

FIGURE 5

Total number of mistakes for three groups of skilled and naive chessplayers over different degrees of information load.

Data in figure 5 reveal small differences between blind and sighted persons and larger differences between skilled and naive subjects. This is especially true in the case of a high degree of the information load, with an outstanding performance for skilled chessplayers. The fine points of these data suggest that vision might contribute, to some extent, to the novices' spatial matching performance. Although the subgroups were compatible with respect to knowledge of chess, it seems plausible that a chessboard is purely an abstract phenomenon for the blind novices. Spatial points of references have presumably been built up for sighted subjects living in a potentially richer milieu. Basically, there were no dramatic changes in the overall pattern, in comparison with the patterns of Figures 3 and 4. One reason for this is that the subjects in each trial have the same pieces on the piece-board in their starting positions as on the search- board. Accordingly, the number of possible mistakes concerning values and colours are reduced. In general, the unskilled blindfolded subjects seem to mix up the pieces more frequently than the rest.

Below, I will continue with a presentation of the average time it took to finish the pre and post-tests. Figure 6 shows the matching-time for skilled chessplayers in the direct matching task prior to the experiment (T1) and after the experiment (T2).

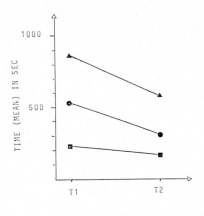

FIGURE 6

Matching-time in a direct matching-task prior and after the experiment for three groups of skilled chessplayers.

Once again, the congenitally blind subjects perform better than the others. It is also interesting to note that blindfolded subjects spend significantly more time on this task than adventitiously blind subjects. Qualitative analyses of the videotapes indicate that congenitally blind subjects use a more economic search strategy, with larger chunks and fewer and shorter stops at single pieces. One question that arises here is whether education might improve tactile information processing or not? In order to obtain a good spatial discriminability, a good strategy might improve this ability, but to become a skilled processor of spatial information takes more than that. Thus, in general, the answer to this question is *no* knowledge without experience seems to be less fruitful. The evidence in the chess literature is plentiful. Firstly, all skilled chessplayers should be aware of the importance of a »holistic approach» to chess problems. Secondly, a lot of the differences between blind and blindfolded subjects cannot be blown away by instructions. For instance, Charness (1982) presents interesting arguments bearing on this issue in a recent book entitled »Chess Skill in Man and Machine». To learn single moves from famous games does not seem to improve chess performance, nor does it seem fruitful to learn an abundance of patterns to become a grandmaster. Curiously, there have been grandmasters who never opened a chess book. Skilled sighted players are less dependent on adjacent pieces of chunking than unskilled players (e.g., Milojkovic, 1982). It is plausible that there is a continuum of distance-dependency related to the amount of practise, which probably also persists for blind subjects. Anyway, my argument is that practise is needed. Data from the present experiment indicate that practising in the short run, during the experimental session, does not contribute to any substantial improvement for skilled players. Figure 7 demonstrates the corresponding matching-time data for the novices.

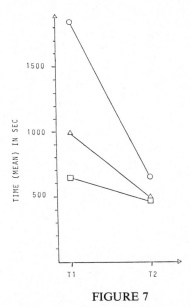

FIGURE 7

Matching-time in a direct matching-task prior and after the experiment for three groups of »naive chessplayers».

In Figure 7, a real improvement can be found for subjects with an acquired blindness. Pertinent to this result is a study by Berlá (1981) who demonstrated that blind students who trained for less than five minutes substantially improved their tactile skills. However, this phenomenon seems to be valid in less complex situations and for less experienced subjects. In our experiment, congenitally blind subjects seem to gain more in an unrestricted time task than blindfolded subjects. But here we have a trade-off effect suggesting that congenitally blind persons do it faster at the expense of more mistakes. On the other hand, practise seems to be more beneficial to blindfolded subjects without any comparable increase in mistakes. The effects of training during the experimental session can be observed in Figures 8 and 9.

The matching-time data for the skilled players are presented in Figure 8. The four trials within each condition are plotted chronologically.

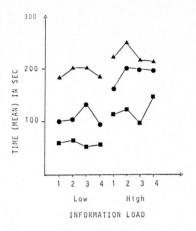

FIGURE 8

Matching-time for three groups of skilled chessplayers over four
replicates of low and high degrees of information load.

By inspection of Figure 8, it can be concluded that the fastest matching-time was
performed by congenitally blind subjects, whereas the blindfolded subjects found at
the top of the figure had the slowest matching-time. The matching-time for the
blindfolded subjects seems to be less affected by varying degrees of information load
compared to the blind subjects. Concerning the effects of training, these are not
reflected in the matching-time data for skilled subjects. The corresponding matching-
timed data for the novices are presented in Figure 9.

The most interesting point to be made from Figure 9 is that blind subjects, in
general, waste more time than sighted subjects in solving this task. Thus, the
blindfolded subjects demonstrate a faster and more accurate information processing
than blind subjects, provided that the subjects are naive in respect to their knowledge
of chess. A second point to be made here is that the largest difference between a high
and low degree of information load is found for the blindfolded subgroup, which is
quite the opposite to the same subgroup among skilled players. The third point to be
mentioned here is the notable training effect for all subgroups. A fourth point of
interest is the expected discrepancy between the high and low degree of information
load.

To conclude this study, I maintain that cognitive compensation as demonstrated
primarily for the congenitally blind-class players must be related to the acquisition of a
certain skill through extensive practise, and must also be separated from their

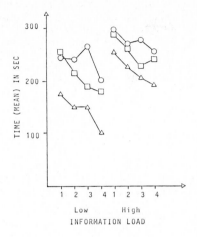

FIGURE 9

Matching-time for three groups of »naive chessplayers» over four
replicates of low and high degrees of information load.

knowledge of chess. In this vein it can also be asserted that knowledge of chess reflects
spatial skills rather than visual skills. According to Foulke and Warm (1967), blind
subjects might acquire tactile skills slower than sighted subjects, but ultimately they
develop more efficient skills. Our data fit nicely into that slot. Furthermore. despite a
presumed extensive utilization of the tactile modality, the unskilled blind subjects were
not able to show any evidence of a genuine compensation. This lack of evidence was
most salient for the adventitiously blind subjects. The fact that blindfolded subjects
surpassed the blind in the unskilled subgroups is conceivable with respect to the
relatively complex task that was implemented. A superior performance in complex
spatial tasks on the part of the blindfolded subjects has been demonstrated elsewhere
(e.g., Millar, 1975; O'Connor & Hermelin, 1976). The present study aimed at
demonstrating not solely the possibility but also the appropriateness of regarding
compensation as skill. Both compensation and skill are still viable concepts in
psychology. As long as other contributors of this volume present what I conceive of as
cognitive compensation, I am convinced that their data will be analysable in terms of
skills, and thus further our understanding of the outlined intricate interactions.
Without dwelling on the concept of skill in the present chapter, it will be necessary in
the future with a refinement of the description of certain skills.

REFERENCES

Bartley, S.H. (1953). The perception of size and distance based on tactile and kinesthetic data. *Journal of Psychology, 36,* 401-408.

Berlá, E.P. (1981). Tactile scanning and memory for a spatial display by blind students. *The Journal of Special Education, 15,* 341-350.

Charness, N.(1982). Human chess skill. In P. Frey (Ed.), *Chess skill in man and machine.* N.Y.: Springer Verlag.

Eaves, L., & Klonoff, H.A. (1970). A comparison of blind and sighted children on a tactual and performance test. *Exceptional Children, 37,* 269-273.

Foulke, E., & Warm, J.S. (1967). Effects of complexity and redundancy on the tactual recognition of metric figures. *Perceptual and Motor Skills, 25,* 177-187.

Furth, H. (1966). *Thinking without language: Psychological implications of deafness.* N.Y.: Free Press.

DeGroot, A.D. (1965). *Thought and choice in chess.* The Hague: Mouton.

Hoemann, H.W. (1978). Perception by the deaf. In E.C. Carterette & M.P. Friedman (Eds.), *Handbook of perception: Perceptual echology X,* N.Y.: Academic Press.

Jones, B. (1975). Spatial perception in the blind. *British Journal of Psychology, 66,* 461-472.

Luria, A.R. (1980). *Higher cortical functions in man.* N.Y. Basic Books.

Marmolin, H., Nilsson, C.-G., & Smedshammar, H. (1979). The mediated reading process for partially sighted. *Visible Language, 13,* 168-183.

Millar, S. (1975). Spatial memory by blind and sighted children. *British Journal of Psychology, 66,* 449-459.

Milojkovic, J.D. (1982). Chess imagery in novice and master. *Journal of Mental Imagery, 6,* 125-144.

Nilsson L.-G., Ohlsson, K., & Rönnberg, J. (1977). Capacity differences in processing and storage of auditory and visual input. In S. Dornic (Ed.), *Attention and Performance VI.* Hillsdale, N.J.: Lawrence Erlbaum Associated.

Nilsson, L.-G., Ohlsson, K., & Rönnberg, J. (1980). Processing and storage explanations of the modality effect. *Acta Psychologica, 44,* 41-50.

O'Connor, N., & Hermelin, B. (1975). Modality-specific spatial coordinates. *Perception and Psychophysics, 17,* 212-216.

Pitman, D. (1965). The musical ability of blind children. *American Foundation for the Blind: Research Bulletin, 11,* 63-80.

Posner, M.I. (1967). Characteristics of visual and kinesthetic memory codes. *Journal of Experimental Psychology, 75,* 103-107.

Rönnberg, J., & Ohlsson, K. (1980). Channel capacity and processing of modality specific information. *Acta Psychologica, 44,* 253-267.

Rönnberg, J., Nilsson, L.-G., & Ohlsson, K. (1982). Organization by modality, language and category compared. *Psychological Research, 44,* 369-379.

Simon, H.A., & Chase, W.G. (1973). Skill in chess. *American Scientist, 61,* 394-403.

Sterritt, G.M., Camp, B.W., & Lipman, B.S. (1966). Effects of early auditory deprivation upon auditory and visual information processing. *Perceptual and Motor Skills, 23,* 123-130.

Warren, D.H. (1978). Perception by the blind. In E.C. Carterette & M.P. Friedman (Eds.), *Handbook of Perception: Perceptual echology, X,* N.Y.: Academic Press.

Communication and Handicap: Aspects of
Psychological Compensation and Technical Aids
E. Hjelmquist and L.-G. Nilsson (editors)
© *Elsevier Science Publishers B.V. (North-Holland), 1986*

TRAVELLING WITHOUT VISION: ON THE POSSIBILITIES OF COGNITIVE AND PERCEPTUAL COMPENSATION

GUNNAR JANSSON

Department of Psychology, Uppsala University
Uppsala, Sweden[*]

It is suggested that the low level of consciousness of the perceptual guidance of locomotion is probably one of the main reasons why this kind of guidance has not been studied very much from a scientific point of view. It is concluded that neither unaided alternative senses nor presently available perceptual travel aids can compensate for the loss of perceptual information for locomotion normally provided by vision. Cognitive compensation is no solution either, since for locomotion there is a need for continuous updating of visual information. More basic knowledge is needed in all the fields of relevance for development of substitutions for normal visual guidance of locomotion.

1   INTRODUCTION

When the Swedish slalom star, Ingemar Stenmark, was once asked by a journalist how he was able to attain such a high quality of this performance, he answered in his northern Sweden dialect with an expression which has nearly got a proverbial character: »D'ä bare te åk». I cannot translate this into English retaining the dialect flavour of it, but the meaning is roughly: »It's only to let go».

---

[*]   My work on these problems was made possible by research grants from the Bank of Sweden Tercentenary Foundation (project No. 75/116, 79/149, 81/96) and from the Swedish Ministry of Health and Social Affairs, the Delegation for Social Research (project No. 82/117, 84/156).

I think this is an adequate answer to a common, but not very perceptive type of question. To ask a person to describe how he performs a complex perceptual motor-task is not very meaningful. I general, the motor behavior is perceptually guided in a way which, to a large extent, we are not conscious of. This is also true of less spectacular ways of locomotion than skiing around poles at high speed, e.g, when we walk along a well-known route. We perform such tasks in a semi-automatic way, making the correct choices along the route and avoiding collisions with obstacles without paying much attention to it.

The low level of consciousness of the perceptual guidance of locomotion is probably one of the main reasons for the fact that this kind of guidance has not been studied very much from a scientific point of view. It has not been thought of as a problem, except when the task is especially difficult, such as slalom skiing at high speed, or when an important perceptual system, such as vision, is missing. In fact, much of the scientific work on the guidance of locomotion has been done in the context of walking without the aid of vision.

It is apparent that vision is normally extremely important for the guidance of locomotion. In most familiar places it provides sufficient information - hearing adding mainly information about sound sources out of sight, dangerous ones being the most important. A totally deaf person can perform most locomotory tasks as effectively as a hearing person, with some added attention to potential dangers.

1.1   A Note on the Terms »Orientation» and »Mobility»

For the totally blind, in contrast to the deaf, the perceptual guidance of locomotion is one of their main problems. Traditionally, this problem area is called orientation and mobility. (For reviews, see Hill & Ponder, 1976; Welsh & Blasch, 1980). These terms are rather vague and their meanings overlap, but they refer to two broad aspects of goal-oriented locomotion: (1) knowing/perceiving spatial relations between the position occupied at each moment and relevant places and objects in the environment, as well as internal spatial relations between these places and objects, and (2) the successful change of position. I prefer to analyze locomotion in aspects cutting across this distinction, each including both orientation and mobility. These aspects will be discussed below.

2 COGNITIVE COMPENSATION

2.1 Increased Relative Use of Cognitive Maps

When travelling in an area visited before, a sighted person combines, in a complex way, immediate perceptual information and earlier acquired information about the surrounding space. The latter information may consist of general knowledge about what can be expected in an area of the kind visited, e.g., about what a townscape generally looks like, as well as more specific knowledge about a special area. A sighted person easily refreshes his memory with the aid of the immediate perception he obtains when he moves around in the area.

The situation for a blind traveller is quite different. His possibilities of immediate perception are always very much reduced, which applies both to earlier visits to the area and to the current visit. Other things being equal, his cognitive map can be expected to be less detailed and less well organized than a sighted person's map. It is probably also more restricted to knowledge about paths and does not contain as much information about the internal spatial relations of the places and objects outside the path (Foulke, 1982).

An increased use of memory, which is sometimes mentioned as a compensation possibility for the visually impaired, is probably the case in a relative meaning, i.e., the blind person's guidance is more relatively based on a cognitive map than on immediate perception, when compared with a sighted person's guidance; a plausible reason for this is the reduction of his/her immediate perception. On general, however, a blind person can hardly have more information, an absolute meaning, in his cognitive map than a sighted person visiting the same area under the same conditions. Visual memory, in all its richness, cannot be expected to be replaced in total.

However, according to many individual reports, it is probably the case that a blind person memorizes, to a higher degree than a sighted person, the sequence of stages of which a travel path consists. Moreover, a blind person's cognitive map often contains other kinds of information than a sighted person's map does, not only because of the lack of visual information to memorize, but also because of the usefulness of this kind of information for non-visually guided locomotion (cf. Brambring's, 1982, study of route descriptions by blind and sighted persons). Thus, it is not meaningful to include in a blind person's cognitive map, landmarks at long distances from the route as the range of the perceivable space is so short. On the other hand, information about the different kinds of surfaces on the ground is important for the visually impaired, both for safety reasons and for guiding purposes, e.g., when walking along a border between two surfaces. The kinds of ground surfaces are important components in a blind person's cognitive map, but often not memorized at all by a sighted person.

2.2   Increased Use of Geographical Maps

One potential way of compensating the visually impaired for their reduced information, both in cognitive maps and in immediate perception of the current environment, would be the increased use of geographical maps over the area visited (for a review of available types, see Bentzen, 1980). The kind of map considered here is a map in a scale useful for locomotion within the area. Such maps are often called mobility maps, orientation maps or safe walking maps. If the maps contained the information necessary for successful locomotion in such a form that it was usable for the visually impaired pedestrian, they would provide forceful substituting information. Unfortunately, this is not the case.

There are many ambitiously produced maps intended as substitutes for visual maps, most of them being tactual maps but they have, so far, not been very extensively utilized. The most probable reason for this is that the maps have not been found sufficiently useful (Jansson, 1983, 1984 a). There are many remaining problems concerning what kind of information they should contain and what form this information should have. Before considering some examples of these problems, let us remember an important piece of information that the map cannot provide.

A map presents a bird's eye view of the area. It contains, in a minified and symbolic form, things such as houses, streets, parks and rivers, and their spatial relations. There is not, however, any information about the location of the observer, with the exception of some (stationary) orientation maps. By only looking at the map, thus, without any additional information, you cannot generally identify the location where you are, on the map. To find this location, you must make a comparison between the map and the environment. You must find corresponding features on the map and in the environment, in both cases by immediate perception. This may sometimes be complicated for sighted observers, but it is still more so for the visually impaired. The tactual map available to them is more difficult to read than a visual map (cf below), and information about the environment is not easily obtained, especially not the environment beyond a few meters' distance.

It should be remembered that the problem, generally, after you have found your location on the map, is to find the direction from the current position to the goal, both on the map and in the environment. Again a perceptual comparison has to be made, and the restriction in the immediate perceptual information available to the visually impaired observer is a formidable obstacle.

With regard to what kind of information a map for the visually impaired should contain, one of the main problems is the necessity of reducing the information in comparison with a common visual map, in order to make the tactual map readable by the finger tips. This is usually achieved by leaving out details, but this has to be done with caution in order not to omit features important for locomotion. There is also a need to add information to a tactual map that is often neglected on a visual map. One example is the kind of sidewalk on the street, as information from the feet and the long cane is important for blind mobility (cf above).

The form of the information presented in tactual maps is probably far from optimal. Touch has a high potential in picking up suitably presented information, as was convincingly demonstrated already by Katz (1925). However, this capacity has not been possible to utilize in the reading of the tactual maps produced so far. The tactual map user has, for example, problems with discriminating more than just a few symbols of the kind invented up until now (cf Jansson, 1984 a). These problems may be possible to solve by the use of other, more discriminable symbols and/or new production methods. A problem harder to solve is the general difficulty in getting an overview with the tactual sense. To read a tactual map will probably always be more time-consuming than to read a visual map. Vision is unmatched in its possibility of giving a rapid overview.

Thus, a visually impaired person has many problems of picking up and comparing information from a map and the environment. It is quite understandable that tactual maps are very seldom used during locomotion. At most, they are used during the planning of a tour. However, the potential of compensating for the reduced spatial information of the visually impaired by using tactual maps is probably high, but our knowledge of how this type of aid should be ideally produced and utilized has to be substantially increased.

3   PERCEPTUAL COMPENSATION

3.1   Types of Perceptual Guidance

The most studied locomotory skill of visually impaired persons is their capacity to avoid obstacles without the use of sight, since the classicalstudies by Dallenbach and his associated (e.g., Cotzin & Dallenbach,1950) known to be an echolocation phenomenon. However, avoiding obstacles is only one aspect of the perceptual guidance of locomotion. There are other important aspects, not yet studied very much that are still more basic (cf Jansson, 1985, in press).

There are, I think, two main types of perceptual guidance of locomotion: moving *towards* a goal and moving *along* an edge. Typically, a total route does not consist of just one section with one type of guidance, but of a sequence of stages each with its own guidance.

Also the handling of obstacles can be described in terms of these two types of guidance. You move *towards* a location to the side of the obstacle, then, maybe, *along* the edge of the obstacle, and finally, directly *towards* the goal. This includes more than the detection of an obstacle. This includes more than the detection of an obstacle; I prefer to call it moving *around* an object.

It should be added that another important aspect of locomotion, not further discussed here, is the keeping of balance which is very much dependent on perceptual information about the surfaces upon which the traveller is moving. Moving *upon* may therefore be added to the list of important aspects of locomotion.

3.2   Perceptual Information for Moving Towards and Moving Along

The perceptual information necessary for moving. *towards* is information about (1) the direction of the goal, and (2) the direction of moving. A difference between these two directions indicates the need to change the direction of moving. The »rule» to be followed is thus: keep your direction of moving identical with the direction of the goal. Gibson (1979, chap. 13) discussed what this means for visual guidance, including a distinction between moving towards an object and moving towards an opening, two types which are visually quite difference.

For moving *along* there are several alternatives. A general one is that the distance to the edge is the important information; and that changes in this distance are an indication that the direction of moving should be changed. The »rule» in this case might then be: keep the distance to the edge constant.

Information for both of these kinds of perceptual guidance is easily obtained visually, and we use both kinds frequently, often changing between them, sometimes using them simultaneously.

3.3   Unaided Perceptual Systems Substituting for Visual Guidance

When vision is missing, hearing and haptics (touch) have to be used instead, with a few contributions of smell. That these perceptual systems can replace vision, at least to an important degree, is demonstrated by the sometimes astonishingly good locomotory skills of blind people, especially when they use a travel aid such as the long cane. An important portion of any rehabilitative program for blind people is to train these other senses to take over as much of the informative task as possible.

What training means is probably not, as is sometimes thought, that the basic sensory abilities are enhanced, but that attention is educated to utilize more of the available auditory and haptic information. Blind people, for example, listen to traffic sounds in order to pick up information about the location and direction of streets, to the sound of a water fountain in order to locate a landmark, to the sounds of their long cane hitting the ground or objects on the ground in order to pick up information about the properties of the surfaces, to haptic information from their feet in order to identify what surfaces they are walking on, and to information from their skin from wind and sun in order to recognize the location of openings between two houses and of shadowing objects. This kind of information is usually neglected by sighted people as vision provides information more easily obtained, but it is important when vision is missing.

The special ability of echolocation which is hardly used at all by sighted people, may appear spontaneously for both blind children and adventitiously blind adults, when locomoting without visual guidance. This means that they can detect and locate objects in their nearest surroudings, but not objects at longer distances and not with a very high spatial resolution.

This restriction of range is one of the most significant features of howthe blind perceive space. Beyond a distance of a few meters, space is not perceivable, except for the sound sources and sound shadows it may form, the situation for the blind being similar to that of a sighted person in thick fog.

A blind person who, for perceptual information, has to rely only on his unaided remaining senses can move *along* an edge if walking close to it and guide himself by either touching or echolocating it. In order to move *towards* something, he has to restrict himself to sound sources or to objects at such a short distance that they are perceived by echolocation. He cannot get perceptual information about silent objects beyond the range of a few meters. That such a restricted preview has important effects for the safety, efficiency and stress level of locomotion has been experimentally demonstrated (Barth, 1978; see also Barth & Foulke, 1979).

3.4   Travel Aids as Perceptual Substitutes

The restrictions in the possibilities of substituting vision with the unaided alternative senses have lead to many efforts to invent devices to make these senses more effective. The now traditional travel aids for the visually impaired, the blind dog and the long cane, are based on ideas which originated centuries ago, but systematically used they belong to our century; these aids and training programs for their use began to be more generally used after the First and Second World Wars, respectively, to a large extent in order to be helpful for the many blinded young war veterans.

The flourishing business of electronics also spread to this area and more than fifty technically advanced travel aids were developed, especially during the sixties and the seventies: ultrasonic torches and glasses, laser canes, TV-based aids, etc. (for a review, see Farmer, 1980). There was sometimes an ambition to invent an aid that would replace the traditional ones. However, it was soon found that none of the aids developed could take over the functions of these aids in a satisfactory way; consequently, these new aids have, so far, primarily been considered as complements.

One main aim for most of the travel aids has been to extend the space perceived by the unaided blind person. The long cane is long just for this reason, it should cover the next step. The range is further increased by the electronic travel aids, but with the exception of optically-based aids, these aids do not increase the range much more than a few meters at the most. The optically-based aids, primarily consisting of a miniature TV-camera with transformation of its picture to a tactile display, have longer ranges, but they are not much more useful at long range because of the low spatial resolution of the tactile display. (However, there are more recent efforts to develop a travel aid with microcomputer analysis of a TV-picture and speech output (Collins & Deering, 1984).

The travel aids increase the range of space perceptually available to the blind to some degree, but it must be remembered that this increase is not very great. The main importance of the enlargements of the perceived space is that objects and openings may be detected at a somewhat greater distance. The increment in preview, for instance, makes better preparations possible for walking around obstacles. It makes it possible to move *along* at a somewhat greater distance from a guiding edge and to start to move *towards* something slightly further away, but this does not mean a very important improvement. The space immediately perceivable for a blind user of travel aids is thus still much smaller than that perceived by the sighted and this restriction is one of the most severe effects of blindness on independent travelling. An increased range is one of the most important features needed for new travel aids (cf. Jansson, 1984 b).

3.5 Compensating by Changing Type of Perceptual Guidance

A sighted person changes without problems between the two main types of perceptual guidance, moving *towards* and moving *along*. Walking a longer tour under ordinary conditions means frequent shifts between them. The visually impaired do not have the same free choice because of the just discussed restrictions of their spatial range. The goals that the sighted can easily walk *towards* are often at too great a distance to be perceivable to the visually impaired. This makes it necessary for them to use the alternative type of perceptual guidance much more often, i.e., to move *along*, In many cases this will not give any problems. You may as well, for example, walk *along* an edge of a lawn to find the opening in a hedge, as walk directly *towards* the opening. In other cases it may be possible to walk *along* instead of *towards,* but it elongates the route considerably, for example, when you have to walk *around* a large market-place to a shop on the other side, instead of walking straight *towards* the shop. In still other cases there may not be any edge available to follow *along,* and the blind pedestrian may then have to walk more or less at random. Thus, change of type of perceptual guidance may, in some cases, be a possible solution, even if it may sometimes be awkward; in other cases it may not be an alternative available for solving the problem of perceptual guidance.

4   CONCLUSIONS

4.1   Increased relative use of cognitive maps

The visually impaired may increase their use of memory at least relatively, but the limited pick-up of perceptual information makes it improbable that this can compensate for the lack of vision more than to a very limited degree.

4.2   Increased use of geographical maps

The tactual map is a potentially important aid, but the visually impaired will have many difficulties in comparing the map and the current environment. There is also a lack of knowledge about both what kind of information should be included and what form this information should take.

4.3   Unaided perceptual systems substituting visual guidance

The blind person uses hearing and haptics to a higher degree than the sighted person by attending more to the available auditory and haptic information. Echolocation is an ability which often develops when vision is missing. Haptics is used, for example, by the feet picking up information about the properties of the ground. In all these cases the range is usually very short.

4.4   Travel aids as perceptual substitutes

The travel aids increase the spatial range available to the blind. This is important because of the increased preview; the long cane gives a preview of the ground and the electronic travel aids of objects above the ground. It must be remembered, however, that the range for a travel aid user is still very restricted, and the information about space available with the travel aids is very attenuated. Sight is substituted by the aids developed so far, only to a very small degree.

4.5   Compensating by changing type of perceptual guidance

A change from moving *towards* to moving *along* is possible in some situations, but it is sometimes awkward and it is not a general solution.

4.6   Some general comments

It should be observed that blind people at present usually locomote only in man-made environments, especially within buildings and in townscapes, with the relatively plane ground surfaces to walk on and relatively regular arrangements of objects, such as streets, sidewalks, blocks, etc. Further, they generally move only in known areas. Most blind people do not walk in unknown environments without special guidance. This is a general indication of the severe restrictions still existing for the independent mobility of blind people.

Neither unaided alternative senses nor presently available perceptual travel aids can compensate for the loss of perceptual information for locomotion normally provided by vision. An increased use of cognitive functions is also only a partial solution concerning locomotion, mainly because of the need for constant updating of the information about the changing spatial relations between the moving travellers and the stationary and moving features of their surroundings. Much more basic knowledge about the perceptual and cognitive processes involved, as well as technical development, is needed before vision used for the guidance of locomotion can be substituted to a degree we consider sufficient.

REFERENCES

Barth, J.L. (1978). *The effects of preview constraint on perceptual motor behavior and stress level in a mobility task.* Unpublished doctoral dissertation, University of Louisville, Louisville, Kentucky.

Barth, J.L., & Foulke, E. (1979). Preview: A neglected variable in orientation and mobility, *Journal of Visual Impairment and Blindess, 73* 41-48.

Bentzen, B.L. (1980). Orientation aids. In R.L. Welsh & B.B. Blasch (eds.), *Foundations of orientation and mobility,* (pp. 291-355). New York: American Foundation for the Blind.

Brambring, M. (1982). Language and geographic orientation for the blind. In R.J. Jarvella and W. Klein (Eds.), *Speech, place and action* (pp. 203-218). New York: Wiley

Collins, C.C., & Deering, M.F. (1984, September). A microcomputer based blind mobility aid. *IEEE Conference Proceedings: Frontiers of Engineering and Computing in Health Care,* Los Angeles, California.

Cotzin, M., & Dallenbach, K.M. (1950). »Facial vision»: The role of pitch and loudness in the perception of obstacles by the blind. *American Journal of Psychology, 63,* 485-515.

Farmer, L.W. (1980). Mobility devices, In R.L. Welsh & B.B. Blasch (eds.), *Foundations of orientation and mobility,* (pp. 357-412). New York: American Foundation for the Blind.

Foulke, E. (1982). Perception, cognition and the mobility of blind pedestrians. In M. Potegal (Ed.), *Spatial abilities.* Development and physiological foundations (pp. 55-75). New York & London: Academic Press.

Gibson, J.J. (1979). *The ecological approach to visual perception* Boston: Houghton Mifflin.

Hill, E., & Ponder, P. (1976). *Orientation and mobility techniques.* New York: American Foundation for the Blind.

Jansson, G. (1983). Tactile maps as a challenge for perception research. In J.W. Wiedel (Ed.), *Proceedings of the First International Symposium on Maps and Graphics for the Visually Handicapped.* (pp.68-74.) Washington: Association of American Geographers.

Jansson, G. (1984 a). Research needed to get more useful tactual maps. *Aids and Appliances Review.* Issue No. 14, 3-6.

Jansson, G. (1984 b) *Theoretical reasons for increasing the range of the next generation of electronic travel aids for the visually impaired.* Paper read at symposium on »Spatial ability», Louisville University, Department of Psychology, Louisville, Kentucky, April 13-14, 1984.

Jansson, G. (1985). Perceptual theory and sensory substitution. In D.J. Ingle, M. Jeannerod, & D.N. Lee (Eds.), *Brain mechanisms and spatial vision* (pp. 451-465). Dortrecht/Boston/Lancaster: Martinus Nijhoff.

Jansson, G. (in press). Implications of perceptual theory for the development of travel aids for the visually impaired. In D.H. Warren & E.R. Strelow (Eds.), *Visual spatial prosthesis: Issues in electronically mediated perception* The Hague: Martinus Nijhoff.

Katz, D. (1925). Der Aufbau der Tastwelt. *Zeitschrift fr Psychologie, Ergänzungsband 11.*

Welsh, R.L., & Blasch, B.B. (Eds.). (1980). *Foundations of orientation and mobility.* New York: American Foundation for the Blind.

Communication and Handicap: Aspects of
Psychological Compensation and Technical Aids
E. Hjelmquist and L.-G. Nilsson (editors)
© *Elsevier Science Publishers B.V. (North-Holland), 1986*

COMPUTERIZED PRESENTATION OF TEXT FOR THE VISUALLY HANDICAPPED

NANCY L. WILLIAMSON, PAUL MUTER, and RICHARD S. KRUK

Department of Psychology, University of Toronto,
Toronto, Ontario, Canada[*]

A method for rapid serial visual presentation (RSVP) is presented and applied
to visual handicaps. The technique entails presentation of words, or groups of
words at a common location. A consequence of certain disorders of the retina
is a loss of peripheral information, resulting in the reader losing track of where
abouts on the page the reader is. Results from studies of one patient indicates
that RSVP might be a useful aid for this type of visual handicap.

1 INTRODUCTION

A method of text presentation which has generated a considerable amount of
research with normally sighted readers may be of benefit to people suffering from a
range of visual impairments. Rapid serial visual presentation, or RSVP, involves the
brief display of consecutive words at a fixed location. Because this technique
eliminates the need for eye movements, readers who experience difficulties executing
these movements would presumably benefit from this type of display. Readers with
retinitis pigmentosa, glaucoma, or other medical conditions which limit peripheral
vision represent such a population, since peripheral vision is thought to be critical in

This work was supported by Research Grant UD 149 from the Natural Sciences and Engineering
Research Council of Canada to the second author.

We thank Pat O'Seaghdha and Kim Wrigley for helpful comments. We also thank Cathleen Drews
and Dr. Barry Skarf for their comments on the clinical aspects of retinitis pigmentosa.

guiding readers' eye movements (O'Regan, 1981). In this chapter, we will first review the RSVP technique. Then, after describing retinitis pigmentos, we will report preliminary data which suggest that RSVP may prove beneficial in assisting readers with this condition read more quickly without a concomitant loss of comprehension.

2   DESCRIPTION OF PRESENTATION TECHNIQUE

Rapid serial visual presentation (RSVP) entails the brief presentation of consecutive words, or groups of words, at a common location. Typically, the rate of presentation per word is set by the experimenter, and each word is shown for an equivalent amount of time. In most of the research with RSVP (Bouma & deVoogd, 1974; Cocklin, Ward, Chen, & Juola, 1984; Forster, 1970; Juola, Ward, & McNamara, 1982; Masson, 1983; Potter, Kroll, & Harris, 1980; Williamson & Muter, 1985; see Potter, 1984 for a review), the display duration of each word is very brief, as implied by the word »rapid» in the acronym. However, there is nothing about the presentation technique that prohibits the use of slower rates. Regardless of the rate of presentation, the functional relevance of RSVP lies in the fact that the reader is not required to make eye movements. Instead, the words are brought to a single fixation point.

There are several aspects of this presentation technique that are essential in displaying the words most effectively. One critical feature of RSVP is the brief presentation of a blank display window at the end of each sentence. Masson (1983) found no difference in comprehension between page-format presentation and RSVP with sentence-end pauses of 500 ms. However, performance was higher with the page-format display when no sentence-end pauses were included in RSVP. Pauses of 1000 ms did not result in any further benefit.

The rate of presentation per word is another factor that influences the readability of RSVP displays. As would be expected, it has been shown that as the presentation rate increases, RSVP reading comprehension steadily declines (Juola et al., 1982; Masson, 1983).

In multiple-word RSVP, the alignment of the words is important. Displays in which English words were vertically aligned, one above the other, yielded worse comprehension performance relative to one-word RSVP, whereas horizontal alignment of multiple-word displays led to comprehension performance equivalent to that obtained with one-word displays (Williamson & Muter, 1985).

The presentation of idea units rather than the strict presentation of 15 characters (on average, three words) in each window has been found to benefit RSVP performance (Cocklin et al., 1984). However, the practical value of this finding is small at present since the availability of text parsers to determine such specific boundaries is limited.

Conversely, there are other factors which seem to have little influence on the effectiveness of RSVP displays. For instance, presenting each word for a duration corresponding to the average length of time spent looking at the words under normal reading conditions was not found to affect RSVP comprehension performance. Equal presentation durations were found to be just as effective as these varible durations (Ward & Juola, 1982).

In addition, RSVP reading has been shown to be possible using a wide variety of display apparatus, ranging from CRT screens (Cocklin et al., 1984; Juola et al., 1982; Masson, 1983; Potter et al., 1980; Williamson & Muter, 1985) and projection screens (Forster, 1970) to cylindrical rollers moving a page of text, with a window of a fixed size being displayed (Bouma & deVoogd, 1974).

The role of the size of the RSVP display is, at best, unclear. Cocklin et al. (1984) showed that the optimal reading size for horizontal RSVP displays was 12 characters, a size considered to be on average, between two and three words. This result was conceptually appealing since the visual span of apprehension has been found to be approximately 12 characters (Rayner, 1983). Contrary to this research, Williamson and Muter (1985) found no difference in performance among consistent one-word, two-word and three-word RSVP displays. Since Cocklin et al. assert that this optimal display size is independent of presentation rate or task difficulty, these two factors cannot be used to account for the apparent discrepancy between experiments. In the Cocklin et al. study, only complete words were shown in each consecutive RSVP display, resulting in a variable number of words per display. As Potter (1984) points out, this method introduces an element of chance since »the change of a single letter in the preceding text could double a word's effective viewing time by causing it to be presented alone instead of with another word». (p.92). In the Williamson and Muter study, a consistent number of words was maintained within each display for each of the different RSVP conditions.

Obviously, a direct comparison of the role of number of characters versus number of words per RSVP display is needed. However, if a consistent number of words per window is to be maintained throughout the RSVP reading, then whether the size of the display is one, two, or three words is apparently irrelevant. All lead to equivalent comprehension performance for a given presentation rate. For readers with little peripheral vision, a window size of one word would seem suitable. A larger window would result in more information appearing outside the foveal area, a region unavailable to such readers.

3   CURRENT EVIDENCE REGARDING RSVP VERSUS PAGE-FORMAT
    READING

There has been a considerable amount of research carried out comparing comprehension performance with RSVP displays to performance with traditional page-format displays presented for the same amount of time (Cocklin et al., 1984; Forster, 1970; Juola et al., 1982; Masson, 1983; Potter et al., 1980; Williamson & Muter, 1985). The majority of these studies have found that readers experience no deficit in comprehension as a result of reading via an RSVP display (Cocklin et al., 1984; Juola et al., 1982; Masson (Experiment 4), 1983; Potter et al., 1980). Given practice with both of the display techniques, readers still reach comparable comprehension levels under the two types of displays (Cocklin et al., 1984). In most of these studies, however, type of display was confounded with presence of pacing. The RSVP technique typically includes computer pacing, whereas in page-format reading, no such externally imposed pacing is present. Perhaps there is some advantage gained with a source of external pacing that compensates for any loss experienced with other features of the RSVP technique. However, Williamson and Muter (1985) found that even when a source of external pacing was provided in both a page-format and RSVP condition, subjects' comprehension of text presented via an RSVP display was at least equivalent to comprehension of traditionally displayed text.

Some qualification to the finding of RSVP and page-format comprehension equivalence is warranted. Cocklin et al. (1984), Juola et al. (1982), Masson (Experiment 4, 1983), Potter et al. (1980), and Williamson and Muter (1985), found no impairment when comprehension was assessed by performance in answering questions. However, Potter et al. found that comprehension as measured by verbatim recall was worse with RSVP as compared to page-format display. Thus, the results of these RSVP studies appear to be somewhat task-dependent, but as long as the reader is not trying to memorize text, the RSVP technique leads to comprehension equivalent to that obtained with page-format display.

It is thought that the effectiveness of the RSVP display lies in the fact that, compared to page-format reading, readers do not have to use valuable processing capacity and time in planning when and where to fixate next (Cocklin et al., 1984). If the Rayner, Slowiaczek, Clifton, and Bertera (1983) finding is correct, that the planning and execution of an eye movement from one location to another takes, on average, 175-200 ms, then elimination of this process in reading using an RSVP display may result in much more time being available for processing of the words themselves. This advantage may offset any disadvantage entailed in being able to see only one word at a time at a fixed rate.

4   RELEVANCE TO VISUALLY IMPAIRED READERS

In normally sighted readers, eye movements from one word to the next during reading appear to be controlled by the length of the next word or two to the right of the word currently being fixated (O'Regan, 1981). Parafoveal information was found to be useful in guiding eye movements from one location to the next in an examination of the effects of restricting foveal and parafoveal information in reading (Rayner & Bertera, 1979). If this information is unavailable, as it is to some visually impaired individuals, then presumably inefficient eye movements occur, the reader loses his or her location on the page, and an unusually large number of regressions and disruptions occur. Since RSVP eliminates the need for readers to move their eyes, it would seem that readers to whom parafoveal information is unavailable or limited would benefit from this presentation technique.

5   RETINITIS PIGMENTOSA

The progressive loss of peripheral vision is one of the primary symptoms of retinitis pigmentosa, a slow bilateral degenerative disorder of the retina. This disease is generally genetically determined. Its onset usually begins in childhood, often resulting in total blindness by middle or old age. The degenerative effect begins near the equator of the eye and gradually spreads both anteriorly and posteriorly, primarily affecting the rods.

Night blindness is the first detectable symptom of retinitis pigmentosa. Dark adaptation ability is attenuated because of the degeneration of the rods, which are primarily responsible for vision under low illumination.

Later, a progressive constriction of the visual field produces a constantly decreasing tube of vision, known as »tunnel vision». The concentric contraction of the field of vision is especially marked under reduced illumination. The degenerative process extends outward toward the peripheral areas, and more slowly inward toward the foveal area in the later course of the disease. Thus, visual acuity is preserved until later stages of the disease. Fifty percent of all patients have an acuity better than 20/50, but by age 50 at least half of patients have a visual acuity of 20/200 or worse (Marmor, 1980). However, rate of loss of central vision, and acuity, varies according to the severity of the disorder (Marmor, 1980).

In comparison with normally sighted individuals whose visual fields extend through 180 degrees, the restricted visual field of a retinitis pigmentosa patient, in later stages, extends about two to three degrees around the fixation point (Marmor, 1980). For further details on retinitis pigmentosa, see Duke-Elder (1970), Merin and Auerback (1980), and Trevor-Roper and Curran (1984).

6   READING AIDS

People with retinitis pigmentosa have good reading vision until the condition reaches an advanced stage. However, with the loss of peripheral information to help guide their eye movements, people with retinitis pigmentosa would be expected to read continuous text with less than optimal efficiency. This is the general observation of clinicians working with these patients. Patients frequently lose track of their place on the page as they read.

A number of reading aids are available for people with retinitis pigmentosa. Magnifiers are helpful in mild cases. The patient is taught to focus on a single fixation point and move the page rather than the eyes while reading continuous text. Other aids include closed circuit television, which is a form of text magnification (Harley & Lawrence, 1977), and reversed telescopes, which increase the number of text characters seen in the patient's limited field of vision. The reading aids described here involve the reader manually manipulating the text page to bring the words into the reader's visual field. RSVP, on the other hand, performs this manipulation automatically.

7 PRELIMINARY INVESTIGATION

A female retinitis pigmentosa patient volunteered to participate in an exploratory experiment. Since she has 10 degrees of vision, she may be classified as suffering from a moderately severe form of the disease. She reported that she read frequently, both at work and for pleasure.

The experiment involved reading 20 self-contained paragraphs, with an average length of 124 words. Ten short-answer questions had been developed for each of these paragraphs and these questions had been found to be a sensitive measure of reading comprehension (Williamson & Muter, 1985). The paragraphs were randomly assigned to one of ten pairs and the method of presentation (RSVP versus page-format) was randomized within each pair of paragraphs.

One-word RSVP was implemented on an Apple Macintosh, which has a white background with black letters. A 14-point font size was used. In the computer-paced RSVP condition, each word was shown for 300 ms, and a pause of 500 ms took place at the end of each sentence. In the page condition, each paragraph was printed out on separate 21.5x28.0 cm sheets of paper in letters of the same font and size as those displayed on the screen. Each paragraph was available to the subject for the same total time as in the RSVP condition, namely: 300 x (number of words) + 500 x (number of sentences) ms. Because the total display duration of each passage was based on the number of sentences in that passage, as well as the number of words, the number of words presented per minute (including pauses) was not the same for all passages because the number of sentences was not uniform. The mean words per minute was 202.4.

Two practice paragraphs in each presentation mode, followed by five test paragraphs in each mode were read under the externally-paced conditions described above. Six further paragraphs (three in RSVP, three in page-format) were self-paced by the subject. In the page condition, the subject initiated the timing of her reading and then indicated when she was finished by stopping the timer. Two keys on the keyboard were identified in the self-paced RSVP condition. By pushing one of the buttons, the reader could reduce the display duration of each word by ten percent, thus increasing her reading speed. Pressing the other key caused the display duration of each word to be increased by ten percent, decreasing reading speed. The initial presentation rate for the self-paced RSVP was the same as that used in the externally-paced display: 300 ms per word. As usual, there was a 500 ms pause at the end of each sentence.

In all conditions, the subject initiated the presentation of the text. After reading a passage, ten comprehension questions were administered. These were read aloud, one at a time to the subject, who recorded her responses on paper. If the subject had not responded to a question within 10 seconds, the next question was read.

When the reading was externally-paced at approximately 200 words per minute, the average comprehension score was 8 out of 10 with the page-format display, and 7 out of 10 with the RSVP display. Because of the limited number of observations, no statistical analyses were performed on the data. However, compre hension levels in these two display formats seemed to be comparable.

The reading rate for the six paragraphs in the self-paced block of the experiment along with their corresponding comprehen sion scores are shown below in Table 1. In the RSVP condition, the subject decreased the rate of presentation twice while read ing the first paragraph. The self-paced RSVP rate of presentation was not altered in subsequent paragraphs. It appears that RSVP allowed the participant to read the paragraph more quickly while still comprehending at the same level as that obtained with the slower page-format. Certainly, with such a small number of observations, no strong conclusions may be drawn from this data. However, these preliminary results are promising.

The participant's comments indicated that she preferred the page-format display to RSVP. She felt that RSVP was more stressful because it did not allow her to return to an earlier word if it had been missed. The ability to make regressions existed in the page-format display. This problem could be overcome within the RSVP paradigm by providing a means of accessing text which had already been presented. In addition, extended practice with the display may allow the reader to become more comfortable with the RSVP technique in general.

TABLE 1
Reading rates and comprehension scores with self-paced reading

RSVP

Trial	Reading Rate	Comprehension Score
16	169.5	7/10
18	164.7	8/10
20	169.1	8/10
Mean	167.8	8/10

Page

Trial	Reading Rate	Comprehension Score
15	134.7	6/10
17	156.5	7/10
19	132.0	10/10
Mean	141.1	8/10

8 CONCLUSIONS

Although the evidence presented here is limited, it is encouraging for the application of RSVP to readers with visual impairments. A retinitis pigmentosa reader was able to increase her reading speed by almost 30 words per minute while experiencing no loss in comprehension. This enhancement of reading performance required no special equipment other than a microcomputer. Perhaps the most promising feature of the present demonstration stems from the fact that the positive effects of RSVP over page-format display were obtained with a reader who had approximately seven to eight more degrees of peripheral vision than individuals in advanced stages of the disease. With less peripheral vision, one would expect to find a greater degree of reading difficulty and thus, a slower page-format reading speed than was observed with the present subject. The benefit obtained with the RSVP display would be even more substantial. Further research is in progress, in the hope of firmly establishing the technique of rapid serial visual presentation as an important aid to readers with little or no peripheral vision.

REFERENCES

Bouma, H., & deVoogd, A.H. (1974). On the control of eye saccades in reading. *Vision Reserach, 14,* 273-284.

Cockling, T.G., Ward, N.J., Chen, H.-C., & Juola, J.F. (1984). Factors influencing readability of rapidly presented text segments. *Memory & Cognition, 12(5),* 431-442.

Duke-Elder, Sir Stewart (1970). *Parsons' Deseases of the Eye (15th ed.).* London: J. & A. Churchill.

Forster, K.I. (1970). Visual perception of rapidly presented word sequences of varying complexity. *Perception & Psychophysics, 8,* 215-221.

Harley, R.K., & Lawrence, G.A. (1977). *Visual Impairment in the Schools.* Springfield, ILL: Charles C. Thomas.

Juola, J.F., Ward, N.J., & McNamara, T. (1982). Visual search and reading of rapid serial presentations of letter strings, words, and text. *Journal of Experimental Psychology General, 111(2),* 208-227.

Marmor, M.F. (1980). Visual loss in retinitis pigmentosa. *American Journal of Ophthalmology, 89,* 692-698.

Masson, M.E.J. (1983). Conceptual processing of text during skimming and rapid sequential reading. *Memory & Cognition, 11(3),* 262-274.

Merin, S., & Auerbach, E. (1976). Retinitis pigmentosa. *Survey of Ophthalmology, 20(5),* 303-346.

O'Regan, K. (1981). The »convenient viewing position» hypothesis. In D.F. Fisher, R.A. Monty, & J.W. Senders (Eds.), *Eye Movements, Cognition & Visual Perception* (pp. 289-298). Hillsdale, NJ: Erlbaum.

Potter, M.C. (1984). Rapid serial visual presentation (RSVP): A method for studying language processing. In D.E. Kieras & M.A. Just (Eds.), *New methods in reading comprehension research* (pp. 91-118). Hillsdale, NJ: Erlbaum.

Potter, M.C., Kroll, J.F., & Harris, C. (1980). Comprehension and memory in rapid sequential reading. In R.S. Nickerson (Ed.), *Attention and Performance VIII* (pp. 395-418). Hillsdale, NJ: Erlbaum.

Rayner, K. (1983). The perceptual span and eye movement control during reading. In K. Rayner (Ed.), *Eye movements in reading: Perceptual and Language Processes* (pp. 97-120). New York: Academic.

Rayner, K., & Bertera, J.H. (1979). Reading without a fovea. *Science, 206,* 468-469.

Rayner, K., Slowiaczek, M.L., Clifton, C. Jr., & Bertera, J.H. (1983). Latency of sequential eye movements: Implications for reading. *Journal of Experimental Psychology: Human Perception and Performance, 9* (6), 912-922.

Trevor-Roper, P.D., & Curran, P. (1984). *The Eye and Its Disorders.* Oxford: Blackwell Scientific.

Ward, N.J., & Juola, J.F. (1982). Reading with and without eye movements: Reply to Just, Carpenter, and Woolley. *Journal of Experimental Psychology: General, 111(2),* 239-241.

Williamson, N.L., & Muter, P. (1985). Rapid serial visual presentation and reading: The role of practice, external pacing, and multiple-word windows. Manuscript submitted for publication.

Communication and Handicap: Aspects of
Psychological Compensation and Technical Aids
E. Hjelmquist and L.-G. Nilsson (editors)
© Elsevier Science Publishers B.V. (North-Holland), 1986

BLIND PEOPLE READING A DAILY RADIO DISTRIBUTED NEWSPAPER: BRAILLE AND SPEECH SYNTHESIS

BRITT-MARIE DROTTZ and ERLAND HJELMQUIST

Department of Psychology, University of Göteborg,
Göteborg, Sweden[*]

Results are reported from a study of five blind subjects' reading a daily newspaper, which they received via radio signals. Empirical results are based on interviews and notes from the subjects' diaries. The users' reactions and attitudes to the new possibility to read a daily paper by Braille or speech synthesis were investigated on different occasions during the research period. Furthermore, the reliability of the technical equipment, with respect to factors that could influence the subjects' possibilities to read the paper, was investigated. The results showed positive or very positive reactions to the new technique, on the whole, and to the possibility it offered to get access to a daily paper. This held true for Braille reading as well as for speech synthesis. The subjects were asked to evaluate Braille and speech synthesis in relation to each other. This comparison indicated certain preferences and differences, to the effect that speech synthesis was preferred if the subject was not a very good Braille reader. The new technique was also judged as giving the best possibilities for searching for information in a paper, compared to other available methods of reading. The report concludes with some suggestions for future research.

The present study is a result of a joint effort by a Swedish daily newspaper (Göteborgs-Posten, the second largest in Sweden), Chalmers University of Technology, Gothenburg, the Swedish Federation of Visually Handicapped, the Swedish Institute for the Handicapped, both in Stockholm and the Department of Psychology in Gothenburg. (See Jönsson, Lindström, & Rubinstein, 1984; The Swedish State Committe on Spoken Newspapers, DsU 1984:8). The project was financed by the National Swedish Board for Technical Development, with contributions from the Federation of Visually Handicapped.

1   INTRODUCTION

There are approximately 200 000 persons with some kind of visual deficiences in Sweden (Lindblad & Weibull, 1984). Among these, there are about 10 000 blind or nearly blind persons (Hedberg, 1984). The age and sex distribution within the group of visually impaired deviate among the Swedish population: about 75% are above 65 years of age and the largest proportion of the group (about 60%) is female (Lindblad & Weibull, 1984). The mean educational and employment level is low compared to the Swedish population.

Visual information amounts to a large proportion of all perceptual information for sighted persons. Sighted people in daily life have the possibility of scanning the surroundings easily to get impressions of other people via non-verbal (visual) information, i.e., by reading texts, advertisements, official notes, etc. Among blind people or persons with visual deficiencies, these possibilities are greatly reduced. Because of this, information must be derived via some external personal help or technical device.

A group within The Swedish Council for Planning and Coordination of Research (1985) considered the difficulties of getting visual information for visually impaired people a basic problem, i.e., a problem which could give rise to other types of problems. A person who has partially or completely lost his/her sight is, therefore, dependent on other persons to get access to the daily flow of information. This forced dependence can be described as a social handicap. The process of creating a social handicap out of a physical deficiency is described and commented on in one of the papers from another group within The Swedish Council for Planning and Coordination of Research (1985). The paper defines a handicap as a social process, where the environment and the personal situation offer the criteria for defining and explaining the degree of the handicap. Individuals are considered handicapped in relation to the environmental and personal situation in which they live. Research should, therefore, direct its efforts, to a greater extent, to studies of the environmental conditions which create handicapped individuals.

As far as blind or visually impaired persons are concerned, this would mean that a visual deficiency could be defined depending on the number of problems the individual encounters in daily life; research is an important aspect from this perspective in order to develop devices available for improving the possibilities for receiving information.

This is the aim of the present project. We have used the perspective on handicap as proposed by a third group within the Swedish Council for Planning and Coordination of Research (1985), where they write: »What a person achieves in a specific situation must therefore be related to the situation in which he/she lives, what he/she already manages and knows, and what intentions and motivations are behind the action (p. 33, our translation).

The information situation for the visually impaired is greatly dependent on the auditory modality. Auditory information includes conversations, listening to TV and radio, cassette recordings, etc. Some visually impaired can read large print or use a strong magnifying glass to read a text. Other technical devices are magnified TV-systems and reading machines. Those who can read Braille or comparable tactile information also have the opportunity of reading books and papers in that format. The latter source of information, however, is space demanding: if paper is utilized, it is about a hundred times more voluminous than ordinary texts (Lindblad & Weibull, 1984).

Altogether there are three main sources of written information which can be combined in different ways for the visually impaired: (1) enlarged texts (2) transmission via speech and (3) transmission via tactile reading. These sources of information can now be enriched due to computer technique. Texts can be read tactually on a terminal display and/or listened to in the form of synthetic speech via a speech synthesis apparatus. This report concerns the actual use of the latter two new devices for reading a daily newspaper.

2 METHOD

2.1 Subjects

The size of the group was limited by the number of available Braille machines, and consequently, in all, five subjects participated; three men and two women. The mean age of the group was 44 years; three persons were under 35 years and two were over 60 years of age. Three persons were blind since birth or early childhood, while two had lost their sight as adults. The younger participants had at least high school education and the older had a compulsory school background. The younger persons also worked full time, whereas the older participants were active sporadically within organizations for the visually impaired. Two of the participants had read daily newspapers before losing their sight, while this possibility was offered to the others for the first time in their lives. The participants knew each other prior to the project, as they were all active in the same organizations. Participation in the project intensified the contact between them during this time.

Needless to say, the participants cannot be regarded as a representative group of visually impaired persons. In fact, they were selectively chosen because of their ability to read Braille and their willingness to spend a great deal of their spare time reading the newspaper throughout the entire project period. However, other criteria such as sex and age were also considered. The selection of participants was based on an arrangement between the organization for the visually impaired in Gothenburg and the project organizers.

2.2   The Device

The technique applied in the present study utilizes the fact that daily papers are being produced more and more by computerized processes. This means that the information in a newspaper is stored, in the first place, in a computer and this information can, in principle, be accessed by anyone with proper equipment. Consequently, each participant had in his or her home an FM-radio through which the newspaper was received, a mass memory (a Winchester disc) where the paper was stored, a Braille terminal (first half of the project) and a speech synthesizer (second half of the project). The equipment was controlled by a microcomputer which also controlled the reading procedures. The transmission of the text started automatically after the ordinary radio programmes had finished at night. This was done by FM transmission to the participants' home receivers. The transmission took approximately 90 seconds, and contained about 600000 characters, i.e., almost the complete newspaper with the exception of photos and logotypes etc. which were not included on the relevant newspaper computer (Rubinstein, 1984). Two types of tactile devices were used, (a) a VersaBraille terminal was used by three of the subjects, and (b) a Schönherr terminal was used by two of the subjects. The VersaBraille required a specific starting routine, i.e., two cassettes had to be loaded before reading was possible, while the Schönherr terminal was easier to start. The displays of the terminals differed: VersaBraille had sharper dots and a reading line with 20 characters, while the Schönherr display had a thin plastic foil covering the 40 characters of the reading line. The speech synthesis apparatus, the SA 101, was produced by INFOVOX AB in Sweden. The entire investigation period was four months, whith two months of Braille reading and two months of speech synthesis reading.

2.3 Search Routines

A search system for the newspaper was developed and organized in a tree-like structure (Rubinstein, 1984). The structure remained the same for the duration of the project, with the addition of some specific speech synthesis commands during the latter project period.

At the top of the hierarchial structure, there were 19 main classes, for example »first page», »culture» and »sports» etc. There was a maximam of four levels in the stucture, but not all main classes contained sublevels. The user could move horizontally within each level by using the commands »f», forewards and »b», backwards. Lower or higher levels could be reached by using the commands »n», downwards and »u» upwards. The main classes could be reached immediately by the command »c», class, linked with the appropriate first three letters describing the requested class. For example, »cspo» was used for reaching the sports main class. From the point where the user was reading, he or she could go to the »next line», »previous line» or directly to another section. It was possible to scan the text or the entire newspaper by only reading the headlines or the initial sentences of an article by using the commands »next article», »next paragraph» or »next graphic change» within the chosen main class. The user could also mark a specific spot in the text by using the command »s», save, and go back to that spot be using the »h», the fetch command. Another command (»find») could be used to look up a certain letter combination in the text. As mentioned above, some commands were added to the described search possibilities used during the speech synthesis part of the project. These were commands regulating the reading speed: »talk faster», »talk slower», »talk in words» and »talk in letters». (See also Rubinstein, 1984).

2.4 Data Collection

Five interviews were conducted with each subject during the project. Data were also obtained from diaries, completed by the participants at least once a week. The questionnaire concerned demographic data, earlier contact with daily newspapers, Braille reading speed and the information situation in general. The subjects were also asked about their expectations concerning participation in the project, expectations generally about the new technology, as well as personal reactions when actually using the new device. We asked what was considered interesting or important reading, as well as what sort of information was of less interest or importance. We tried to understand how subjects used the stucturing of the text described above, for reading, based on questions concerning frequency of use of available commands. We asked how they searched for specific material and how they developed their reading skill.

Some questions were asked at every interview in order to make comparisons possible over time. Towards the end of the four-month project period, the participants were asked to compare the two reading modalities as well as other information media with respect to aspects of access to specific text material, ease in handling the device and reading satisfaction. They were also asked general questions concerning different aspects of the communication and work within the group of participants and within the whole project. In the diary questionnaire, (which was a tape-recorded collection of questions sent to the participants at the start of the project), we tried to capture the actual use of the commands, what had been read, comments about interesting, uninteresting or difficult text materials, if the subjects had encountered any technical problems and, if so, a description of these problems and their solutions.

3 RESULTS

Questions about expectations concerning the new technology, in general, and the equipment used, in particular, gave rise to positive judgements. The attitude to the current technical development in society was colored by the experiences of participating in the project and closely connected to the enthusiasm due to access to a daily newspaper. The participants used expressions such as »very good», »gives hope», »sensational» etc. concerning the device and the reading possibilities, at the first interview. Generally speaking, high expectations and hope were expressed for the future concerning the technical development of equipment for the visually impaired. The participants were encouraged by and positively surprised that the sighted world had put such an effort and spirit into blind people's information situation as demonstrated by the project. A sense of fascination and surprise were among the emotions mentioned with regard to handling the apparatus and the reading ability, mixed with confessions about prior doubts about being able to handle it all. One person pointed out that one does not have to be an engineer to be able to read the news.

We also noticed a carefulness in the initial enthusiasm. All participants commented on the cost aspects and mentioned future possibilities for making information available via the technique, in relation to future priorities of decision makers. A possible interpretation of these comments is that the participants wanted to dampen their enthusiasm, as they were well aware that the reading possibility was only for the limited time of the project. This interpretation was supported by the fact that the participants even at the first interview commented on their fears of future negative reactions, when the time came for their reading opportunity to cease.

Apart from the negative aspect of the considerable current costs for the apparatus, the participants emphasized the advantages of handling information using computers, their storage possibilities and the advantages of the method for searching in a large text material. Huge Braille text books or hours of listening to tape recordings were characteristic of their normal information situation. Regarding the possible interest among the blind and the visually impaired in general, it was agreed that this new technical approach could be frightening or less interesting for most of the elderly, but would in due time be discovered and appreciated among active and young persons. These comments had generally greater relevance concerning the speech synthesis apparatus, while the tactile device also requires Braille reading skills, a skill managed only by about 1700 persons in Sweden. However, there was some hope that greater availability of texts and daily news would encourage more active interest in learning to read Braille and thereby maintain and develop the written language.

The equipment in the project was evaluated mainly in the light of its information distributing function, as the participants all agreed that getting in touch with normal, everyday news and available information was the most important aspect when developing new aids. Apart from this, they also gave specific examples and advice for the ideal equipment. First of all it must function well and all the parts in the distribution chain must be well organized. When a well-established habit of having access to a daily newspaper (or other kinds of material) is disturbed, dissatisfaction is only to be expected. Secondly, the equipment, ideally, should be combined into one small, portable and noiseless unit. Thirdly, there was an explicit wish to be able to choose reading modality, or better still, have a combined speech synthesis and Braille reading possibility. Some suggestions for developing the search routines were also made, and comments were given on the layout and content of the newspaper.

Technical disturbances, as reported by the participants, occurred in approximately 21% of the total project time, (prolonged reading time is included here). Fifteen percent of this time was due to sending or transmission functions, whereas about 5% of the total time reduced the reading possibility due to receiver or apparatus deficiences. The reaction to these interruptions was mainly irritation, mixed with hopes for the transmission to be quickly resumed. The participants were clearly aware of the explorative nature of the project, consequently, these disturbances were to be expected. Nevertheless, they worried about the interruptions, since these interfered with their access to the newspaper, and in their perspective, precious time.

The participants agreed that the starting and reading procedures were relatively simple to handle. After one to two weeks they felt familiar with these procedures. No one mentioned any severe difficulties in the handling of the apparatus, though initially questions were raised concerning what actually happened when the commands were given. This knowledge, though interesting in its own right, would not be necessary for users, but the participating men expressed interest in deepening their knowledge in that respect. It was interesting that these comments were mentioned first at the third interview, showing the changing character of problems confronting the participants.

The VersaBraille terminal was regarded by its users as superior to the two other Braille machines, though complicated. The advantages of the apparatus were attributed to the dots on the display which could be easily read, and to the speed with which the new line was received. The Schönherr users were content with their terminal, even though the plastic foil which covered the display was considered to be somewhat inconvenient, which made it a bit difficult to read the produced signs.

Another source of comments from the participants was the computer-Braille language. This formalization of Braille differed in certain repects from that hitherto used, and signs for capital letters and numbers were unfamiliar to the users. The initial reading speed was therefore slightly slower.

At the second interview, after about six weeks, all participants seemed to have got used to the apparatus and the reading techniques, and from then on their interest was mainly directed towards the content of the newspaper. The reading procedures seemed automatized and the users discovered or made more frequent use of the available commands.

The extra apparatus which was installed after two months for the speech synthesis period was not specifically commented on. The experience was mainly one of continuity, but using another modality. During this period the participants kept the terminals for giving commands, but the text was read via the speech synthesis apparatus.

At this point in time, those who had never read a daily paper said that one previous problem had been to discover the structure of the newspaper. When the speech synthesis was installed, they knew what to expect and approximately where to find an expected text in the paper. Because of this, the change of apparatus was of less importance. The previously sighted participants already had an idea of the structure of a newspaper, so the problem of what to expect was less important to them, even though they explicitly mentioned comparisons with the picture they held with regard to the contents. Comments on the quality of the synthetic speech was surprisingly positive. Even those participants who were hesitant to its use before starting the speech synthesis part of the project, changed their minds and found the speech quality acceptable. Later on, more specific criticism was expressed concerning the speech quality, to the effect that although the speech was acceptable it was important for it to be improved further. A suggested improvement was to include bass and treble adjustment. This could be important for users with hearing deficits. It should also be possible to be able to choose a male or female voice.

The speech synthesizer used had some inadequate pronounciations and stressed some words in a »funny» way. When heard in its context there were seldom any problems in understanding the meaning, but it took some time to get used to the specific »dialect». The speech sounded metallic and closed up and would not be enjoyable for reading novels or poetry. However, it was clearly pointed out that it was preferable to listen to this speech than not to be able to read the material at all. It was also pointed out that news material, dictionary information and other kinds of current text would be convenient to listen to in this way and would also fit perfectly the type of storage and retrieval system used.

At the end of the project, four of the five participants said that if they had to choose between the Braille device and the speech synthesis device they would choose the latter. With the speech synthesis device, one could read more text during the same time, do other things while listening, as well as listen together with the family. Although Braille was favored for certain purposes, e.g., certain types of text comprehension, spelling and immediate access to numbers, these aspects were generally considered less important for news information. The fifth person considered Braille reading advantageous, taking into consideration the immediate access to the material read and better concentration while reading. This person was an excellent Braille reader.

One good piece of advice to beginners of the new technique is to be patient. It should be understood that it takes time to get used to the procedures and search system, and learning the main classes and the specific commands comes in due time. The technique is nothing to be afraid of and should be investigated and explored. It was suggested that a start be made by exploring a specific part of the text closely, getting to know the structuring and search system to get a feeling of familiarity and control, and then continue with other text materials. Another suggestion was to learn to scan the material as soon as possible and in this way be able to survey the entire content and thus avoid stops and routine-like reading of articles of little interest.

It was also considered important to learn something about the functioning of the device, for example how to connect cables if they were accidentally disconnected.

In an ordinary newspaper there are often page references indicating continuation of an article inside the paper. In the computerized paper, the material was classified according to the previously mentioned main classes, not pages, resulting in initial difficulties to find the following text. After a certain amount of reading, the users developed a sense of what kind of material they were reading and could frequently guess in what main class the continuing text belonged. Another way of finding material was to use the contents specification where pages were indicated, and go to the class approximately indicated by the page numbers. The command »find» would also facilitate the search, provided that the relevant letter combination was given within the right class. The participants agreed that their ability to find the continuing text of an article developed in accordance with their knowledge of the structure of the paper.

When asked what kind of information was interesting to read, the subjects gave diverse answers. The information from the diaries and interviews indicated the development of favorite subjects, such as general news, local politics, sports or family news, etc. However, this more specialized reading occurred much later on. In the beginning, everyone read all kinds of material, interesting or not, as much as time permitted as they wanted to get a good overall view of the contents.

In such a newspaper as the one used in this project, which covers many different types of subjects, the possibility to read all different kinds of material was available and the participants agreed upon the importance of this aspect. Their everyday experience of information had hitherto been of material selected for them by other people.

When asked to describe the importance of the available information, the results can be summarized in the concepts of Equality, Choice and Communication. The equality stands for having access to the same material as other people, being able to form an opinion based on the source itself, instead of via second-hand information. It also stands for being able to enjoy or participate in a chosen activity, such as the cinema, local politics or sports events. The possibility of choice was stressed specifically as being dependent on information. To have access to information gave freedom of choice. Newspaper information was seen as an important source in this respect. The communication aspect stressed the opportunity it gave to be able to talk to others about current news, after reading about it oneself. Newspaper reading helps to initiate a conversation, forming an opinion and actively taking part in social life. These aspects highlightened and exemplified the handicap process mentioned earlier.

Questions were also asked concerning the comparisons of the two different modalities. The aspects compared were memory, access to material, ease of handling and satisfaction from reading. The kind of information best memorized, according to the subjects reports, was the main news items, events which were sensational and prominent. Material which was of personal interest was also easy to remember, such as a political argument, a report, or comments about sports events. Memory retrieval was described as more passive than active in the sense that when a topic was discussed it was easy to remember the material one had read and participate in the discussion.

Memory of texts during the tactile and auditive project periods were experienced differently. Three persons were of the opinion that reading Braille gave a better memory of the text. The main argument was that reading tactually was a more active and involving activity, while listening could easily be disturbed and interrupted, especially if one chose to do other things while listening. Two persons did not mention any differences concerning memory retrieval with respect to the two reading possibilities, as far as newspaper reading goes. One of them read any kind of material on the speech synthesis, the other preferred reading specialist literature in Braille.

Those who preferred the tactile modality pointed out that the information assimilated in this way was registered immediately and that it was difficult to read Braille passively. One person strongly emphasized that speech synthesis was easier to understand and memorize because the reading speed was higher, giving larger chunks of information. The text was therefore kept together better.

All the participants agreed that reading was much faster on the speech synthesis apparatus. There were different opinions, however, concerning the amount of information which could be handled and how soon one reaches an information overload.

It seems, therefore, that memory for text material presented in a tactile or an auditory modality may depend, firstly, on Braille reading speed and, secondly, on the kind of material to be read. The habit of listening to recorded text materials in general could also be of importance.

Questions concerning access to other kinds of information material were asked, even though it was difficult to make comparisons between the technique used and tape-recordings or Braille books. There was agreement that the new technique had great advantages with respect to storage capacity and in finding information in a vast information base. These advantages were related specifically to material where one wanted to scan or get a review of a lot of available information. On the other hand, it may be preferable to use tape-recordings with high speed or speech synthesis when reading specialized literature from beginning to end.

When handling text materials, the speech synthesis was preferred. This was partly due to the less difficult and less time consuming procedures to find relevant material, compared to ordinary tape recordings. On the whole, however, the participants were reluctant to make comparisons between the new technique and other media. This reluctance was mostly due to the fact that no other media presented, or could possibly present, a complete daily newspaper. The comparisons requested were therefore hard to conceive. Every medium has its own special advantages, usually containing specific kinds of information and therefore useful and necessary in their own rights. The new technology offered yet another kind of reading-searching possibility, unique in its own way.

As mentioned, there were diverse opinions as to what modality was preferred when reading different kinds of material, but satisfaction was nevertheless generally high.

4   DISCUSSION

We have described and discussed attitudes, ideas and problems reported on various occasions during a four-month investigation period, where the opportunity to read an almost complete newspaper was given to five blind persons. The participants' reactions were positive, but they also mentioned possible future improvements of the equipment. Participants in the project were not representative for the group of visually impaired in Sweden, mainly due to their Braille reading ability. Nevertheless, they were a group of blind persons clearly evidencing the importance and need for greater availability of current information.

Research within the frame of the work presented here will now concentrate on studies of basic psychological aspects as well as development of practically useful solutions for future users of the new type of technique. The psychological aspects are related to research within communication and cognitive psychology. Related research topics are discussed in Hjelmquist (1984), Kintsch and van Dijk (1978), Mandler and Johnson (1977), and Singer (1982).

There are both practical and theoretically interesting aspects in studies of text processing, with respect to comprehension and memory. Particularly interesting is the relation between text reading in tactile and auditory modes, such as comprehension and memory for the same information, presented in the different modalities.

An example of another interesting research topic is the possibility to study acquisition of skill when listening to speech synthesis. In spite of the advanced technique, there is still a long way to go before the speech synthesis sounds like an ordinary voice. There is little knowledge, as yet, concerning how learning and familarity to speech synthesis are developed.

Yet another topic concerns how individuals develop search strategies when using the tactile and auditory modalities, respectively. Their development of mental strategies for handling and using the available system can be followed in detail, since the subjects' use of the different commands is stored in the computer.

Finally, the type of material preferred in different modalities, could also be studied. Among the comments from the participants in this study, there was a request for a combined reading possibility, as the auditory modality was preferred in certain respects (long text passages, whole articles etc.) and the tactile modality in other respects (reading tables, numbers and names etc.).

The method of transmitting text via radio signals seem effective and could be of great importance to blind people, and potentially to sighted people as well. Therefore it is important to investigate the psychological consequences of this new technique. The study reported here is a first attempt to accomplish this.

REFERENCES

DsU (1984). Om stöd till radio och kassettidningar. (About support of radio and cassette newspapers). Betänkande från taltidningskommittén, 8.

Hedberg, R. (1984). Studier av taltidningsläsning. (Studies of reading cassette-recorded newspapers). C-uppsats i informationsteknik, Statsvetenskapliga institutionen, Göteborgs universitet.

Hjelmquist, E. (1984). Memory for conversations. *Discourse Processes, 7,* 319-334.

Jönsson, I., Lindström, J.-I. & Rubinstein, H. (1984). RAPS-projektet. En kort beskrivning. (The RAPS-project. A brief description). Chalmers tekniska högskola, Göteborg.

Kintsch, W., & van Dijk, T. (1978). Toward a model of text comprehension and production. *Psychological Review, 85,* 363-394.

Lindblad, A., & Weibull, L. (1984). Kassettidningar i Sverige. Innehåll och läsning. (Casette-recorded newspapers in Sweden). Forskningsrapport till taltidningskommittén, Sociologiska institutionen, Umeå universitet, och Avd. för Masskommunikation, Göteborgs Universitet.

Mandler, J.M., & Johnson, N.S. (1977). Remembrance of things parsed: Story structure and recall. *Cognitive Psychology, 9,* 111-151.

Rubinstein, H. (1984). Radio-distributed digital daily newspaper for the blind. *Proceedings of the 2nd International Conference on Rehabilitation Engineering,* Ottawa.

Singer, M. (1982). Comparing memory for natural and laboratory reading. *Journal of Experimental Psychology: General, 111,* 331-347.

The Swedish Council for Planning and Coordination of Research (1985). *Forskning om Handikapp* (Research on Handicaps). Report 85:3.

Communication and Handicap: Aspects of
Psychological Compensation and Technical Aids
E. Hjelmquist and L.-G. Nilsson (editors)
© Elsevier Science Publishers B.V. (North-Holland), 1986

WORKING MEMORY, READING AND DYSLEXIA

ALAN BADDELEY

MRC Applied Psychology Unit, Cambridge, England

Working memory is suggested as a framework for understanding some aspects of the complex skill of reading, together with hypothetical specific strategies. An articulatory loop model is outlined, comprising a store and a recycling system. The implications of the working memory model are discussed, and it is claimed that cognitive psychology is of value for understanding normal as well as impaired cognitive functioning.

1   INTRODUCTION

The alleviation of handicap offers a challenge that demands the skills of many different disciplines. The contributions of the engineer in designing prostheses, or the psychoacoustician in helping the deaf, or the educationalist in aiding the learning disabled are all obvious; almost as obvious is the value of an applied experimental psychologist in measuring the effectiveness of any proposed aids to the handicapped. It is however much less clear that the psychological theorist can make any contribution, and it is this issue that I plan to address. I shall argue that a conceptual understanding of the processes underlying normal cognition offer a valuable framework, not only for conceptualis ing deficits, but sometimes also for suggesting methods of alleviation. It would of course be foolish to pretend that our understanding of cognition is at anything other than a very early stage of development, but even so, I would like to argue that it can provide valuable background for work on the alleviation of handicap. I shall do so by describing a theoretical model or framework with which i have been working for about 10 years; I shall then discuss my attempts at applying it to the understand ing of normal reading and dyslexia. The model in question is concerned with *Working Memory,* a hypothetical system involved in storing and manipulating information in the process of performing such important cognitive tasks as reasoning, learning, comprehending and reading (Baddeley, in press).

2   COMPONENTS OF MEMORY

While this remains a somewhat controversial area, I think that most people currently working in the field would accept that certain distinctions are useful. One is a distinction between long-term memory and what used to be called short-term memory, which is now more frequently called 'working memory'. Long-term memory is a system which is concerned with storing information needed on a semi-permanent basis. Short-term, or working memory, is concerned with temporary storage of information (Baddeley, 1983). In listening to a sentence, for example, you need to remember the wording, at least until you get to the end of the sentence. On the other hand, four or five or six sentences later you do not need to know specifically which word appeared in which position in that sentence. What is then needed is the gist or general meaning. Working memory provides a temporary storage system which is responsible for accurately holding the surface information, while the gist is more dependent on long-term memory.

In what sense is this concept of working memory different from the older concept of short-term memory? One way of illustrating this is to describe some experiments performed about 10 years ago by a colleague, Graham Hitch, and myself, which were concerned with the rather simple question of »what is short-term memory for?» There were many suggestions about this but not much evidence. Most views assumed that short-term memory is used for the temporary storage and manipulation of information and that it plays a central role in learning, comprehending, reasoning, and many other cognitive tests. We decided that we would try and test this view directly (Baddeley & Hitch, 1974).

It was generally assumed that short-term memory was involved in memory span tasks, such as recalling a telephone number. We therefore decided to use up the short-term memory capacity of our subjects by giving them a telephone number to remember, while at the same time, requiring them to do one of the many tasks which are supposed to be dependent on short-term memory. The logic behind this is as follows: most theorists assumed that the short- term memory system has a limited amount of capacity, and cannot absorb and hold more than a small amount of information. It was also generally assumed that a 6 digit telephone number would use up most of the available capacity. So with very little of the available capacity left, our subjects should show great difficulty in comprehending, in reasoning or in learning.

We therefore carried out an experiment in which we gave our subjects a reasoning task comprising a series of sentences that purport to describe the order of two letters, A and B. They can either be very simple sentences like, *»A follows B - AB»,* which is false, or include a passive, such as *»B is followed by A - AB»,* or a negative, *»A is not followed by B - BA».* We had our subjects solve problems of this sort as quickly as they could, and at the same time we gave them a telephone number to remember. The results are shown in Figure 1: response time increases systematically with memory load from approximately 2 sec for a simple sentence to about 3 sec for our most complex items, a reliable but far from dramatic increase.

Secondly, and perhaps more strikingly, regardless of how many numbers the subjects were remembering, the error rate on the reasoning task was approximately constant at about 5%. The fact that a six digit number approaching memory span, did not serious ly disrupt reasoning is hard to explain in terms of the existing theory. Either we had to assume that remembering a telephone number does not fill up the short-term system, or else that the system is not used in reasoning. But both of these must be to some extent false. If they were true, we would not expect the observed relationship. It is clear then that the situation is more complicated than appeared. A more complicated short-term memory system is suggested, not just by this, but by quite a lot of other sources of information.

We therefore opted to split the concept of the unitary short-term memory into several separate components. We assume first of all a system which we call the central executive. This is the part of the system that is responsible for controlling attention, for selecting strategies and for operating strategies. We split off from this a number of what we termed »slave systems», which are less clever, more specialised, and allow the central executive to get on with the more important things, helping it by storing information. One of the two systems which we have so far explored in details is the *Visuo-spatial Scratch Pad,* or *Sketch Pad* which is involved in creating and maintaining visual imageas. I will not comment about this because, although there is some evidence that it is involved in reading, its role in reading has been explored very little.

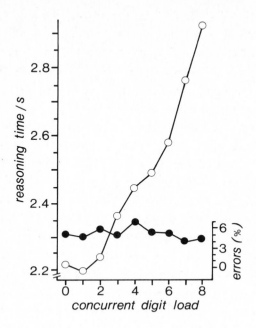

FIGURE 1

Relationships between reasoning time, concurrent digit load and error rate.

The other system is termed the *Articulatory Loop*. Essentially it is related to sub-vocal speech or sub-vocal rehearsal. If you look up a telephone number and have to walk across a room before dialling it, most people tend to say the number to themselves, utilising the articulatory loop. In recent years we have attempted to explore this process, which appears to be important in reading.

I think the importance of the articulatory loop for fluent adult readers is different from its role in children learning to read. Before examining reading I shall discuss the evidence for a separate articulatory loop system. Supportive evidence is extensive and will be examined in some detail. This may help in understanding what the system is and also I hope to give it greater credibility. The essence of this approach to theorising is to try to tie together a substantial body of related work in such a way that, although perhaps any individual experiment can be explained in several different ways, the sum total is very hard to explain in any way other than the one proposed. The whole enterprise therefore is one of trying to tie together a great deal of related evidence and in order to convey the flavour of this approach it is necessary to discuss this evidence. One of the most striking phenomena associated with the articulatory loop is the effect on memory of acoustic or phonological similarity. As Conrad and Hull (1964) showed, repeating a string of letters that sound alike (e.g. *B T C D G*) is more likely to produce a mistake than if they sound dissimilar (e.g. *H Y W M R*). Similarly with words; a sequence of five dissimilar words, like *pit, day, dog, bar, sup* will be easier than a phonological sequence such as *mad, cat, map, tax, can.* This result points to a system for temporarily storing information that is based on speech.

Two pieces of further evidence support this view. One is that if I were to present you with these words visually the effect would remain. However if instead of allowing subjects to say the items to themselves, I keep their articulators busy by requiring them to say something else like *'da da da da da'*, then the amount remembered drops because the subject is not able to use the sub- vocal system. Secondly the effect of similarity of sound disappears. Another phenomenon that reflects the articulatory loop is that based on word length. If I give subjects five short words to remember, like *sun, peg, ham, wit, bond,* this task will cause little difficulty. If instead I present *association, opportunity, representative, organisation, considerable,* people have much greater difficulty in remembering them accurately. This is because of the semantic characteristics of the various words. In other experiments we have used, for example, names of countries that are short like *France, Chad* or long like *Tanganyika, Switzerland.* Again a very big difference accours in favour of the short words. The crucial factor is not the number of syllables but how long it takes you to say each word. Another experiment used two-syllable words; in one case the two syllables were long with words like *Friday, harpoon* in the other they were short with words like *bishop* and *wicked.* We found that the words that take a long time to say also lead to poorer memory (Baddeley, Thomson, & Buchanan, 1975).

The word length effect produced an interesting spin-off in cross cultural research. Nick Ellis at Bangor Unviersity became intrigued by the fact that the norms for digit span in the Welsh version of the WISC were systematically lower than the American norms. Thinking about this, it occurred to him that the Welsh digits all seem to have longer vowel sounds, and he ran an experiment with bilingual students, testing their memory span in Welsh - which was their preferred language - and in English, as their second language. He found that when analysing their span in terms of the time it takes to speak sequences, then the difference vanishes. When he stopped his subjects saying the material to themselves by having them say *'da da da da da'*, to keep their articulators busy, the difference re-appeared (Ellis & Hennelly, 1980). So it looks as though there is a rehearsal system that operated at a certain speed. Long words take longer to process and are therefore less well remembered.

One final piece of evidence related to the functioning of the articulatory lopp I came upon accidentally. I was working with a visiting colleague from France, Pierre Salamé, on the effect of noise on memory. He had previously worked on white noise and had found very small effects. He was interested in looking at the effects of unattended speech on memory. He predicted that there would be much larger effects because the meaning of the speech would, he thought, interfere. I postulated that this would not happen because the phonological memory system does not seem to be very dependent on meaning. In fact we were both wrong. We ran an experiment in which the subject sits in front of the screen and a series of numbers appear. The subject's task is to wait until the sequence has finished and then write the numbers down in the correct order. In one condition whilst memorising the incoming digits irrelevant spoken information is presented comprising either words or nonsense syllables. Unattended speech impaired memory performance as Pierre Salamé had predicted but I was correct in predicting that meaning would be unimportant since the disruption was as great for nonsense syllables as it was for words (Salamé, & Baddeley, 1982).

What are the implications of this pattern of results? I will begin by outlining a simple model, then briefly go through the various effects which have been described and examine how they can be explained. The model assumes two separate components, the first of which is a store which holds speech-based phonological information. The second component is a control process based on articulation or sub-vocal rehearsal, a process that serves two functions. It can take material that is written and convert it into a speech-based code; this enhances memory by feeeding it into the phonological store. As this is a relatively durable store, such a strategy is often helpful. A second useful function of the articulatory process is that it can act as a way of maintaining items in the store. An item in the phonological store will fade over time unless refreshed by means of the articulatory rehearsal process which can pick out an item and recycle it, boasting the fading trace in a way that resembles the refreshing of a fading visual trace on a TV screen by the scanning process.

The articulatory loop model hence comprises a two-process system: a store and a re-cycling system that can put information into the store, or pick it out and refresh it. The phonological similarity effect occurs because the items within this store are stored in terms of their speech-based or sound characteristics. Two more items are very similar in sound, they will tend to be confused when the store is searched, with the result that errors will appear. The word length effect does not arise in the store itself but comes from the rehearsal process. If the subject is rehears ing something, the longer it takes to say the slower the process of rehearsal, and the greater the chance that an item will fade before its memory trace is refreshed.

The unattended speech effect is explained by assuming that, when information is spoken, it goes directly into the phonological store, whether the listener attends to the spoken material or not. This is why unattended speech causes so much trouble. The subject is using the store to try and remember visual material while at the same time a voice feeds irrelevant material into the store, corrupting it and hence reducing its efficiency. The process of articulatory suppression prevents the subject trans ferring the visually presented items into the phonological store hence making the corruption of the store by unattended speech irrelevant. The subject is relying on a different memory store.

Having given a brief overview of the articulatory loop component of working memory, I would now like to examine the implications of the working memory model for understanding reading and dyslexia.

I shall begin by briefly discussing adult fluent reading. Is there any evidence for a general involvement of working memory in the performance of normal adults? There certainly is some. In particular there is evidence from a number of studies that have used a measure known as »working memory span», whereby a person has both to remember information and to manipulate it at the same time. One such test requires a subject to process a number of sentences and then the first or last word of each sentence. So a subject might hear *'Dogs eat meat, Sheep climb trees, Policemen wear large boots'* and then be asked what the first word was in each. A correct response would be *'dogs, sheep, policemen'*. Performance on this task correlates surprisingly highly, with comprehension score on a standardised reading test in normal fluent reading adults. Those who have a good span on the test also tend to be good at comprehending spoken prose (Daneman & Carpenter, 1980).

While this technique suggests that working memory is involved in fluent reading it is not very analytic in revealing which components of working memory are important, or why. Some of the experiments which I have been doing with colleagues have been connected with the more specific question »Does the articulatory loop help in fluent reading in adults?» We ran one experiment using a technique that has become colloquially known as the silly sentences test. It involves presenting subjects with a series of simple statements about the world that any reasonable person ought to be able to answer, such as *»Robins have red breasts», »US Presidents hold political office».*

Negatives are produced by crossing over the subject and object of two sentences, sometimes producing rather bizarre items such as *»US Presidents have red breasts»* and *»Robins hold political office»,* hence the name »silly sentences». It has the advantage that it is a task that people enjoy doing and perform at a rapid rate. It has proved to be sensitive to many stressors ranging from alcohol to performance at depth in sea divers. One experiment that we ran looked at the extent to which working memory in general and the articulatory loop in particular were involved in sentence comprehension. The role of working memory in general was assesssd by loading up the memory, giving subjects a six-figure telephone number to remember while they were verifying sentences. The articulatory loop was investigated by having them repeatedly utter the digits 1, 2, 3, 4, 5, and 6 so as to suppress articula tion, while involving a minimal memory load. We found that the time required to verify the sentences increased with memory load very consistently. However, simply stopping subjects articulating had no effect on performance. They were just as fast as when they were free to sub-vocalise. Error rates were uniformly very low. So initially we concluded that adults do not use sub-vocal coding in comprehension.

There was however other evidence which seemed to be inconsistent with this conclusion and we decided to use a rather more demand ing test involving longer passages. We presented our subjects with passages of prose which contained occasional errors. The errors involved reversing the order of two words within passages comprising several hundred words. Hence, instead of *There was an abundance of food and water* the subject was given *There was an abundance food of and water.* Subjects were asked to put a ring round the error. We found that this task was very sensitive to the effects of articulatory suppression in terms of error rate though not speed. This suggests that for certain tasks which demand high accuracy, such as checking an insurance policy then sub-vocal representation is probably important. If you are read ing a novel, it probably does not make a great deal of difference to your ability to follow the plot (Baddeley, Eldridge, & Lewis, 1981).

Our evidence therefore suggests that sub-vocalisation may be helpful in adult reading, but is probably not at all essential. But what of learning to read in children? Here, I think there is much stronger evidence for the importance of the articulatory loop. One of the key observations was made by Conrad (1972), who noted that the acoustic similarity effect starts to appear in children at about the time they begin learning to read. He also pointed out that phonological coding in deaf children often does not occur, and that deaf children frequently have difficulty in learning to read. This stimulated work by Liberman and her co- workers Haskins laboratories in the

USA. They observed that the children who were particularly poor at reading, despite having normal intelligence, tended not to show the phonological similarity effect, whereas good readers did. This particular result has caused a certain amount of controversy; for example Ellis, Miles and I have looked at dyslexic fourteen-year-olds in Britain and found that, although their memory span is low, they do show evidence of phonological coding. Age of testing may be an important factor. Phonological coding of visually presented material is something that does not occur in very young children, it develops later (Hitch & Halliday, 1983). It may be the case that children who exhibit reading disabilities are even later in showing phonological coding effects. However, having developed a phonological strategy, and having shown every sign of using sub-vocal coding, their memory span is still poorer and they still show verbal learning problems (Jorm, 1983). It seems therefore that such children do use the articulatory loop system, but that the system does not function as effectively as in normal children.

There seems to be very strong evidence that children with reading disabilities very often have impaired memory span, or difficulty in retaining sequential order information (Jorm, 1983). Many phenomena arise which at first sight do not appear to be related to language but which, when examined more closely, suggest that sub-vocal coding of some sort could be involved. For example a joint study with Ellis and Logie looked at various aspects of reading in dyslexic children on a wide range of tasks. We found that the best predictor of their reading ability was the rate at which they could count rapidly from 1 to 10, a task that was used in order to estimate how quickly they could sub-vocalise. There is evidence from other sources which again suggests that the rate of sub-vocalisation may be a crucial factor (Baddeley, in press, Chapter 9); but I think at the moment it is too soon to specify just what aspect of the articulatory loop system is defective in dyslexic children. The evidence points in the direction of some form of phonological deficit in many children with learning disabilities, but not necessarily all (Temple & Marshall, 1983). We ourselves have, however, found a surprising consistency in the pattern of performance in the children with reading disabilities that we have examined.

If one assumes then that the articulatory loop is important in learning to read, why is it important? One answer was suggested by listening to children trying to read out loud a word that was unfamiliar. They tended to process each individual letter in turn, say the letter to themselves, try to remember it while they pick off the next one, finally trying to blend together all the letters and search for a real word resembling that composite blended sound. I would argue that the system which is used to store and blend this information is the articulatory loop.

If the articulatory loop interpretation is tentatively accepted, can anything useful be concluded from it? In order to remember consonant sounds, what we typically do is to add a dummy vowel sound, an »uh» sound. If you want to say a »B» sound or a »P» sound or a »T» sound without any vowel after it, there's virtually nothing to hear unless such a vowel is added hence producing sounds such as »buh» and »tuh». Notice that when pronounced in this way, a sequence of consonants becomes a string of highly phonologically similar syllables. Note also that Conrad and Hull's work on phonological similarity in memory span indicates that this is the worst possible sequence for remember ing. This sort of sequence is maximally likely to produce errors of order and hence is something that it would be wise to avoid. How? One way would be to teach children to combine consonant and vowel pairs hence both reducing number of sounds to be maintained and also making the sound sequences easier to remember.

A further problem with the single letter strategy is that picking off each individual letter may create problems when a later letter changes the pronunciation of an earlier one, as in the case with the terminal »e» in *made*. A memory task in which the subject encodes a sequence of letters in memory and then must go back and change one of them is obviously difficult and demanding. How can one avoid this problem? It may be advisable to discourage children from simply starting at the left and working through, perhaps encouraging them to start with a quick scan, looking for vowels that change the pronunciation of earlier items or combinations, before beginning their systematic letter decoding.

3   CONCLUSION

The concept of working memory therefore offers both a broad framework for understanding at least some aspects of the complex skill of reading, together with suggestions about specific strategies. It should be pointed out that these strategies have not been empirically validated, and hence should be explored with caution. Indeed, a recent review of the possible contribution of cognitive psychology to the study of reading suggested that a letter-by-letter decoding strategy might be preferable to decoding in consonant-vowel cluster (Anderson, Hiebert, Scott, & Wilkinson, 1985). However the authors admit that evidence on this point is lacking, and do not discuss the problems with letter-by- letter decoding just discussed, probably because such problems only become obvious when the task is considered from the view point of the working memory demands of reading.

In conclusion then I would like to suggest that cognitive psychology does have a useful contribution to make to the understanding and remediation of handicap, not only because the skills of the applied cognitive psychologist contribute to the evaluation of techniques, but also because our developing models of cognitive processing provide a useful framework for the understanding of both normal and impaired cognitive functioning.

REFERENCES

Anderson, R.C., Hiebert, E.H., Scott, J.A., & Wilkinson, I.A.G. (1985). *Becoming a nation of readers: The report of the commission on reading.* Washington: National Institute of Education.

Baddeley, A.D.(1983). *Your memory: A user's guide.* Harmondsworth: Penguin.

Baddeley, A.D. (in press) *Working memory.* Oxford University Press.

Baddeley, A.D., Eldridge, M., & Lewis, V. (1981) The role of subvocalisation in reading. *Quarterly Journal of Experimental Psychology, 33A,* 439-454.

Baddeley, A.D., & Hitch, G.J. (1974) Working memory. In G. Bower (Ed.), *Recent advances in learning and motivation Vol. VIII* (pp. 47-90). New York: Academic Press.

Baddeley, A.D., Thomson, N., & Buchanan, M. (1975). Word length and the structure of short-term memory. *Journal of Verbal Learning and Verbal Behavior, 14,* 575-589.

Conrad, R. (1972). Speech and reading. In J.F. Kavanagh & I.G. Mattingley (Eds.), *Language by Ear and by Eye.* Cambridge, Mass.: M.I.T. Press.

Conrad, R., & Hulls, A.J. (1964). Information, acoustic confusion and memory span. *Brittish Journal of Psychology, 55,* 429-432.

Daneman, M., & Carpenter, P.A. (1980). Individual differences in working memory and reading. *Journal of Verbal Learning and Verbal Behavior, 19,* 450-466.

Ellis, N.C., & Hennelley, R.A. (1980). A bilingual word-length effect: Implications for intelligence testing and the relative ease of mental calculation in Welsh and English. *British Journal of Psychology, 71,* 43-52.

Hitch, G.J., & Halliday, M. (1983). Working memory in children. *Philosophical Transactions of the Royal Society London* B, *302,* 325-340.

Jorm, A.F. (1983). Specific reading retardation and working memory: A review. *British Journal of Psychology, 74,* 311- 342.

Salamé, P., & Baddeley, A.D. (1982). Disruption of short-term memory by unattended speech: Implications for the structure of working memory. *Journal of Verbal Learning and Verbal Behavior, 21,* 150-164.

Temple, C.M., & Marshall, J.C. (1983). A case study of developmental phonological dyslexia. *Brittish Journal of Psychology, 74,* 517-533.

Communication and Handicap: Aspects of
Psychological Compensation and Technical Aids
E. Hjelmquist and L.-G. Nilsson (editors)
© Elsevier Science Publishers B.V. (North-Holland), 1986

THE READING/SHORT-TERM MEMORY RELATIONSHIP: IMPLICATIONS OF AN EXCEPTION

RONALD L. COHEN

Department of Psychology, York University,
Canada*

It is suggested that reading and short-term memory are related through the use of a common processing system dealing with phonological information. This supposition allows for children with difficulties in: reading, arithmetic, STM, or any combination of these skills. Irrespective of the particular model favoured, it is shown that children with deficient STMs can become proficient readers. The precise explanation of this phenomenon, however, remains to be given.

1 INTRODUCTION

That there is a correlation between reading ability and auditory short-term memory (STM) performance, there is little doubt. The poor performance shown by dyslexics on serial STM tasks such as digit span, is an established finding in the literature (see, for example, Cohen, 1982; Coltheart, 1980; Jorm, 1983). Nor is this relationship limited to comparisons between competent readers and dyslexics; it also extends to the upper end of the reading ability distribution (Cohen, Netley, & Clarke, 1984).

---

* The author is grateful to Melissa A. Clarke and Toni Mantini-Atkinson for their invaluable help in the preparation of this chapter. Thanks are also due to Anne Russon for her helpful comments on an earlier draft of the manuscript. The project was supported by grant A7023 from the Natural Sciences and Engineering Research Council of Canada.

The doubt arises in the interpretation of this correlation. The purpose of this chapter is first to review some of the explanations given for the reading/STM relationship, and second to consider the implications for these explanations, of an exception to the rule, with special emphasis on possible compensatory operations.

2   SOME EXPLANATIONS FOR THE READING/STM RELATIONSHIP

These can be conveniently classified into explanations which favour a common operation for reading and STM and those which favour a common system, but not a common operation. I will deal first with possible common operations.

Limited short-term memory capacity has been invoked as a cause of poor reading. So-called real reading, that is the read ing of sentences to extract mening, is thought to involve the use of STM to retain early words, presumably in phonemic form, in order to provide a guide for extracting meaning from later words (see Baron, 1977). Consequently, a sound STM would appear to be a prerequisite for real reading, according to this hypothesis. The argument against this hypothesis comes from studies in which subjects have to extract meaning from sentences either with or without a concurrent articulatory loading task. For example, Baddeley (1979) reports that articulatory suppression has no effect on meaning extraction. This result indicates that even if the articulatory system of working memory is normally used for the phonemic retention of the early words in a sentence, this is not a necessary operation for meaning extraction.

Causality in the other direction, namely that learning to read develops serial STM, could appear to be improbable since poor serial STM has been found to temporally precede poor reading (Cohen, 1982; Hull, as cited in Baddeley, 1979).

While dyslexics are undeniably handicapped in real reading, this may not be their basic difficulty. Dyslexic children also have an impairment in reading individual words. In such tasks, the meaning of the words is extraneous to the main objective, which is simply to pronounce the words. Two possible routes to word pronunciation have been proposed, namely the direct access ing of the word in the mental lexicon from the visual pattern of the printed word or letter string, or else the translation of individual letters or graphemes to phonemes and the blending of these phonemes into a word (see, for example, Baron, 1977; Jorm, 1981; Mitterer, 1982; Saffran & Martin, 1977; Shallice & Warrington, 1975; but see Henderson, 1982, and Kay & Marcel, 1981, for one-route alternatives to the two-route model of reading). The individual grapheme-phoneme-blending strategy has commonly been supposed to be especially important in the normal development of reading skills (Baddeley, 1979; Nelson, 1980; Snowling, 1980; Williams, 1984), although again there are dissenting views (see Bryant & Bradley, 1980). In this view developmental dyslexics owe their initial reading problems to an impairment in some aspect of the grapheme-to-phoneme-to-word operation, and it is here that the link between reading problems and poor STM is thought to lie (Baddeley, 1979; Jorm, 1983; Nelson, 1980). This is also thought to be the case for acquired deep dyslexics , who appear to have a specific graphemic-phonemic reading deficit (Shallice & Warrington, 1980) and also exhibit STM impairment (Coltheart, 1980).

One way of interpreting the reading/STM correlation, at least in the case of developmental dyslexics, follows directly from these findings. Baddeley (1979) argues that the letter-phoneme-blending route to recognizing a word requires that the early letters in the word, having been translated into phonemes, have to be maintained in working memory through the use of an articulatory loop, until the remainder of the letters are trans lated. If there is an impairment the reader will have to devote all of the articulatory system to retention and will thus be unable to decode the remainder of the letters. This view of the reading/STM connection can, for example, explain why dyslexics make more errors on the final than on the initial conconant in word identification. Incidentally, this would also account for the finding that in serial recall, dyslexics show a more reliable inferiority on the final than on the initial items in serial STM tasks (Cohen, 1982).

After reviewing some relevant literature in the area, Jorm (1983) extends Baddeley's notion somewhat. For Jorm (1983), the use of the articulatory loop plays an important role in learning to read, but a deficient loop is not the basic problem dyslexics suffer, since this depends in turn on a phonological deficit in long-term memory.

There are, however, some findings in the literature which create problems for this approach. First, dyslexic children show inferior STM ability in a running memory test in which long lists of digits of varying length are presented auditorily. In one such study the children were required to repeat the final three items in each list (Cohen & Netley, 1981). Given that the target set was unknown to the children until presentation was complete, and given that the dyslexic children showed their most marked inferiority at a presentation rate of 7.2 digits/sec, it is difficult to see how subvocal rehearsal can be invoked as an explanatory mechanism. Surely, the last thing subjects require for success on this task is the retention of early list items.

Second, dyslexic children have also demonstrated an impairment on a short-term probed paired associate task, where each list contained four digit-CVC word pairs. In this task, the STM deficit appeared on the primacy and not on the recency pairs (Cohen & Netley, 1978). This finding does not, of course, fit Baddeley's (1979) view of an overloaded articulatory loop exerting its effect on later items into store, although it could be made to fit a more general rehearsal explanation.

And third, if an articulatory loop impairment in dyslexic children manifests itself as sluggish articulation, then the data do not support Baddeley's (1979) hypothesis. Dyslexic children with a clear serial STM deficit proved to be able to recite the alphabet and count to 50 just as fast as normal readers (Cohen, 1983).

Another explanation for the reading/STM connection takes a sequential processing tack. Witelson (1977), for example, suggests that dyslexic children may have a left hemisphere dysfunction which affects both reading and serial STM, since both of these tasks involve the sequential processing of items. Here again, it is the grapheme-phoneme-blending aspect of reading which is of interest. This approach also runs into problems, however, Nelson (1980) has argued that if dyslexic children have a general sequential processing deficit, this should show up in their spelling. In analysing the spelling errors made by dyslexic children, however, Nelson (1980) found no evidence of increased sequencing errors. And second, although the Witelson (1977) suggestion of a left hemisphere dysfunction is certainly compatible with the incredible difficulties dyslexic children have in learning how to read it is not really compatible with the ease with which a group of dyslexic children were able to improve their STM capability over a series of weekly one hour practice sessions (see Cohen, 1982). In this study, the dyslexic children performed as well as competent readers, who had received no practice, by the fourth session and continued to improve their performance over the remaining sessions. This finding not only raises a problem for Witelson's (1977) rather specific view, but also for the more general notion that reading and STM impairments depend on a weakness in a common operation, namely why such an operational impairment is so readily overcome in STM but not in reading.

A more general approach to the reading/STM relationship is to suppose that it stems, not from a weakness in a common operation, but from an impairment in a common system, more specifically the phonological system (see, for example, Coltheart, 1980). In a review article, Williams (1984) tackles the question of the importance of phonemic operations in reading, concluding that phonemic segmentation and phonemic synthesis are important in learning to read. This conclusion dovetails rather nicely with the apparently reliable finding that dyslexic children show little in the way of a phonological similarity effect in STM, an effect which is very marked in nondyslexic children (Liberman, Shankweiler, Liberman, Fowler, & Fischer, 1977; Byrne, & Shea, 1979; Mark, Shankweiler, Liberman, & Fowler, 1977). The relationship between a phonemic weakness in a reading context, and the absence of a phonological similarity effect in the memory context receives further support by the twin findings that the absence of a phonemic effect in STM is limited to young dyslexics (Olson, Davidson, Kliegl, & Davies, 1984; Siegel & Linder, 1984), and that poor readers who showed a phonemic segmentation problem in first grade showed no signs of this problem in a follow-up 3 years later although they were still poor readers and poor phonetic spellers (Fox & Routh, 1980, 1983). Consequently, a good case can be made for reading and STM being related through the use of a common processing system which deals with phonological information. A more precise connection between the phonological aspects of reading and STM will be suggested in the next section.

Before going on to consider the implications of an exceptional case, it is perhaps worthwhile to review briefly the current state of the developmental literature in STM, in order to provide a broader perspective to our views on individual differences.

3   THEORIES OF STM DEVELOPMENT

An early explanation of IQ-related differences in STM capability used the decaying neurological activity view of STM inherent in the models of Hebb (1949), Broadbent (1958) and, more recently, Shiffrin and Schneider (1977). Developmentally retarded subjects were considered to be poor at STM tasks because their short-term traces decayed too rapidly (Ellis, 1963). This quasi- physiological approach to developmental STM was superceded not too many years later by a more cognitive approach. Borrowing from Atkinson and Shiffrin (1968), developmental changes in STM capability were attributed to the use of strategies such as rehearsal (Belmont, & Butterfield, 1969; Ellis, 1970; Flavell, 1970).

Both of the above approaches blamed developmental changes in STM performance on differences in the actual retention of information. Lately, however, the emphasis has shifted somewhat, and such changes in STM have been attributed to differences in item processing efficiency (Case, Kurland, & Goldberg, 1982; Dempster, 1981; Huttenlocher, & Burke, 1976). The STM system is considered to have a fixed attentional capacity. Subjects showing poor STM capability (young children, in the studies referred to above) have to direct a relatively large portion of their available attention to the identification of incoming items which reduces the amount of attention available for storage operations. Thus, although this model does talk of a retention problem, the basic cause of an underdeveloped STM capability is inefficient item processing. Baddeley's (1979) articulatory loop approach to the reading/STM relationship has some correspondence with the earlier rehearsal hypothesis of developmental STM, while Jorm's (1983) extension of that approach brings it more into line with the current item identification hypothesis.

The item processing view of developmental STM implies that item identification during encoding is a necessary operation for competent performance in serial STM tasks. This has been challenged both by Cohen and his colleagues (Cohen, 1982; Cohen, & Netley, 1981; Cohen, Quinton, & Winder, 1985) and by Hulme, Thomson, Muir, and Lawrence (1984). Cohen et al.s' argument against the item identification hypothesis rests on a failure to find reliable correlations between identification of items presented in an auditory string and serial STM performance (see Cohen, 1982) except in a sample of first grade children (Cohen, Quinton, & Winder, 1985). Furthermore, reliable age differences in running memory (recalling the final 3 digits in lists of varying length) were obtained even when presentation was too fast to allow for the identification of items during encoding (Cohen, Quinton, & Winder, 1985). In view of these findings Cohen et al. favour an explanation of the relatively poor serial STM capabilities of young children, retarded subjects, and dyslexics in terms of an impairment in handling speech sound patterns or nonsegmented speech (see models proposed by Neisser, 1967, and Aaronson, 1974).

Hulme and his colleagues have been pursuing the possible causal connection between STM capability and speech rate. These two skills show a high degree of correlation across children of various ages, which leads Hulme to suspect that speech rate is a determiner of STM capability. Hulme (1984) suggests that speech rate may be an index of rehearsal rate in STM. Young children, having a slow speech rate, will presumably be unable to rehearse as proficiently as older children. In a variation on this theme, developmental changes in speech rate are envisaged as affecting STM by varying the amount of attention required for articulation (Hulme et al., 1984). An attempt to establish a causal relationship between speech rate and STM by training up speech rate in young children and looking for improved STM capability unfortunately yielded equivocal results (Hulme & Muir, 1985). In a sense, then, the Hulme approach to the age/STM correlation bears some similarities to the Baddeley approach to the reading/STM correlation.

To sum up, explanations of developmental changes in STM capability in terms of changes in rates of neurological trace decay or of changes in rehearsal proficiency have lost favour (see Dempster, 1981), although Hulme still retains some of the flavour of the earlier rehearsal explanations. The item identifi cation notion which replaced the rehearsal explanation has been challenged on empirical grounds. The speech sound pattern view of individual differences in STM capability has so far not been challenged, but then it is formulated in a rather vague form, although it clearly differs from many other views of serial STM by supposing that an important source of recall information is representational nonsegmented speech. There is, of course, no difficulty in reconciling this latter view with the view that dyslexics have a general impairment of the phonological system which causes their poor showing in reading and in serial STM tasks.

Assuming that the recall of recency items from a serial list is based, at least in part, on nonsegmented speech or speech sound patterns, a case can also be made for an operational connection between grapheme-phoneme-blending in word identification and the performance of serial STM tasks. Foreit (1977) has suggested that adults are superior to young children in STM capability because they are superior decoders in the sense that they are better able to produce a correct response from a faded, and thus degraded, trace. If this proposition is combined with the notion that dyslexics can have a problem in accessing phonological aspects of verbal material from LTM (see review in Jorm, 1983), an obvious connection between grapheme-phoneme-blending and serial STM results.

Recall in a serial STM task is based on a speech sound pattern, which will be of varying degrees of degradation depending on, for example, the recency of the input. Children who show good STM capability can make use of the degraded pattern by translating it into (say) a string of digits by accessing phonological representations of digits in LTM. In dyslexic children, who also have a STM impairment, this accessing operation is defective, which means that some of the degraded pattern which is of use to unimpaired children is not usable by the dyslexics. In essence, phonological access impaired children base their recall solely on the intact contents of STM whereas unimpaired children can compensate for degradation to some extent by using information from LTM.

Similarly, in beginning readers, an important operation is presumably the blending of phonemes into syllables or words. If the phoneme blending operation received no help from the mental lexicon, words would never be produced since the concatenation of phonemes yield distorted approximations of words. By analogy with the STM scenario just described, competent readers are able to remove these distortions by accessing word representations in LTM. This use of LTM to clean up the noise inherent in our far from perfect phoneme blending can also be regarded as a compensatory mechanism. Dyslexics, having an access problem, will receive less help from LTM, and consequently be less able to make sense of their blends.

As already mentioned, there is a fair amount of data in the literature which point up the access problems of dyslexics. And, of course, the compensatory mechanism proposed in the context of serial STM can explain the differential effects of phonological similarity in dyslexic children and controls. Increasing the phonological similarity of items in a serial list would severely limit the usefulness of the compensatory mechanism since a degraded trace would access too many items in LTM. Since dyslexic children do not compensate, phonological similarity would have little or no effect on their performance. Although some of the data do not agree with the use of this compensatory mechanism as an explanation of individual differences in the developmental context for older children, data obtained with grade 1 children were not inconsistent with the LTM compensation hypothesis (Cohen, Quinton, & Winder, 1985).

4   AN EXCEPTIONAL CASE

Mitterer (1982) has pointed out that a good reader is flexible in her approach to reading, using both the direct route (whole word identification) and the indirect route (grapheme-phoneme-blending). It follows, then, that any person who is deficient in either of these operations should be a less than competent reader. Consequently, an individual can have an unimpaired phonological system, but still have reading problems. Also, although deep dyslexics appear to have intact direct access to their mental lexicons they still have reading problems, presumably on account of a dysfunction in their phonological system as evidenced by their poor STM showings. And in the area of developmental dyslexia, Snowling (1980) has concluded that whereas competent readers improve their reading skills over time partly through an increase in grapheme-phoneme-blending proficiency, developmental dyslexic children improve by increasing their sight vocabulary. Having set the stage, let me now describe the strange case of A.B.

During the course of a longitudinal study of STM and reading we tested over 100 children once a year for three years. The first testing was conducted when the children were just finishing senior kindergarten and had not yet begun formal reading lessons. The second and third testings were conducted near the end of the children's years in first and second grade, respectively. Only the latter two testings are of interest here.

The tests used included a running memory test, a probed serial recall test using lists of fixed length, and the Wide Range Achievement Test (WRAT) of reading, spelling, and arithmetic. These are described below:

The following two memory tests were administrered during the course of one session in grade one.

4.1 Running Memory

Nine lists of digits ranging in length from 10 to 20 items, were presented by audiocassette. The first 3 lists were presented at a rate of 1.5 digits/sec, the second 3 lists at a rate of 3 digits/sec, and the final 3 lists at a rate of 5 digits/sec. The children were instructed to repeat the last 3 digits in each list, as soon as presentation was complete. Given that the children had no idea of the length of each list, until presentation was complete, performance on this test should be minimally affected by the possible use of rehearsal strategies.

4.2 Probed Serial Recall

Twelve 6-digit lists were presented by audiocassette, at a rate of 2 digits/sec. Following each list, on the audiotape, was the word FIRST or LAST, which were post-cues for the children to recall either the first 3 or the last 3 digits from the list. Each half of the list was probed 6 times, using a fixed random order. Since these lists were of fixed and predictable length, this task was more open to the use of strategies than was the running memory.

4.3 Achievement Tests

The Wide Range Achievement Test (WRAT) of reading, spelling and arithmetic was also administrered, on a second testing session. These subtests were administered in accordance with the WRAT Manual of Instructions, Revised Edition (Jastak, Bijou, & Jastak, 1978) with some slight modification. For example, a certain flexibility with regard to the strict time limits in reading and dictation was found to be necessary.

The same tests were given in grade 2, except for two changes. First, the running memory task used 12 digit lists, 3 presented at each of the four rates 1.5 digits/sec, 3 digits/sec, 5 digits/sec and 7 digits/sec. And second, the length of the probed serial recall lists was increased to 7 digits, although the children were still cued to recall either the first 3 or last 3 digits in any given list.

With regard to the group data, it is sufficient to report that the expected correlations were obtained between the two STM tasks. and between each STM task and number of words correctly read on the WRAT. What is of prime interest here are the reading score for the children who showed signs of a weak phonological system in the form of poor STM performances. Specifically, the reading scores for all subjects performing more than one standard deviation below the sample mean on either STM test were scrutinized. In the first grade testing, 25 children fell into this category. Of these, only 3 children gave a reading score which was equal to, or better than, the sample mean. And of these 3 children, only one child (A.B.) performed more than one standard deviation below the sample means on both STM tests. In the second grade testing, the findings were very similar. Of 21 children who scored more than one standard deviation below the sample mean on one or other of the STM tests, only 3 read at the average level or better, one of whom was A.B.. And again A.B. was the only child to perform poorly on both STM test. Table 1 gives the actual performance data for A.B. and for the total sample. A comparison of these sets of scores reveals that A.B. performed not simply poorly on the STM tests - she performed atrociously.

TABLE 1

STM performance scores (proportion correct) for A.B. and for the total sample (N = 101). Standard deviations are in parenthesis

	Running memory		Probed serial recall	
	1st gr.	2nd gr.	1st gr.	2nd gr.
sample means	.58(.23)	.76(.17)	.38(.20)	.45(.21)
scores from				
A.B.	.11	.19	.03	.19

In addition to the WRAT measure of reading ablity, estimates of the children's school reading skills were solicited from their teachers. These estimates, made on a 5-point scale, correlated around 0.7 with the WRAT scores.

A.B.'s grade 1 and grade 2 teachers both rated her as an average reader. Consequently A.B. could not only pronounce individual words competently, she was also able to cope successfully with reading in her everyday school life.

Reading and spelling usually correlate rather highly in children and our study proved to be no exception, yielding coefficients of .85 and .81 in grades 1 and 2 respectively. Spelling appeared to present no great problems for A.B., who scored about half a standard deviation lower than the sample mean on the spelling portion of the WRAT.

The third achievement measure taken was arithmetic. This correlated with both reading and spelling, yielding coefficients in the range of .40 - .48 at both grade levels. Arithmetic also correlated with STM performance, yielding r-values in the range of .33 to .45. Here A.B. did show signs of an impairment. Although she scored only a few points lower than the sample mean on the arithmetic portion of the WRAT, these few points translated into 2.6 standard deviations below the means for both grades 1 and 2, because of the rather narrow ranges of scores within the sample.

It should be stressed that A.B. fell into our net by accident, as it were, and she was not administered any supplementary tests. Post-test enquiry did, however, reveal that A.B. suffered from petit mal.

There appears to be little in the way of hard data dealing with cognitive capability in petit mal children. The picture I have managed to put together is as follows. Generally petit mal is associated with the temporal lobe and is characterized by a selective difficulty in mathematics (Bradley, 1951). A study of a non-differentiated sample of epileptic adults showed among other cognitivie deficits, a weakness in digit span albeit not a very marked one (Brittain, 1980). Epileptic children were found to more likely to have a substantial reading deficit, although on average these children were only about 12 months retarded in reading (Yule, 1980). Again this observation was based on a heterogenous sample. In addition, Yule (1980) writes that »... impairment in spelling and arithmetic may be more pronounced (than in reading), but this conclusion rests on very weak data.« (p.165). Consequently, A.B. could be said to conform to the rather vague picture we have of individuals with epileptic disorders.

In the present context the main interest lies in A.B.'s ability to read despite an obvious impairment in serial STM. Ellis (1979) has stated that no-one has yet demonstrated that a poor STM capability is a necessary condition for a reading impairment. While A.B.'s data do not answer this challenge they clearly show that poor reading is not a necessary *outcome* of poor STM.

What, then, does this conclusion imply for the various explanations of the STM/reading relationship reviewed in Section I? First, it would appear to falsify the common operations explanations, unless further assumptions are made. Thus the notion that poor STM depends on an impairment in the articulatory loop is untenable in A.B.'s case, since this impairment should also affect grapheme-phoneme-blending thereby causing a reading deficit. A.B.'s data present a similar problem for the hypothesis that poor STM and poor reading depend on a failure to use phonological aspects of verbal material in LTM to augment degraded memory traces and imperfectly blended phonemes, respectively. Obviously, if we are prepared to suppose that A.B. is really an exceptional case in the sense that her STM problem has a different origin from that observed in dyslexic children, then both of the above hypotheses could survive A.B.'s results.

The other obvious solution to the problem raised by A.B. is to simply assume that she does indeed have an impairment in her grapheme-phoneme-blending route to reading, but has managed to compensate for this by establishing a greater than average sight reading vocabulary for use in the more direct lexical route.

5   CONCLUSION

When I began writing this chapter, I was under the impression that A.B. was, if not unique, then at least a very rara avis. A recent article by Siegel and Linder (1984) has shown that this is far from being the case, however. These authors report an investigation which involved two samples of learning disabled (LD) children, one sample consisting of 45 children with reading but not arithmetic problems and a second sample of 38 children with arithmetic but not reading problems. Not only did both samples of children show a serial STM deficit as compared with control groups, but the younger children in both LD samples showed the same peculiarity, namely the absence of a phonological similarity effect (see Section 1). If A.B.'s results are to be interpreted as a compensation effect, this raises the question of why A.B. and presumably Siegel and Linder's (1984) acalculic children were able to compensate for an impairment in one reading route by overdeveloping the other whereas dyslexic children, even of superior intelligence, are apparently unable to do this. There is also the question of how A.B. and the acalculics could manage to build up their superior sight vocabularies with only limited help from grapheme-phoneme-blending (Jorm, 1979). And thirdly, there is the question of whether Siegel and Linder's, 1984) dyslexic children have managed to compensate for their STM deficit by using an STM independent method of doing arthmetic, and if so what this method might be.

In sum, then, the data of A.B. and Siegel and Linder's (1984) acalculics raise a number of problems for a common operations approach to the reading/STM relationship, not least that of how some children, but not others, manage to compensate for a weakness in grapheme-phoneme-blending by increasing sight vocabulary. Given these problems it is tempting to abandon common operations in favour of a common system notion. Thus it could be supposed that children can have a malfunction in the linguistic system, albeit in different areas of the system. This supposi tion, although somewhat less than satisfying, would allow for children with difficulties in reading, or artihmetic, or STM, or in any combination of these skills.

Whichever hypothesis we favour, it is clear that children with deficient STMs can become proficient readers. Whether or not these children represent genuine cases of compensation, however, is still an open question.

REFERENCES

Aaronson, D. (1974). Stimulus factors and listening strategies in auditory memory: A theoretical analysis. *Cognitive Psychology, 6,* 108-132.

Atkinson, R.C., & Shiffrin, R.M. (1968). Human memory: A proposed system and its control processes. In K.W. Spence & J.T. Spence (Eds.), *The psychology of learning and motivation: Advances in research and theory,* Vol. 2 (pp. 89-195). New York: Academic Press.

Baddeley, A.D. (1979). Working memory and reading. In P.A. Kolers, M.E. Wrolstad & H. Bouma (Eds.), *Processing of visible language,* Vol. 1 (pp. 355-370). New York: Plenum Press.

Baron, J. (1977). Mechanisms for pronouncing printed words: Use and acquisition. In D. Laberge & S.J. Samuels (Eds.), *Basic processes in reading: Perception and comprehension* (pp. 175-216). Hillsdale N.J.: Erlbaum.

Belmont, J.M., & Butterfield, E.C. (1969). The relation of short-term memory to development and intelligence. In L.P. Lipsitt & H.W. Reese (Eds.), *Advances in child development and behavior,* Vol. 4 (pp. 29-82). New York: Academic Press.

Bradley, C. (1951). Behavior disturbances in Epileptic Children. *Journal of the American Medical Association, 32,* 436-441.

Brittain, H. (1980). Epilepsy and intellectual functions. In B.M. Kulig, H. Meinardi, & G. Stores (Eds.), *Epilepsy and behavior '79* (pp.2-13). Lisse: Swets & Zeitlinger B.V.,

Broadbent, D.E. (1958). *Perception and communication.* New York: Pergamon Press.

Bryant, P.E., & Bradley, L. (1980). Why children sometimes write words which they do not read. In U. Frith (Ed.), *Cognitive processes in spelling* (pp.355-370). London: Academic Press.

Byrne, B., & Shea, P. (1979). Semantic and phonetic memory codes in beginning readers. *Memory & Cognition, 7,* 333-338.

Case, R., Kurland, D.M. & Goldberg, J. (1982). Operational efficiency and the growth of short-term memory span. *Journal of Experimental Child Psychology, 33,* 386-404.

Cohen, R.L. (1982). Individual differences in short-term memory. In N.R. Ellis (Ed.), *International review of research in mental retardation* (pp. 43-77).Vol. 11. New York: Academic Press.

Cohen, R.L. (1983). Reading disabled children are aware of their cognitive deficits. *Journal of Learning Disabilities, 16,* 286-289.

Cohen, R.L., & Netley, C. (1978). Cognitive deficits, learning disabilities, and WISC verbal performance consistency. *Developmental Psychology, 4,* 624-634.

Cohen, R.L., & Netley, C. (1981). Short-term memory deficits in reading disabled children, in the absence of opportunity for rehearsal strategies. *Intelligence, 5,* 69-76.

Cohen, R.L., Netley, C., & Clarke, M. (1984). On the Generality of the short-term memory/reading ability relationship. *Journal of Learning Disabilities, 17,* 218-221.

Cohen, R.L., Quinton, C., & Winder, S. (1985). Critical processes in serial short-term memory: A developmental study. *Intelligence, 9,* 171-188.

Coltheart, M. (1980). Deep dyslexia: A review of the syndrome. In M. Coltheart, K. Patterson, & J.C. Marshall (Eds.), *Deep dyslexia.* (pp. 22-47). London: Routledge & Kegan Paul.

Dempster, F.N. (1984). Memory span: Sources of individual and developmental differences. *Psychological Bulletin, 89,* 63-100.

Ellis, A.W. (1979). Developmental and acquired dyslexia: Some observations on Jorm (1979). *Cognition, 7,* 413-420.

Ellis, N.R. (1963). The stimulus trace and behavioral inadequacy. In N.R. Ellis (Ed.), *Handbook of mental deficiency: Psychological theory and research* (pp. 134-158). New York: McGraw-Hill.

Ellis, N.R. (1970). Memory processes in retardates and normals: Theoretical and empirical considerations. In N.R. Ellis (Ed.), *International review of research in mental retardation,* Vol. 4. (pp. 1-32). New York: Academic Press.

Flavell, J.H. (1970). Developmental studies of mediated memory. In H.W. Reese & L.P. Lipsitt (Eds.), *Advances in child development and behavior,* Vol. 5. New York: Academic Press.

Fox, B., & Routh, D.K. (1980). Phonemic analysis and severe reading disability in children. *Journal of Psycholinguistic Research, 9,* 115-119.

Fox, B., & Routh, D.K. (1983). Reading disability, phonemic analysis, and dysphonetic spelling: A follow-up study. *Journal of Clinical Child Psychology, 12,* 28-32.

Foreit, K.G. (1977). Developmental differences in short-lived auditory memory for various classes of speech sounds. *Journal of Experimental Child Psychology, 24,* 461-475.

Hebb, D.O. (1949). *The organization of behavior.* New York: Wiley.

Henderson, L. (1982). *Orthography and word recognition in reading.* London: Academic Press.

Hulme, C. (1984). Developmental differences in the effects of acoustic similarity on memory span. *Developmental Psychology, 20,* 650-652.

Hulme, C., & Muir, C. (1985). Developmental changes in speech rate and memory span: A causal relationship? *British Journal of Developmental Psychology, 3,* 175-181.

Hulme, C., Thomson, N., Muir, C., & Lawrence, A. (1984). Speech rate and the development of short-term memory span. *Journal of Experimental Child Psychology, 38,* 241-253.

Huttenlocher, J. & Burke, D. (1976). Why does memory span increase with age? *Cognitive Psychology, 8,* 1-31.

Jastak, J.F., Bijou, S., & Jastak, S. (1978). *Wide range achievement test.* Washington, Delaware: Jastak Associates, Inc.

Jorm, A.F. (1979). The nature of the reading deficit in developmental dyslexia: A reply to Ellis. *Cognition, 7,* 421-433.

Jorm, A.F. (1981). Children with reading and spelling retardation: Functioning of whole-word and correspondence-rule mechanisms. *Journal of Child Psychology and Psychiatry, 22,* 171-178.

Jorm, A.F. (1983). Specific reading retardation and working memory: A review. *British Journal of Psychology, 74,* 301-342.

Kay, J., & Marcel, A. (1981). One process, not two, in reading aloud: Lexical analogies do the work of non-lexical rules. *Quarterly Journal of Experimental Psychology, 33A,* 397-413.

Liberman, I.Y., Shankweiler, D., Liberman, A.M., Fowler, C., & Fischer, F.W. (1977). Phonetic segmentation and recoding in the beginning reader. In A.S. Reber & D.L. Scarborough (Eds.), *Toward a psychology of reading: The proceedings of the CUNY Conference* (pp. 207-255). Hillsdale, N.J.: Erlbaum.

Mark, L.S. Shankweiler, D., Liberman, I.Y., & Fowler, C.A. (1977). Phonetic recoding and reading difficulty in beginning readers. *Memory & Cognition, 5,* 623-629.

Mitterer, J.O. (1982). There are at least two kinds of poor readers: Whole-word poor readers and recoding poor readers. *Canadian Journal of Psychology, 36,* 445-461.

Nelson, H.E. (1980). Analysis of spelling errors in normal and dyslexic children. In U. Frith (Ed.), *Cognitive processes in spelling* (pp. 475-494). London: Academic Press.

Neisser, U. (1967). *Cognitive Psychology.* New York: Appleton-Century-Crofts.

Olson, R.K., Davidson, B.J., Kliegl, R., & Davies, S.E. (1984). Development of phonetic memory in disabled and normal readers. *Journal of Experimental Child Psychology, 37,* 187- 206.

Saffran, E.M., & Marin, O.S.M. (1977). Reading without phonology: Evidence from aphasia. *Quarterly Journal of Experimental Psychology, 29,* 515-525.

Shallice, T., & Warrington, E.K. (1975). Word recognition in a phonemic dyslexic patient. *Quarterly Journal of Experimental Psychology, 27,* 187-199.

Shallice, T., & Warrington, E.K. (1980). Single and multiple component central dyslexic syndromes. In M. Coltheart, K. Patterson, & J.C. Marshall (Eds.), *Deep dyslexia* (pp. 119-145). London: Routledge & Kegan Paul.

Shiffrin, R.M., & Schneider, W. (1977). Controlled and automatic human information processing: II. Perceptual learning, automatic attending, and a general theory. *Psychological Review, 84,* 127-190.

Siegel, L.S. & Linder, B.A. (1984). Short-term memory processes in children with reading and arithmetic learning disabilities. *Developmental Psychology, 20,* 200-207.

Snowling, M.J. (1980). The development of grapheme-phoneme correspondence in normal and dyslexic readers. *Journal of Experimental Child Psychology, 29,* 294-305.

Williams, J.P. (1984). Phonemic analysis and how it relates to reading. *Journal of Learning Disabilities, 17,* 240-245.

Witelson, S.F. (1977). Developmental dyslexia: Two right hemispheres and none left. *Science, 195,* 309-311.

Yule, W. (1980). Educational achievement. In B.M. Kuling, H. Meinardi, & G. Stores (Eds.), *Epilepsy and behavior '79* (pp. 162-168). Lisse: Swets & Zeitlinger B.V.

Communication and Handicap: Aspects of
Psychological Compensation and Technical Aids
E. Hjelmquist and L.-G. Nilsson (editors)
Elsevier Science Publishers B.V. (North-Holland), 1986

COMPENSATION IN READING DISABILITIES

INGVAR LUNDBERG and CHE KAN LEONG

Psychology Department, University of Umeå, Sweden and Department for the Education of Exceptional Children, University of Saskatchewan, Saskatoon, Saskatchewan Canada.*

The concept of compensation in reading disabilities relates to additional expenditure of attention and mental effort. There are intra- and inter-individual differences in utilizing oral language to access print language. The components of decoding and comprehending are inter-related levels of processing print. Difficulties in processing at one level can be compensated for by a greater use of information from other levels. Studies by the authors and others show that rapid, automatic decoding is necessary, though not sufficient, for comprehending. While deficient in »higher« levels of text processing, disabled readers benefit more by context utilization, under certain conditions. Technical aids to enhance performance include the use of audio-visual equipment, microcomputers as »tutor, tool, tutee« and Lundberg's research into on-line, real-time »textwindow« technique using the computer to study components of reading and individual difference.

Preparation of this paper was supported in part by the Social Sciences and Humanities Research Council of Canada Leave Fellowship No. 451-84-2280 awarded to the second author. Parts of this paper were written while the second author was visiting the Psychology Department, London University, Birkbeck College, England and the Psychology Department, University of Umeå, Sweden. Library facilities and other forms of assistance given by Arthur Summerfield, Max Coltheart at Birkbeck, The Reading Research Group and Lars-Göran Nilsson in Umeå are greatly appreciated. Any shortcomings are necessarily our own.

1   INTRODUCTION

Any kind of task can be accomplished in various ways where the end product of the performance is the same. In reading, for example, there is always a constructive and reconstructive interaction between the reader and the text. Two readers may approach one and the same text with widely different prior knowledge or schematic frames in relation to the demands of the text. For the skilled reader the reading will run smoothly, automatically and with low expenditure of mental resources, while the unskilled reader has to pay careful attention and work hard to reach the same level of understanding. In one sense, we could then say that the reader has to *compensate* for his or her lack of prior knowledge with more expenditure of energy. Usually, such a reader also has to spend more time on the reading task. Thus, it seems as if the expenditure of mental effort and time is closely related to the concept of compensation. It also seems necessary to establish some kind of *norm* or criterion as a reference for compensatory behavior.

This reference yardstick for compensation in reading disabilities should be cast within a developmental context because reading consists of an integration of components or subskills and children acquire these subskills at different rates and with varying degrees of success. In a recent »modest proposal» Chall (1983) has schematized reading as a kind of problem solving behavior in which readers progress through different stages - logographic, alphabetic, orthographic and conceptual - and interact with the environment through assimilation and accommodation. At each stage, a balanced experience is needed so that readers are sufficiently challenged and can move on to the next stage. This stage of development concept states that skilled readers at any one stage have mastered the subskills in the earlier stage and disabled readers lag behind in the antecedent subskills as compared with their peers. Thus disabled readers require more than the traditional remedial teaching to make up for their deficiencies. Rather, they need some kind of developmental teaching which should take into account not only linguistic and reading subskills, but also strategies for flexible cognitive processing as well. From the compensation point of view, the stage concept is a useful one, but the precise nature and characteristics for each stage will need to be delineated in relation to chronological age and grade placement. There is also considerable intraand inter-individual differences in readers.

On the *intra-individual* level, various extraneous factors such as unfavorable reading conditions (e.g. poor lighting, high noise level, poor handwriting, degraded typography, and internal physical states) affect the same readers differentially, and at different times. More attention, effort and time are needed to compensate for these adverse conditions.

On the *inter-individual* level, compensation is also reflected in dissociations or interactions (in the statistical sense) among variables conceived as relevant to the task. Suppose there are theoretical reasons and empirical evidence for a generally strong relation between reading ability and general intelligence (as measured by conventional tests). If we then found individuals with a comparatively low level of intelligence but with unimpaired or even well developed reading ability, we have to account for this dissociation by assuming some kind of compensation. An example of this situation is illustrated in Figure 1 which presents the results of an AID-analysis (Sonquist, Baker, & Morgan, 1973). The data are obtained from a study by Lundberg (1985).

The variance of the criterion measure (basic skills in reading and spelling) is analyzed in such a way that a nonsymmetric branching process is developed to partition the population into a series of subgroups with maximum homogenity with respect to the dependent variable. The computer program looks for the predictor variable which, after dichotomization yields the lowest within group sums of squares. Starting again from the obtained subgroups, the program proceeds by looking for the next subgrouping with the lowest within group sums of squares. The progressive splitting continues until specified criteria concerning group size and sums of squares have been met. It should be noted that the subgroups on a given split level are different in at least two ways: first, they have different means on the criterion measure, and second, they are different on some critical predictor variable, specified at the split point (scale values are indicated above each box within parenthesis). Group 18 contains individuals with superior basic skills in reading and spelling. However, their Raven scores are low. These children seem to have been able to offset or *compensate* for their limited cognitive abilities with very good socio-emotional adjustment and with a high level of language comprehension. Thus, the AID-analysis has helped us to detect the factors which can explain the unexpected dissociation of general intelligence and reading for a subgroup of individuals.

Within the above context, we can discuss two concepts, only directly related to reading disabilities. One is accessing print language from oral language. The other is the inter-relationship between rapid, automatic decoding and comprehending including the role of metacognitive aspects of reading.

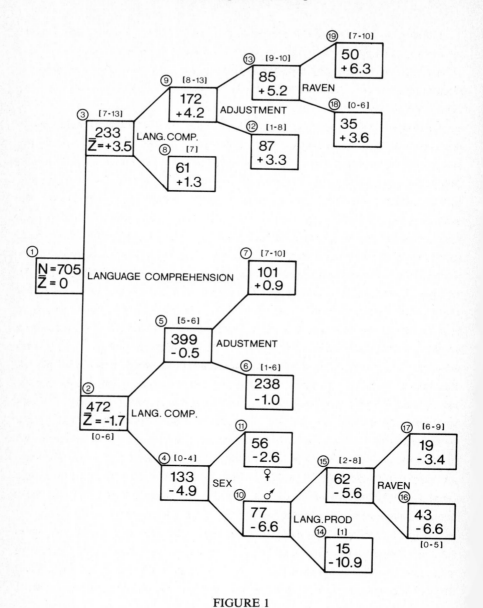

FIGURE 1

AID analysis of basic skills measured in grade 1 and 2 (Lundberg, 1985).

2   FROM ORAL TO PRINT LANGUAGE

The differences and similarities between oral and written communication have recently been subjected to careful analyses (e.g. Olson, 1977; Rubin, 1980; Tannen, 1982). Syntactic, semantic and pragmatic differences have been particularly emphasized. However, there is also a low-level difference relevant to decoding which deserves closer attention. In oral communication a message can be more or less clearly articulated, mainly depending on the closeness of speaker and listener. We can conceive of a continuum of articulatory precision extending from *under-articulation* to *over-articulation*. Owing to a general biological principle of minimizing the expenditure of physiological energy at muscle movements, the speaker tends to underarticulate the message. The listener, however, normally wants to hear what is said and tends to force the speaker upwards on the articulation-continuum by signalling his or her dissatisfaction (»What?», »Speak louder!»). This competition typically ends with a point of equilibrium satisfactory to both parts. In natural, spoken conversation, where speaker and listener stand in a close, complementary relationship, the speech signal is most often treated towards the underarticulation end of the continuum. Written language, in contrast, is always located at the over-articulation endpoint. Here the full architecture of a word must be displayed. Regardless of context a written word must be spelled out fully. The spelling must be invariant with surrounding words and communicative context and purposes. Written language is typically decontextualized and appears in clear, detailed morpho-phonemic from materialized in sharp, visible typography. Spoken words, however, which are often expressed in noise, are under-articulated and not clearly separated from surrounding words. There is also much more redundant information in oral communication through the use of prosodic elements such as intonation, stress, pause and extra-linguistic information such as gesture, facial expressions, etc.

These fundamental differences between written and oral language should also be reflected in the way words are perceived in the two modalities. Thus, there are reasons to assume that the perception of oral speech, to a greater extent, is conceptually driven (top-down processes) than the decoding of written words, which, at least for skilled readers and with clear typography, is a data-driven process (bottom-up). Concept-driven and data-driven processes are mutually supportive and mutually facilitating. We will now discuss some experimental evidence.

3   DECODING AND COMPREHENDING

Most people have had the experience of reading aloud to children and how, perhaps with some embarrassment, they have discovered during their reading that they have not the slightest idea of what they have actually read. Their minds have been preoccupied with other thoughts. Apparently, however, they have been decoding the text with sufficient fluency and prosody to please the audience. This is a case of decoding without comprehension. A perhaps still more common experience is silent reading of a boring textbook, when the reader suddenly discovers that he/she has not paid attention to the content of the text. If we had recorded the eye movements during this period of day dreaming, we had probably not been able to detect any significant deviations from normal reading. The decoding process had proceeded smoothly and automatically, despite the absence of comprehension. These examples point to the relevance of making a conceptual distinction between decoding and comprehension in reading research.

The current theories and empirical studies of the inter active and reciprocal nature of bottom-up and top-down processes provide a great deal of insight into reading and individual differences. Research programs by Perfetti and his associates in Pittsburgh (see Perfetti & Roth, 1981, for representative find ings); Stanovich in Rochester (Stanovich, 1980; Stanovich & West, 1981), Carr in Michigan (1981) have clearly shown the inter dependence of rapid, automatic decoding and comprehending. Haines and Leong (1983) have also obtained similar results in their investigation of skilled and less skilled readers. Typically, the experimental paradigm is that of pronunciation latency and lexical decision. In these experiments subjects are asked to pronounce a word or to decide if a string of letters is a word or a nonword as quickly and as accurately as possible and their reaction times are taken as an index of their verbal efficiency.

An example is the analysis of pronunciation latency reaction times from Experiment 1 of the Haines and Leong (1983) study with 72 children from grades 4, 6, and 8, who were dichotomized as skilled and less skilled comprehenders in reading. The stimulus materials were three-letter, four-letter and five-letter predictable or regular English words, unpredictable or irregular words and pseudowords as defined by Venezky (1970). Predictable words are those words with a vowel or vowel cluster mapping onto its most frequently occurring phoneme correspondence (e.g. SUN,

RUSH, BROOM). Unpredictable words are those with a vowel cluster mapping onto a less frequently occurring phonemic correspondence (e.g. WON, POUR, HEART). For the purpose of the study, pseudo-words (e.g. JOP, POUD, TROAK) matched the vowel or vowel cluster of the predictable or unpredictable words. The rationale for using these stimuli are as follows. A predictable word such as CLEAR could be pronounced either *pre-lexically* or »assembled» from subcomponents of the letter string *(post-lexical phonology).* Unpredictable words like SEW could be pronounced via either route but would be liable to mispronunciations by analogy with FEW. Pseudowords like STOOM could only be pronounced pre-lexically. Vocalization latencies for these different letter strings thus reflect the processing routes used by the readers.

Results of a 3 (grade level) x 2 (reading ability) x 3 (stimulus type) x 3 (stimulus length) analysis of variance with repeated measures on the last two factors are displayed in Figure 2.

The main effects for grade, reading ability, stimulus type and stimulus length and the stimulus type x reading ability interaction all reached statistical significance. The decline in performance on the unpredictable words and pseudowords is greater for less skilled readers than for skilled ones. Inspection of error rates and also statistical testing across grades do not reflect a speed-accuracy trade-off. The general finding of this experiment and also Experiment 2 on lexical decision is that less skilled comprehenders, more than skilled ones, tended to rely more on phonological coding in word processing. Paradoxically, less skilled readers also experienced their greatest difficulty in processing through the phonological route, as evidenced by the relatively longer latencies on pseudowords and also the greater number of errors made on unpredictable than predictable words.

In general, the results of the various studies of rapid, automatic word processing suggest:

1. Less skilled readers showed longer vocalization latencies to context-free printed words and pseudowords.
2. Less skilled readers showed slower lexical access. This is probably related to their difficulty with recoding letter strings and not so much to a poor lexicon.
3. Less skilled readers were less efficient with phonological coding so essential to comprehension.

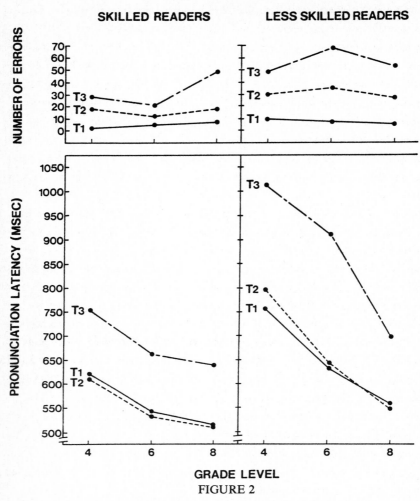

FIGURE 2

Mean pronunciation latency and number of errors on stimulus type as a function of grade level for skilled readers and less skilled readers (T_1 = predictable words, T_2 = unpredictable words, T_3 = pseudowords) (Haines & Leong, 1983).

To some extent, the findings of longer vocalization latency or slower lexical access in less skilled readers can be explained by the very powerful *automaticity* model proposed by LaBerge and Samuels (1974). In essence, this model implies that readers have to be alert to the source of information, to be selective and to use the limited capacity of attention to advantage. LaBerge and Samuels assumed that a person can attend to only one task at a time but can perform other activites simultaneously if these activities do not require attention or if they have attained automaticity. The criterion for deciding if a skill is automatic is whether or not it can function while attention is focussed on other acts. Another criterion is that if two tasks are to be performed at the same time and each requires attention, can the tasks be performed simultaneously? If so, then at least one of the tasks is operating automatically. When readers attain auto maticity in reading subskills, they can concentrate on the mean ings of what is read rather than on the mechanics of reading itself.

The various studies provide some support for the LaBerge-Samules postulate of automaticity. However, the focus of current literature in this area is more on the speed of lexical access, on verbal knowledge from print rather than on overcoming competing attention. In one sense, we are coming back to the great debate-- the code emphasis and the meaning emphasis in reading. Both could be right as reading is interactive and draws information from multiple sources. The crux is how *fast* and how *automatically* children could decode or could comprehend. If they decode accurately but very slowly, then their attention is directed away from comprehension.

One possibility in remediation is practice on fast word recognition, but more evidence is needed to support the long-term efficacy of this approach. What is important is to follow a systematic strategy of teaching word recognition subskills. In particular, a balanced code and meaning emphasis is needed to remedy the poor readers' inefficiency in using a phonological code. In this connection, Lesgold and Perfetti (1981) aptly sum up the role of coding in lexical access:

> A less awkward model would assume that lexical access always activates phonemic codes. The only relevant strategic factor is whether a reader recodes in subword units and then uses that code to consult meaning and to place it in the text representation. The attractive feature of this proposal is that the activated phonemic code is available for later memory scanning. A name code is thus available for securing reference. By this proposal, reading skill includes the rapid activation of all lexical information, including phonemic information. In any given situation, activation of phonemic information may precede or follow activation of semantic information depending upon the depth of semantic analysis required and the familiarity of the word. (pp. 404-405)

Thus word recognition is derived from information from multiple sources and poor readers may well use context to compensate for inefficient word coding or recoding abilities (Perfetti, 1980; Stanovich, 1980). Put another way, the Perfetti and associates' model of rapid lexical access in reading and the LaBerge and Samuels' automaticity model of word encoding can be utilized to enhance semantic processes. This was demonstrated by Beck, Perfetti, and McKeown (1982) in a systematic, long-term vocabulary instruction study. They instructed 27 grade 4 children in 104 words over a five-month period and compared these children with 39 controls matched on vocabulary and comprehension. The keynote of the study was on automaticity of word processing and the development of network of meanings. After instruction, the experimental subjects were found to be superior to the controls on tasks ranging from semantic decisions to simple verification and memory for discourse. Thus, the compensatory-facilitative process could work either way - with context facilitating lexical access and word knowledge contributing to comprehension.

3.1   Context Utilization

From the studies discussed in the preceeding section, evidence is strong that poor comprehenders tend to be verbally deficient in decoding context-free printed words. The question is whether or not poor readers also fail to use context to aid word recognition. Here, the results from a study by Lundberg (1985) of reading accuracy in two measures of grade 5 dyslexics (according to a statistical criterion) compared with a control group is pertinent. One task was oral reading of small, coherent stories, while the other task was oral reading of lists of unconnected words. The dyslexic group had an average error rate of 20% on the word reading task, while the mean for the control group was 7%. The dyslexic students also showed far more hesitation and rereadings and their reading speed was only half as fast. However, the difference between dyslexic and controls was not of such a dramatic kind in the context condition. For both groups, the error rate decreased considerably (dyslexics: from 20% to 3%; controls: from 7% to 1%) but to a much greater extent for the dyslexic group (although the ratio of noncontextuel /contextual errors is virtually identical for both groups). A large number of dyslexic children seem to read quite fluently under context condition and could not be discriminated from normal children, probably to the satisfaction of most teachers. However, their comprehension was often still poor. It is also doubtful whether their superficial graphic information processing and their heavy dependance on contextual cues is an acceptable reading strategy in the long run when unexpected and less familiar words are encountered. Their poor utilization of word-internal cues, the architecture of words, was also reflected in their spelling. In a spelling task, only 6 of the 40 dyslexic students reached the mean level of the control group, most of them being far behind. Although we may have a case of compensa tion, it is not a full compensation in all relevant aspects of literacy.

Ongoing research by Stanovich and associates (Stanovich & West, 1979; Stanovich, West, & Feeman, 1981; West, Stanovich, Feeman, & Cunningham, 1983) is also illuminating. The typical kind of study of context effect on word recognition is along the following lines. Subjects are asked to read aloud a sentence context with its final (target) word missing. When the subjects finish reading the incomplete sentence context, they are asked to name quickly and accurately the target word which then appears. The kind of sentences might be as follows:

CONDITION	CONTEXT	TARGET
Congruous	The soldier flew in the	plane
Neutral	They said it was the	plane
Incongruous	The cowboy fired the	plane

With the different contextual conditions (congruous, neutral, and incongruous) the prediction is that recognition time in the congruous condition should be faster than the times in the neutral condition (context facilitation effect), if context is indeed used to speed up word recognition. Conversely, an incongruous context might slow down word recognition relative to the neutral condition (context inhibition effect). The general finding is that poor readers do not seem less likely to use context to facilitate word recognition when the context is adequately understood and that overall context effect diminishes as developmental level increases. Further, the word identification performance of poor readers is greatly speeded up when the word is predictable from context and slowed down when the word is unexpected. Thus the paradox is that context effects are much more pronounced in less skilled readers and yet the greatest facilitation of word recognition by meaningful context is also observed consistently with these poor or younger readers rather than with skilled or older ones.

The above kinds of reasoning and empirical findings have led to the formulation of the *interactive compensatory* model of reading (Stanovich, 1980; Stanovich, West & Feeman, 1981). This is based on the assumption that difficulties in processing at one level can be compensated for by a greater use of information from other levels and this compensation takes place regardless of the level of the deficient process. The important consideration is that the context be properly understood. Failure of poor readers is not so much with the »psycholinguistic guessing game», but more with the fast, accurate decoding of words to the automotic level. It is this deficiency with verbal processing that affects discourse comprehension.

The findings in grade school children of significant facilitation effect (recognition time in the congruous condition subtracted from recognition time in the neutral condition) and inhibition effect (recognition time in the incongruous condition minus recognition time in the neutral condition) have been interpreted as support for a *two-process* model of sentence context effect on word recognition (Stanovich & West, 1979). In essence, the dual contextual mechanisms suggest that there are effects due to fast, automatic spreading activation and effects due to slower, conscious, capacity-demanding processes. Children, more than adults, may be slow enough in word recognition to allow the conscious-attention mechanism to take effect and this explains both the contextual facilitation and inhibition effects in reaction times found with children. Similarly, poor readers are slower than good readers in processing words and thus rely more on contextual facilitation from both fast, automatic spreading activation and the slower conscious-attention mechanism.

3.2   Higher Level Processes of Reading

When a reader is confronted with an unfamiliar text it is often necessary to make a conscious effort to activate relevant schemas or prior knowledge which might help to clarify the meaning and significance of the facts presented in the text. The reader must monitor his or her comprehension and discover when gaps in understanding or problems in the text occur and develop repair strategies to overcome the difficulties. This is the *metacognitive* aspect of reading (see e.g. Brown, 1980; Wong, 1982). The reader may have the potential or the necessary prerequisites for the reading task, but for some reason they are not always spontaneously accessible. Compensation in this context would mean helping readers to utilize their latent resources.

Typical for many poor readers is their tendency not to use active strategies in their reading. They read passively without self-regulating controls of their own understanding and without activating their prior knowledge. In one sense, reading is a question of *cognitive economy*. Mental resources are invested in the reading process. The use of strategies costs time and effort. However, such mental investments must yield a corresponding pay-off, e.g. richer and more interesting reading experience, enjoyment, success, increased clarity, better fulfillment of reading goal, personal significance, emotional satisfaction. The cost-benefit analysis then indicates two dimensions of the remedial measures. On the one hand, it is a question of guiding the students to use simple and effective strategies to minimize the necessary investments of time and energy or effort (e.g. automatization). On the other hand, it is a question of maximizing utility, thus providing the students with opportunities to experience the personal significance of the reading task. They need help to see the limitations of their habitual and non-efficient information processing and realize how it can be improved.

A nice example of this approach is given by Bransford, Stein, and Vye (1982, p. 146): The students are presented with a list of sentences of the following type:

> The kind man bought the milk.
> The short man used the broom.
> The funny man liked the ring.
> The hungry man purchased the tie.
> The bald man read the newspaper.
> The tall man used the paint brush.

The first task then is to answer questions of the type: Which man did X? Only a few questions can be answered correctly. The next step is to discuss why the material is difficult to memorize. The arbitrary relation between the two parts of a sentence is demonstrated. There is no logical or inherent association between being kind and buying milk. However, by active and constructive elaborations a meaningful relation can easily be created. For example, in the first sentence a possible elaboration could be »The kind man bought the milk for the poor children». After elaborating all sentences in similar way, the children will experience a dramatic increase in their recall performance. The students have learnt to understand why one type of material is more difficult than another. They have also learnt that they can, to some extent, control their own understanding and their own mental processes. They have seen how it is possible to overcome the learned helplessness which often characterize students with learning disabilities. The Bransford et al. study is intriguing, but it is not yet clear to what extent learning experiences of this kind will transfer to more typical text processing tasks.

4   TECHNICAL AIDS

The cost-benefit analysis of reading mentioned above indicated two related strategies for remedial teaching of reading for disabled students: (a) minimizing the necessary investment of mental resources (time and effort) in the decoding process and (b) maximizing the pay-off or utility of reading. One technique where both of these remedial aspects are considered is *listening while reading*. Students are encouraged to read texts at the same time as listening to the same texts recorded on tape, where the speed of the spoken text is varied systematically. Word recognition is assumed to develop painlessly through the repeated prompting provided by the voice on the tape. Comprehension is facilitated by the prosodic support given by the leading voice. The student is also helped to discover the excitement and personal significance inherent in many texts and is thus encouraged to go on independently. After all, you can only learn to read by reading.

This kind of procedure has been recommended, among others, by Carbo (1978), Chomsky (1978), Gamby (1983), Hollingworth (1978), and Schneeberg (1977). Carbo (1978) reported an average gain of eight months in reading level after a three month treatment period. Schneeberg (1977) reported that her four year study using reading while listening with educationally disadvantaged students in an innercity school resulted in high gain scores.

One technical breakthrough which may have a profound impact on reading instruction is the development of machines which, when attached to computerized speech synthesizers, can read printed text aloud with minimal phonological and prosodic distortions.

4.1   Computers in Remedial Teaching

The computer is a versatile tool, well suited to serve as an aid in special education. Although computers are widely used in schools now, it seems as if their real potentials have not been utilized to any great extent. The International Reading Association (IRA) has recently published an annotated bibliography on the use of computers in reading instruction (Mason, Blanchard, & Daniel, 1983). It contains some 900 references of which some are bibliographies. Thus, the literature on computers in reading is indeed already of a considerable size. Properly used, the computer goes beyond the »drill and practice» level and can help in problem solving (see Papert, 1980). Moreover, computers are capable of doing much more; for example, they can measure reaction time and can be used to record physiological reactions, eye movements, voice onset etc. Here, we illustrate the use of computers in writing instruction and in developing appropriate strategies in reading.

A word processor can be a useful tool in helping to teach disabled students to develop writing skill. It allows the writer to take risks, to be tentative, to consider organization and word choices more freely. It can foster a metacognitive style or attitude in relation to the writing process and develop a sense of control. In a dialogue with the teacher, the student can revise his/her work and correct spelling and punctuation, work on sentence structure and cohesion of sentences without fear of having to produce a new copy every time his/her work is reviewed. A word processor should also be particularly helpful to students with difficulties in handling a pencil.

Unfortunately, systematic research or evaluation of this powerful tool has not, to our knowledge, been reported.

As a final illustration of technical aids we would mention the text-window technique developed in Umeå (Bromley, Jarvella, & Lundberg, 1985). Subjects read text on a cathode-ray tube (CRI) with their field of vision limited by a simulated moving window which passes through the text. The system allows the reader to control the speed of the window. It also has a look-back function and a set of on-line methods (e.g., probing signals) which tests comprehension keyed direct of the readers knowledge of whereabouts in the text he/she is. The system opens up a possibility of a reading diagnosis which is far more sophisticated than those normally in use (performance indicators are: Variation in window speed, look-back frequency, oral reading accuracy under various window widths and speeds, reaction times and accuracy at dual tasks like auditory signals, word probes, reference monitoring and detection of misspellings, eye-voice span, etc.). The reader's manipulation of the window speed, his or her look-back behavior together with the exact text environment when these options are used will be registered and recorded in the computer's history of each subject's reading protocol. One and the same text can be read very differently depending on the purpose of reading. The effect of various task demands can be assessed by studying how subjects distribute their reading times over different parts of the text. This flexible system for studying reading in real time can also be used as a remedial teaching tool for helping students develop useful reading strategies.

It has been found that poor readers lack flexibility in their reading. They seem to keep the same speed regardless of text requirements, reminding us of a car driver who drives at the same speed on a straight highway as on a narrow, winding, busy street downtown. In contrast, good readers are characterized by adjusting their reading to text demands. When propositional density increases or when references are potentially ambiguous, they slow down, perhaps even stop and look back, in order to secure relevant information.

The text-window technique offers a possibility of strategy training for poor readers. The computer can provide readers with exact feed-back on their reading process and how it changes during the course of training. Texts can be read under various instructions, such as following directions, looking for specific information, recalling main ideas, verbatim recall, summarizing and other strategies. To many readers, a page of text may sometimes appear as an overwhelming amount of information where you can easily go astray. They »play with» the text lines in an erratic or chaotic way. Such uncoordinated reading behavior is not necessarily an expression of some basic disability to monitor eye movements. It looks rather like a lack of mobilization of mental resources in reading. A linear scanning along the text lines seems to require a certain amount of effort and sustained attention. It does not seem unlikely that text-window practice would be helpful for these students in providing them with external guidance and restrict a behavior which unsupported could easily be totally disorganized. In a planned series of experiments the strategy-training potential of the text-window system will be evaluated.

5   NEURONAL ASPECTS OF COMPENSATION

There is yet another aspect of compensatory mechanisms in reading disabilities that merit attention. The irregular performance of disabled readers with deficits in the academic areas of reading, writing, spelling and arithmetic but with possible (if often latent) strengths in visual-spatial tasks including the arts has a biological basis (Geschwind, 1984). This relates to the diversities and variations in human abilities and also the observations that groups affected by certain risk factors for certain conditions may have lower risk factors for other conditions. The finding in a small number of dyslexics of anomalies of cortical organization characterized by abnormal folding (micropolygyria) involving predominantly the temporo-parietal (Tpt) architectonic field, an important part of the substrate for language, may be viewed in this light.

It will be recalled that in the first architectonic analysis (an analysis of dividing the cerebral cortex into areas based on differences in cellular arrangements of layers and columns) of the twenty-year old dyslexic brain, Galaburda and Kemper (1979) found abnormality at the gross anatomical level with larger and more white matter on the left side and abnormality in the development of the cortex in the left hemisphere only, probably because of disordered neuronal migration (failure of the neurons reaching their final cortical destination). Further studies confirm that anomalous lateralization and distortion of cortical architecture may be a characteristic of the dyslexic brain (Galaburda, 1982, 1983).

These findings permit the notion that at least for some developmental dyslexics there is the *potential* for right hemisphere substrate developing more fully than for some nondyslexics. This notion may help to explain the asymmetry of abilities found in some dyslexics. There is an optimistic (as of writing) side. Goldman (1978) has shown that altering the cortex of one side in the monkey in intrauterine life leads to superior growth of corresponding regions on the other side of the areas near the affected region. Could it be that factors in brain changes that bring about disabilities could also produce some abilities or even superior abilities?

This principle of compensatory growth during fetal life may hold some promise in research and remediation of reading disabilities. Recently, Geschwind and associates (Geschwind, 1983; Geschwind & Behan, 1982) found an association between left handedness, learning disorders and autoimmune disorders including migraine, allergies, asthma and diabetes. Since more males than females are affected by these disorders, Geschwind speculated that during intrauterine life males are exposed to greater amounts of testosterone and this excess of male sex hormone may delay the growth of the left hemisphere, thus contributing to dyslexia, other learning disorders and impairment in the development of the immune system. Obviously, research will need to be carried out on animals and even pregnant women to substantiate these findings. If indeed disordered cortical development relate to disordered neuronal migration in some disabled readers it may be possible to block or adjust the levels of testosterone during pregnancy (Geschwind, 1983). There is a further optimistic note while we await these exciting developments. Technological advances of the kind outlined in the earlier sections can help to ameliorate some of the difficulties. What is more, the helping professions will need to recognize latent, untapped talents in disabled readers and encourage their development.

REFERENCES

Beck, I.L., Perfetti, C.A., & McKeown, M.G. (1982). Effects of long-term vocabulary instruction on lexical access and reading comprehension. *Journal of Educational Psychology, 74,* 506-521.

Bransford J.D., Stein, B. S., & Vye, N.J. (1982). Helping students learn how to learn from written texts. In M.H. Singer (Ed.), *Competent reader, disabled reader: Research and application* (pp. 141-150). Hillsdale, NJ: Erlbaum.

Bromley, H.J., Jarvella, R.J., & Lundberg, I. (in press). From Lisp machine to language lab. *Behavior Research Methods, Instruments, and Computers.*

Brown, A.L. (1980). Metacognitive development and reading. In R.J. Spiro, B.C. Bruce & W.F. Brewer (Eds.), *Theoretical issues in reading comprehension: Perspectives from cognitive psychology, linguistics, artificial intelligence, and education* (pp. 453-481). Hillsdale, NJ: Erlbaum.

Carbo, M. (1978). Teaching reading with talking books. *The Reading Teacher, 32,* 267-273.

Carr, T.H. (1981). Building theories of reading disability: On the relations between individual differences in cognitive skills and reading comprehension. *Cognition, 9,* 73-114.

Chall, J. (1983). *Stages of reading development.* New York: McGraw-Hill.

Chomsky,C. (1978). When you still cannot read in third grade: After decoding, what? In S.J. Samuels (Ed.), *What research has to say about reading instruction.* Newark, DE:IRA.

Galaburda, A.M. (1982). Neuroanatomical aspects of language and dyslexia. In Y. Zotterman (Ed.), *Dyslexia: Neuronal, cognitive & linguistic aspects* (pp. 3-10). New York: Pergamon.

Galaburda, A.M. (1983). Developmental dyslexia: Current anatomical research. *Annals of Dyslexia, 33,* 41-53.

Galaburda, A.M., & Kemper, T.L. (1979). Cytoarchitectonic abnormalities in developmental dyslexia: A case study. *Annals of Neurology, 6,* 94-100.

Gamby, G. (1983). Talking books and taped books: Materials for instruction. *The Reading Teacher, 36,* 366-369.

Geschwind, N. (1983). Biological associations of left-handedness. *Annals of Dyslexia, 33,* 29-40.

Geschwind, N. (1984). The brain of a learning-disabled individual. *Annals of Dyslexia, 34,* 319-327.

Geschwind, N., & Behan, P. (1982). Left-handedness: Association with immune disease, migraine and developmental learning disorder. *Proceedings of the National Academy of Sciences, USA, 29,* 5097-5100.

Goldman, P. S. (1978). Neuronal plasticity in primate telencephalon: Anomalous projections induced by prenatal removal of frontal cortex. *Science, 202,* 768-770.

Haines, L.P., & Leong, C.K. (1983). Coding processes in skilled and less skilled readers. *Annals of Dyslexia, 33,* 67-89.

Hollingsworth, P.W. (1978). An experimental approach to the improved method of teaching reading. *The Reading Teacher, 31,* 624-626.

LaBerge, D., & Samuels, S. J. (1974). Toward a theory of automatic information processing in reading. *Cognitive Psychology, 6,* 293-323.

Lesgold, A.M., & Perfetti, C.A. (Eds.) (1981). *Interactive processes in reading.* Hillsdale, NJ: Erlbaum.

Lundberg, I. (1985). Longitudinal studies of reading and reading difficulties in Sweden. In G.E. Mackinnon & T.G. Waller (Eds.), *Reading research: Advances in theory and practice, Vol. 4,* (pp. 65-105). New York: Academic Press.

Mason, G.E., Blanchard, J. S., & Daniel, D.B. (1983). *Computer application in reading* (2nd ed.). Newark, DE: IRA.

Olson, (1977). From utterance to text: The bias of language in speech and writing. *Harvard Educational Review, 47,* 257-281.

Papert, S. (1980). *Mindstorms: Children, computers, and powerful ideas.* New York: Basic Books.

Perfetti, C.C. (1980). Verbal coding efficiency, conceptually guided reading, and reading failure. *Bulletin of the Orton Society, 30,* 197-208.

Perfetti, C.A., & Roth, S. (1981). Some of the interactive processes in reading and their role in reading skill. In A.M. Lesgold & C.A. Perfetti (Eds.), *Interactive processes in reading* (pp. 269-297). Hillsdale, NJ: Erlbaum.

Rubin, A. (1980). A theoretical taxonomy of the differences between oral and written language. In R.J. Spiro, B.C. Bruce, & W.F. Brewer (Eds.), *Theoretical issues in reading comprehension: Perspectives from cognitive psychology, linguistics, artificial intelligence, and education* (pp. 411-438). Hillsdale, NJ: Erlbaum.

Schneeberg. H. (1978). Listening while reading: A four year study. *The Reading Teacher, 32,* 629-639.

Sonquist, J.A., Baker, E.L., & Morgan, J.N. (1973). *Searching for structure.* Ann Arbor, MI: Survey Research Center, University of Michigan.

Stanovich, K. E. (1980). Toward an interactive-compensatory model of individual differences in the development of reading fluency. *Reading Research Quarterly, 16,* 32-71.

Stanovich, K.E., West, R.F., & Feeman, D.J. (1981). A longitudinal study of sentence context effects in second-grade children: Tests of an interactive-compensatory model. *Journal of Experimental Child Psychology, 32,* 185-199.

Tannen, D. (Ed.). (1982). *Spoken and written language: Exploring orality and literacy.* Norwood, NJ: Ablex.

Venezky, R.L. (1970). *The structure of English orthography.* The Hague, Netherlands: Mouton.

Wong, B.Y.L. (1982). Strategic behaviors in selecting retrieval cues in gifted, normal achieving and learning disabled children. *Journal of Learning Disabilities, 15,* 33-37.

West, R.F., Stanovich, K.E., Feeman, D.J., & Cunningham, A.E. (1983). The effect of sentence context on word recognition in second- and sixth-grade children. *Reading Research Quarterly, 19,* 6-15.

Communication and Handicap: Aspects of
Psychological Compensation and Technical Aids
E. Hjelmquist and L.-G. Nilsson (editors)
© Elsevier Science Publishers B.V. (North-Holland), 1986

APHASIA THERAPY RESEARCH: METHODOLOGICAL REQUIREMENTS AND ILLUSTRATIVE RESULTS

SALLY BYNG and MAX COLTHEART

Department of Psychology, Birkbeck College
London, England

A rehabilitation approach to aphasia is described and tested on one aphasic patient. This approach seeks to restore, partially or fully, the impaired specific communicative ability. The patient's sentence comprehension deficit and deficit in abstract-word comprehension were treated by specially developed methods, and it is concluded that the positive effects noted for both these deficits, can only be ascribed to the treatment given.

1   INTRODUCTION

The ways in which a person's communicative capacities can be handicapped are many and various. It may be the ability to receive communications from others that is affected, or it may be the ability to generate communications for others to receive. It may be that one modality of communication (for example, the spoken) is affected and others (for example, the written, the gestural) are not.

Also heterogeneous are the varieties of approaches that can be taken to the treament of communicative handicap. There is a basic distinction here which may perhaps be described as the distinction between compensation and rehabilitation. Even if these two terms may not be the most appropriate ones to describe the distinction we have in mind, the distinction itself seems real enough. What we are referring to by the term *compensation* is any approach which assumes that the specific communicative function which is impaired will remain so; here the treatment approach is to seek to minimise the consequences of this permanent impairment, by, for example, developing the affected person's ability to make use of alternative modes of communication, or by manipulating the person's environment so that the communicative disability will have fewer or less servere effects on the person's wellbeing.

In contrast, what we are referring to by the term *rehabilitation* is any treatment approach which seeks to restore, partially or fully, the impaired specific communicative ability, rather than trying to circumvent the consequences of its impairment.

It is obvious that there are circumstances in which a rehabilitation approach as we have defined it is quite inappropriate as a way of assisting someone with a communicative handicap: for example, cases where deafness or blindness are due to irreversible damage to peripheral sensory systems. If someone has permanently impaired vision and the treatment aim is to improve the person's ability to travel around, then a compensation approach - for example, the provision of technical aids such as tactual maps, as described in the chapter by Jansson in this book - is appropriate. But the situation is not always so clearcut. Consider the dysarthric person. Should one attempt to alleviate this condition by a compensation approach, such as making adjustments to the acoustic environment of the home that will reduce background noise and so make the dysarthric speech less unintelligible to other members of the family? Or might one adopt a rehabilitation approach, attempting to improve the person's ability to articulate accurately?

Even less clear is the situation with respect to aphasia. One thing that is certain is that, in any aphasic patient except the very rare very severe global aphasic, some communicative abilities will have been retained, even though others are impaired or even abolished. As discussed in the chapter by Ahlsén, nonverbal communicative abilities can be well preserved in people with otherwise rather severe aphasia. It follows that in cases of aphasia there is likely to be much scope for attempts at compensation - attempts at improving overall communicative performance by emphasising the use of alternative communicative channels to replace those affected by the aphasia.

But in this paper we wish to argue that there is much scope for a remediation approach too - that is, an approach which seeks to restore specific linguistic functions which have been damaged in a particular aphasic person, an approach which seeks to confront rather than curcumvent the communicative handicap.

For at least two basic reasons, this approach to dealing with communication disorder often meets with scepticism. There is a practical reason: if the consequences for the aphasic of his or her disorder can be appreciably alleviated by compensatory procedures, then the value of embarking upon time-consuming therapeutic regimes of unproven efficacy is open to doubt. And there is a scientific reason: if a specific linguistic function has been impaired by damage to a specific region of the brain, and this neurological damage is permanent, must it not be the case that the damage to the linguistic function is permanent too?

One might reply to the first of these points simply with the observation that no compensation for a lost or impaired linguistic function could be as satisfactory as the complete restoration of the function if that were possible. And one might reply to the second point by arguing that it is an empirical question whether intact regions of brain tissue are capable of acquiring cognitive abilities formerly subserved by now damaged regions - and it is a question to which the answer is not known.

But this scepticism concerning the possible efficacy of the rehabilitation approach to dealing with aphasic disorders is both widespread and not unreasonable. Certainly there are few examples of convincing demonstrations of treatment efficacy. On the other hand, of the many studies which have sought to investigate the efficacy of aphasia therapy, there are quite extraordinarily few which meet even the most elementary methodological criteria. Hence the situation at present is that we have almost no useful evidence concerning the efficacy of aphasia therapy.

Exactly what would count as worthwhile evidence? What are the elementary methodological criteria for research on the efficacy of aphasia therapy? We will consider these issues, and after having done so will go on to give two examples of current work on the efficacy of aphasia therapy, work which satisfies these criteria and provides a little direct evidence concerning potentialities of the rehabilitation approach to the treatment of communication disorder in aphasia.

2   THE METHODOLOGY OF RESEARCH ON THE EFFICACY OF APHASIA THERAPY

A first and obvious point is that one cannot begin to consider whether a particular treatment of an aphasic communicative disorder has been effective unless measurements of the severity of the disorder before and after treatment are available. A second and equally obvious point is that if there is no improvement in performance between the pre-test and the post-test then there can be no suggestion that the treatment has been effective.

Let us suppose, then, that measurments of language performance are made before and after treatment, and that performance at the post-test is superior to performance at the pre-test. This might have come about because the specific treatment regime applied was efficacious. However, there at least two other possibilities. The first is spontaneous recovery: the aphasic patient might have improved between pre-test and post-test even if no treatment had been applied. The second is the nonspecific treatment effect: the improvement might have occurred simply because some treament - any treatment - was applied. If the aim is to determine whether the specific treatment applied was efficacious, then one has to provide evidence that the improvement between pre-test and post- test was not due to spontaneous recovery, and was not simply a general effect of application of treatment. It is rare for efficacy research to be designed in such a way that studies are capable of providing such evidence - yet to design research meeting such aims is not especially difficult.

Attempts are sometimes made to deal with the problem of spontaneous recovery by applying treament to people whose aphasia is of relatively remote onset, the argument being that spontaneous recovery will have reached a plateau before the commencement of therapy. However, we know very little about the time-course of spontaneous recovery from aphasia, so this way of meeting the problem is simply unsatisfactory - especially since much more rigorous methods are available.

An alternative way of dealing with the problem of spontaneous recovery is to take multiple baseline measures before treatment begins, since if performance is stable across these baselines then spontaneous recovery is not happening. However any subsequent improvements could be either specific or general effects of therapy: the multiple baseline approach does not allow us to distinguish between these two possibilities.

A third way of assessing the contribution of spontaneous recovery to any improvements between pre-test and post-test, which also allows one to distinguish between general and specific effects of treatment, is to make use of the fact that in any aphasic patient it is usually the case that a number of different linguistic functions are impaired. If one obtains pre-test and post-test measures on all of these functions, but applies treatment only to some or even only to one of the functions, and if the outcome is that the pre-test-post-test differences are larger for the treated functions than for the untreated functions, then one has obtained solid evidence that a specific effect of treatment is operating. If instead it is claimed that spontaneous recovery or some general treatment effect has been responsible for the improved performance between pre-test and post-test, we are left with no explanation for the finding that the improvements are greater with the treated than with the untreated functions.

This reasoning can be made even more persuasive if there is a second phase of treatment in which previously untreated language functions are now subjected to treatment and previously treated functions are no longer treated. Particularly clear evidence for the existence of specific treatment effects is obtained if in this second phase the newly treated functions improve more rapidly than the previously treated ones. This particular design has an additional virtue, because it provides a way of measuring the permanence of any effects of the first treatment phase. The first-treated function can be measured at the beginning and at the end of the second treatment phase. If any improvements present at the end of the first treament phase are still evident at the end of the second phase (during which there has been no further treatment of the first-treated function), then the first treament's effects have been shown to be more than merely transitory.

Failure to design efficacy research along lines like these is one of the common deficiencies of studies of the treatment of aphasia; that is, there are very few published studies in which positive outcomes of treatment can confidently be interpreted as specific treatment effects and not as general treatment effects or consequences of spontaneous recovery.

A second very common deficiency of research on the efficacy of aphasia therapy is that in such research language functions are usually defined and measured far too broadly. Here it is the *negative* outcome of efficacy research that is uninterpretable. One cannot expect any single treatment method to be appropriate for all patients classified simply as having a disorder of language: the category of »disorder of language» is simply too broad. So we are very unlikely to learn anything useful about the efficacy or inefficacy of aphasia treatments by studying the effects of applying any one treatment to a group of patients categorized broadly as aphasic. Such a group will inevitably be extremely heterogeneous with respect to the particular types of language disorders present, and so different types of treatment will be appropriate for different patients in the group. If we wish to investigate the efficacy of a particular specific treatment method, then it is essential that all the patients to whom the treatment is applied are in fact suffering from the specific linguistic impairment at which the treatment method is directed. Selecting patients in terms of broad categories of language impairment will inevitably mean that some or even most of the patients in the treated group are inappropriate as candidates for the treatment being applied. Hence negative outcomes are to be expected in this kind of research on aphasia therapy; but they tell us little or nothing about whether specific treatment methods can be effective when applied to patients selected on the basis of sufficiently narrow categories of linguistic impairment.

How narrow must such categorizations be? It is easy to show that they must be very narrow indeed. »Disorder of spoken language» is too broad, since it includes both receptive and expressive aphasia, for which, surely, different treatment approaches are appropriate. »Disorder of spoken-language production» is also too broad: one would not expect the same treatment to be effective in cases of non-fluent (Broca's) and in cases of fluent (Wernicke's) aphasia. »Broca's aphasia» is also too broad: patients classified as Broca's aphasics exhibit a variety of impairments of the ability to produce spoken language (for example, non-fluency, effortful articulation, abnormally simple syntax, difficulties with grammatical morphemes) and, crucially, these symptoms do not invariably co-occur (see, e.g., Berndt, 1986; Parisi, 1986). Since the symptoms do not invariably co-occur, they must have different causes; but if they have different causes, they will require different treatment. Hence there cannot be a treatment for Broca's aphasia. Even the individual symptoms of the syndrome of Broca's aphasia just listed are divisible into narrower categories: for example, the apparently extremely specific symptom »difficulty in producing grammatical morphemes correctly» is divisible, because difficulties with function words, prefixes, and affixes do not invariably co-occur (Parisi, 1986).

The existence of these extremely fine-grained dissociations between narrowly-defined linguistic capabilities certainly provides considerable complications for attempts to formulate approaches to the treatment of aphasic disorders. But these complications need to be met head-on: to ignore them will mean that one will be applying treatments which can be at best only partially appropriate to the set of patients being treated, and this minimises the chances of obtaining any evidence of positive effects of treatment.

An obvious difficulty arises here. As we have already argued, efficacy research requires that there be pre-test and post-test measurements of patients' linguistic capabilities. There are many standardised aphasia tests available, and it is such tests that are normally used in efficacy research. But none of these tests provides anything adequate in the way of narrow categorizations of patterns of impairment. Even in those tests which contain subtests aimed at fairly specific linguistic functions, such as comprehension of concrete nouns or knowledge of letter-sound rules for reading, the numbers of items in such subtests are always so small that the subtests are entirely inadequate as a basis for statistical pre-test - post-test comparisons. This means that, at least at present, researchers and therapists have no alternative but to make up their own sets of testing materials.

Enormously helpful here are prior theoretical analyses of the disabilities exhibited by individual patients. Even the crudest thoughts about how some particular linguistic activity is *normally* performed provide insights for the interpretation of patterns of impairments of that activity seen in aphasic patients and ideas about what materials are most appropriate for measuring these impairments.

We will illustrate the approach to efficacy research discussed here by describing, fairly briefly, applications of this approach in the treatment of two patients, one with an acquired dyslexia and the other with a sentence comprehension impairment affecting both written and spoken sentences.

3   TREATMENT OF SURFACE DYSLEXIA

Models of the processing mechanisms used by readers of alphabetic scripts generally distinguish two different processing routines for reading aloud, a *lexical* and a *non-lexical* routine (see, e.g. Coltheart, 1985, 1986), both of which are available to the normal skilled reader. The non-lexical routine depends upon access to a system of rules describing correspondences between orthography and phonology, and reading aloud via this routine takes the form of *assembling* a phonological representation of a letter-string from the phonological segments derived from application of the rules. The lexical routine depends upon access to word-specific representations in an internal lexicon, so reading aloud via this routine takes the form of *addressing* a phonological representation already existing in the internal lexicon. The lexical routine cannot be used for reading nonwords aloud (because they do not exist in the internal lexicon) and is required for the correct reading aloud of irregularly-spelled words such as *yacht* or *pint* (because such words would be wrongly read by the non- lexical routine, since they do not obey the rules used by this routine).

One line of evidence for such »dual-route« models of reading is provided by studies of acquired dyslexia. In some patients with acquired dyslexia, the ability to read words aloud is well- preserved whilst nonword reading is severely impaired or even abolished - this is »phonological dyslexia« (see, e.g. Beauvois & Derouesné, 1979; Funnell, 1983). In other patients, nonwords and regularly-spelled words are read relatively well, whilst irregularly-spelled words are read badly - this is »surface dyslexia« (see, e.g., Patterson, Marshall, & Coltheart, 1985). A very natural interpretation of these observations is that phonological dyslexia arises when the non-lexical routine is selectively damaged, whereas surface dyslexia arises when the lexical routine is selectively damaged.

This theoretical interpretation has immediate consequences for the selection of treatment methods. A »phonics» approach - teaching letter-sound rules, for example - is appropriate where it is the non-lexical routine that is impaired, and indeed this approach can be extremely successful in such cases (de Partz, in press). Such an approach is not appropriate for treating an impairment of the lexical routine, however, because this routine uses word-specific lexical knowledge rather than general rules about correspondences between orthography and phonology. Instead, some form of »whole-word» treatment is appropriate here. Hence with E.E., the case of surface dyslexia we discuss here, the technique used to improve the accuracy with which he read single words aloud involved attempts to restore word-specific representations which his neurological damage had abolished.

This patient, a 40-year-old left-handed postman, sustained a skull fracture in a fall in October 1980. An initial dysphasia resolved into anomia and surface dyslexia. Tested in March 1981, he exhibited a selective difficulty in reading irregularly- spelled words. Given 39 irregular words and 39 closely-matched regular words (from Coltheart, Besner, Jonasson, & Davelaar, 1979), he read correctly 12/39 irregular words and 23/39 regular words ($p<.02$ by McNemar's Test). The imperfect performance with regular words showed that his ability to use the non-lexical routine was not intact (which has been true for many but not all surface dyslexics), but the important point here is that the significantly worse performance with irregular words implies a major impairment of the lexical routine.

As a way of assessing the course of any spontaneous recovery, these 78 words were given to the patient for reading aloud on seven occasions, from March 1981 (5 months after his injury) to July 1981 (9 months after the injury). The results are given in Table 1.

TABLE 1

EE: Results of repeated re-testing of single-word oral reading

Date	2/3/81	25/4/81	5/5/81	12/5/81	21/5/81	27/5/81	7/7/81
Proportion of words correctly read ($N = 78$)	.42	.53	.56	.67	.59	.69	.71

As is clear, although there was some improvement across early occasions, performance on this test had stabilised by mid-May 1981 and scores across the last four occasions showed no suggestion of any improvement. Hence there is evidence that spontaneous recovery of reading ability was no longer occurring after May 1981. Nevertheless, the treatment (which was begun in mid-July 1981) was administered in such a way that spontaneos recovery effects, if present, would be distinguishable from specific treatment effects.

The first of the three treatment programmes carried out with E.E. involved words containing the sequence <vowel/vowel/GH> - words like *though, through* and *cough.* This category of word was selected because this spelling pattern is the most irregular in English: not only are there no predominant pronunciations for the vowel digraph and the GH sections of such words, but there are a large number of different pronunciations across words having this spelling pattern. Not surprisingly, E.E. was extremely bad at reading these GH words aloud: of the 24 such words used, he was correct with only 5 of them in a pre-treatment test of reading aloud.

The 24 GH words were divided into two matched groups of 12; call these group 1 and group 2. Once a week for 5 weeks (from 14 July 1981 to 11 August 1981), he was given this set of 24 words to read aloud. The first of these 5 sessions was a pre-test session. After this the group 1 words were treated throughout the following two weeks, whilst the group 2 words were not treated. Then, for the final two-week period, the group 2 words.

For each of the words, a mnemonic aid was provided: a card containing the printed word plus a picture representing the meaning of the word. The word *borough,* for example, was accompanied by a small map of part of London, and the word *bough* by a drawing of a tree. The use of these cards was explained to the patient, and it was arranged that he would spend 15 minutes per day at home, every day, reading aloud the treated words from their cards with the help of the mnemonic pictures, recording his daily progress on a chart provided for this purpose. As mentioned above, all 24 words were tested under normal conditions (i.e., without the mnemonic cues) once a week for 5 weeks.

Averaged over the first 3 testing sessions, proportion of correct reading responses was .68 for the treated words and .31 for the untreated words, and this advantage for the treated words was significant by Mann-Whitney test ($Z = 2.53$, p<.01). What was unexpected, however, was that the *untreated* words also improved across the three sessions (1/12, 3/12, and 7/12 correct respectively). Application of Cochran's Q test revealed not only that performance with the treated words improved significantly across the first three testing occasions (chi squared = 10.9, p<.01), but that this was also true for the untreated words (chi squared = 8.0, p=.02).

The superiority of the treated over the untreated words indicates that there was a specific treatment effect here: the mnemonic method did specifically improve the reading of the words with which this technique was used. But there was also an additional effect operating, which affected the untreated words (and, presumably, the treated words, to the same degree). This could have been either spontaneous recovery (and we have already provided a reason for doubting this), or else a generalisation effect of some kind. This was studied further in the second and third treament programmes carried out with E.E.; we discuss these shortly.

In the last two weeks of the first treatment programme, the treatment was applied to the group 2 words (which had previously recieved no treatment) and the treatment of the group 1 words was discontinued. At the end of this period, performance was perfect with both sets of words.

The second programme was begun by giving E.E. a set of 485 single words to read aloud, the 485 most-frequent words in the count of Kucera and Francis (1967). He misread 54 of these words. This set of 54 words was divided at random into two groups of 27, and the mnemonic method described above was used with one of these sets, over a period of weeks in November 1981. The period of treatment was preceded by two pre-test sessions of reading the 54 words, and followed by two post-test sessions. The results are given in Table 2.

Pre-test performance was no different for T versus U words (Z = .388, p = .7). At post-test, the T words were superior (Z = 6.10, p<.001). However, for both sets of words, post-test performance was better than pre-test performance (Z = 4.315, p<.001 for U words; Z = 4.73, p<.001 for T words). Just as with the first treatment programme, then, there were two effects: a specific treatment effect (T words better than U words) and a nonspecific effect (U words improve, although not as much a T words). However, the design of the second study allows us to investigate the nonspecific effect in more detail, because we used two rather than only one pre-tests. If the nonspecific effect is due to spontaneous recovery, or if it is simply a practice effect, then one would expect performance to be better in the second pre-test than in the first. However, this was not so; as Table 3 shows, neither for the T words nor for the U words was there a significant difference between the two pre-tests. Hence the nonspecific effect appears to be *produced by the treatment* - the mnemonic technique benefits treated words more than untreated words, but it does improve the reading of untreated words to some degree too.

TABLE 2

E.E.: Effects of a mnemonic therapy on single-word oral reading (high-frequency words)

	PRE-TREATMENT		POST-TREATMENT	
	Pre-test 1	Pre-test 2	Post-test 1	Post-test 2
Treated words	.19	.44	1.00	.96
Untreated words	.47	.44	.85	.74

Very similar results were obtained in the third and final treatment programme, which took place in the period after the completion of the second programme. The third programme used the next 388 words in the Kucera-Francis norms. E.E. misread 101 of these. The misread words were divided at random into two groups (51 T words and 50 U words). After two pre-test sessions reading the 101 words, the mnemonic therapy was used with the T words. Then there were two post-test sessions reading all 101 words. The results are given in Table 3.

Pre-test performance was not different for the two groups of words ($Z = .57$, $p = .56$). The T words were superior to the U words at post-test ($Z = 8.46$, $p < .001$). However, both groups of words improved between pre-test and post-test (for U words, $Z = 3.5$, $p < .001$; for T words, $Z = 5.6$, $p < .001$). The difference between the two pre-tests was not significant for the U words ($Z = .447$, $p = .65$) but was just significant for the T words ($Z = 2.07$, $p = .04$).

These three studies of rehabilitation in acquired dyslexia provide evidence that it is possible to use a whole-word technique to restore at least partially the ability to use the lexical procedure for reading aloud after the use of this procedure has been impaired by neurological damage. The effects observed cannot be ascribed to spontaneous recovery or practice; the treatment has a highly specific effect (assisting only the particular words treated) and in addition a second, more general, effect (giving some assistance to untreated words and treated words alike).

TABLE 3

E.E.: Effects of a mnemonic therapy on single-word oral reading
(low-frequency words)

	PRE-TREATMENT		POST-TREATMENT	
	Pre-test 1	Pre-test 2	Post-test 1	Post-test 2
Treated words	.45	.63	1.00	.96
Untreated words	.48	.52	.78	.70

4   TREATMENT OF A SENTENCE COMPREHENSION DISORDER

Models of sentence comprehension are not currently as well developed as
processing models for reading, so it is more difficult to interpret impairments of the
sentence comprehension process in the same model-based way as the impairment in the
reading process was interpreted for the patient described above. However, patients
who demonstrate an impairment in comprehending reversible sentences have been well
documented in the literature (see, e.g., Schwartz, Saffran, & Marin, 1980, and Kolk &
van Grunsven, 1985), and, despite the lack of a precise theoretical model of the
sentence comprehension process, an outline of some of the necessary procedures can
be provided for use in interpreting the performance of such patients.

The sentence comprehension process would appear to involve three major
components. One of these is the parsing component which is responsible for carrying
out a syntactic analysis of the incoming sentence so as to produces a hierarchical
representation of the syntactic structure of the sentence. A second component involves
consulting the lexical entry for the verb, to establish what thematic roles (Jackendoff,
1972) are the properties of that particular verb. These two procedures on their own
are, however, insufficient to allow comprehension of a sentence - the syntactic parse

provides only a labelled description of the constituents of the sentence, and the lexical entry of the verb provides only an indication of the thematic roles which are the properties of that particular verb. A third procedure is critical for comprehension: the integration of the two types of information yielded by the first two procedures. This third procedure might accurately be described as a *mapping* of syntactic functions on to thematic roles. This final procedure enables the interpretation of »who is doing what to whom» to be made. Figure 1 provides a schematic outline of these ideas about the sentence comprehension process.

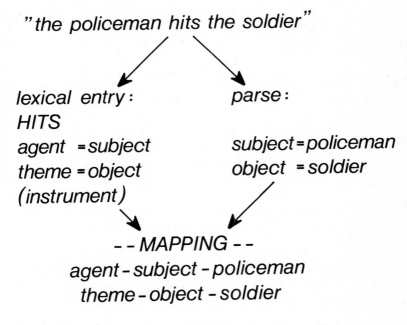

FIGURE 1

Schema for comprehension of sentences.

The reversible sentences used in many tests of sentence comprehension demand the application of all three procedures for correct comprehension to be accomplished, as there is no possibility for the use of any pragmatic strategies to be implemented to assist comprehension, precisely because the sentences are reversible.

It is clear that, according to this analysis, there will be at least three potential sites within the comprehension process where a sentence comprehension deficit could arise: in the parsing procedure, in consulting the lexical entry, or in the mapping procedure, and a further possibility would be a deficit in working memory. An assessment of the sentence processing abilities of a patient will therefore need to include some means of evaluating the intactness of each of these three components, in order to determine which component of the process is impaired, and therefore what aspect of the impairment the treatment programme should be aimed at restoring. An impairment in the *mapping procedure* was isolated for the next patient we discuss, B.R.B., and the technique used to restore this ability will be described.

This patient suffered a cerebro-vascular accident, involving an extensive left middle cerebral artery infarct, in 1979, when he was 41 years old. Until his stroke, B.R.B. had worked as a businessman. An initial aphasia examination diagnosed a moderate/severe expressive dysphasia and a mild receptive dysphasia, characteristic of Broca's aphasia. Tested in early 1984, he performed poorly on comprehension of reversible active declarative sentences (such as »The vicar photographs the policeman») and reversible locative sentences (such as »The cup is in the box») - see Figures 2 and 3.

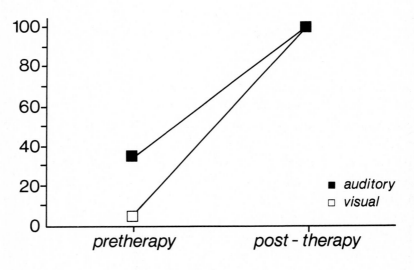

FIGURE 2

Comprehension of locative sentences.

His ability to parse was assessed by asking him to carry out grammaticality judgements, wich do not require comprehension of the sentence, but rather are a

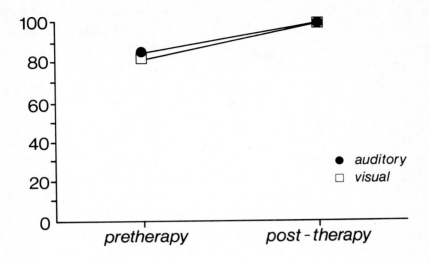

FIGURE 3

Comprehension of reversible sentences.

measure of ability to detect syntactic illegalities. B.R.B. had no difficulty with these types of tasks. Mapping in isolation from parsing was tested using a test of comprehension of single verbs (choosing which of two videotaped scenes matched the verb). Here comprehension of the verbs depends upon the ability to map thematic roles onto the visual representation. Parsing is not required because only one word is presented. B.R.B. had difficulty on this test (see Figure 4), suggesting that the locus of his sentence comprehension deficit was his inability to map; the pattern of his difficulties suggested relatively intact lexical retrieval.

Further support for the notion of a mapping deficit underlying B.R.B.'s poor performance came from an analysis of his sentence *production,* as his speech contained very few instances of combined arguments and functions. This deficit might be expected if mapping thematic roles onto any representation is impaired. Testing of other aspects of his language processing ability revealed that he also had a reduced

S. Byng and M. Coltheart

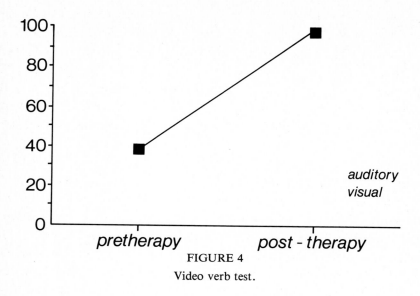

FIGURE 4

Video verb test.

short term memory matching span, an impairment in comprehension of printed or spoken abstract words and a complete inability to read aloud non words.

A treatment programme was commenced which aimed at teacing B.R.B. the ralationship between the two noun phrases in the sentence, i.e. what the thematic role of each of the noun phrases in a particular position in the sentence is. The locative sentences were selected for treatment, for two reasons. One was that B.R.B. was more impaired with locative sentences, and the second was that the relationships between the noun phrases are less predictable with this type of sentence. A constraint from the start on the design of this programme was that B.R.B. would not be able to attend for testing/therapy sessions more than once a week because of travelling distance. It was considered that if he was going to be able to relearn or reaccess some principle or strategy about language processing, a single session each week was inadequate. Therefore the therapy had to be designed in such a way that he could practise at home, monitor his performance, and do this without any assistance, so as a) to ensure that the treatment method would not be interfered with, and b) to preserve B.R.B.'s sense of self esteem by arranging that he could carry out a task without any outside help.

The therapy task consisted of twenty reversible locative sentences. Each sentence was accompanied by two pictures, the correct picture and a picture depicting the two noun phrases in the reverse relationship. For example, the sentence might be »the marmalade is behind the butter,» so the correct picture would show the marmalade behind the butter, and the reverse role distractor picture would show the butter behind the marmalade. The patient's task was to select the correct picture for the sentence. In order to help him make the correct choice, he was given certain clues. For each of the four prepositions included in the sentences he was given a »meaning card» which diagrammatically depicted the relationship between the two noun phrases in the sentence containing the preposition. For example »in» was represented as:

$$\text{↘①}\ \mathbf{2}$$

In addition the »1» was written in red, and the »2» in blue. The next clue was a »meaning card» which also contained a sentence »1 is in 2» and the »1» and »2» were written in the same colours again. This illustrated to B.R.B. that the first »thing» (=NP) in the sentence was located in the second »thing» (=NP). The third clue consisted of the »practice cards,» which had the therapy sentence printed on them with the two pictures, but with the sentence written in colours to correspond with the »meaning card» cue, i.e. the first NP was written in red, and the second in blue. The two pictures were also drawn in colour; for the sentence »the pan is in the jug,» the correct picture would have a red pan in a blue jug, and the reverse role picture would have a red jug in a blue pan. By matching up the colours in the sentence with the colours in the picture, B.R.B. could detect the mismatch if he interpreted the sentence wrongly. This enabled him to have an aid to comprehending the way to interpret the sentence, and to monitor his own progress. The final stage for him was the »test cards.» These comprised the same sentences written in black, so that B.R.B., having gone through the coloured cards, could test himself by selecting a coloured picture to go with the uncoloured sentence i.e. no clues were available for assistance. Then he could find the corresponding coloured sentence to go with the black sentence, and check that he had selected the correct picture.

B.R.B. understood what the task required very easily. In total he had five sentences with ten pictures for each of four prepositions, which gave him a total of twenty sentences and forty pictures. After the procedure had been explained to him, B.R.B. went home to practice the sentences. He was instructed to practice as much as he felt he needed to, and to return in one week to check on his progress. When B.R.B. returned after one week, the therapy sentences were retested, using black and white pictures and sentences. He made three out of twenty errors, and at his own request, returned home with the original set of cards to consolidate the first week's learning.

On his return the following week, performance was not only perfect but also rapid, in contrast to his previously very slow performance.

It was predicted that if this improvement happened because B.R.B. could now once again map thematic roles onto syntactic structures, the effect will not be confined just to visually presented sentences, the modality in which the treatment had been carried out, nor just to locative sentences, nor just to active sentences. The improvement ought to generalise all the way to comprehension of auditory, non-locative passive sentences, such as »The soldier was pushed by the policeman». When B.R.B. was re- tested on sentences such as these he was found to have improved to 100%. He had thus achieved perfect performance in all comprehension tasks involving mapping (see Figures 2, 3 and 4). When sentence production was also analysed after therapy had taken place, that too had improved considerably, but this improvement was not wholesale; rather, only structural aspects of his speech had improved (see Figure 5). Other aspects such as the underrepresentation in his speech of function words, had not improved (see Figure 6.)

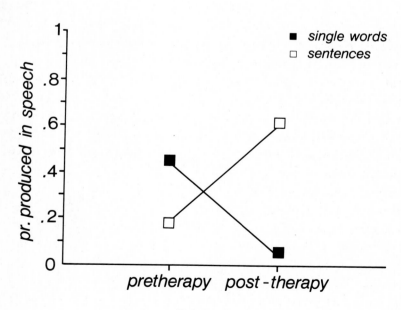

FIGURE 5
Quality of speech production.

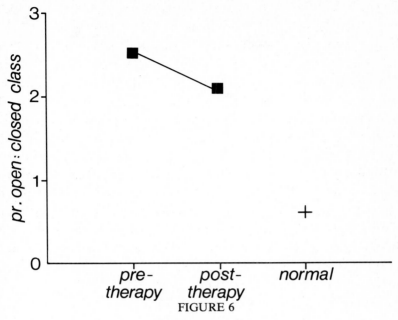

FIGURE 6

Speech production.

It is unlikely that B.R.B.'s improvements in sentence comprehension and production were spontaneous-recovery effects, unrelated to the application of treatment, for two reasons. The first reason is that the treatment began five years after his stroke, and there are no reasons to believe that spontaneous recovery is still continuing so long after the initial neurological damage. This is a slightly speculative argument, since the evidence about the time-course of spontaneous recovery is fragmentary and methodologically inadequate in several ways. The second reason is the more compelling. As mentioned before, B.R.B. exhibited a variety of different language impairments before the treatment was instituted. At re-test after the end of the treatment period, only one of these impairments had improved significantly - namely, the one which had been treated. This is illustrated in Table 4.

However, there may be those who would be prepared to argue that, by chance, this rehabilitation study had selected for treatment that particular linguistic function which happened still to be spontaneously recovering, whilst other impaired linguistic functions had stabilised at an impaired level. As noted by Coltheart (1983), this possibility can be assessed by using a crossover-treatment design. Let X be a linguistic function which was treated (and improved) and Y be a linguistic function which was not treated (and did not improve). Suppose after this first treatment phase there is a

TABLE 4

B.R.B.: Summary of impairments pre- and post-treatment

	Percentage Correct	
	Pre-treatment	Post-treatment
Comprehension of reversible sentences	60.0	100.0
Production of structurally complex speech	20.6	75.4
Comprehension of relative clauses	54.2	50.0
Oral reading of abstract words	63.4	67.9
Synonym judgment with abstract words	76.0	71.0
Oral reading of non-words	6.0	17.0
Short-term memory matching span	4 digits	4 digits

second treatment phase in which Y is treated and X is not. If Y, which did not improve during the first phase (when it was not treated) improves during the second phase, it seems virtually assured that the treatments of X and Y did specifically improve the linguistic functions at which treatments were directed. Furthermore, one can assess the durability of effects of the first treated function, X: if X improved during the first phases, did it remain at the same high level after the second phase (during which it was not treated), which could indicate some durability of the treatment?

These methodological desiderata were applied by selecting for treatment a linguistic function which was impaired in B.R.B., and which had not been improved by the treatment which raised his scores on sentence comprehension tests to 100%. This function was the comprehension of abstract words. He was good at judging whether two concrete words (e.g., sack/bag) had the same meaning, but poor at a matched task involving pairs of abstract words (e.g., safety/security). As Table 5 indicates, his performance at abstract word comprehension was no better after the mapping treatment than before.

TABLE 5

Results of two different treatment procedures for two different comprehension disorders

	Percentage Correct		
	Before all treatment	After treatment for reversible sentences	After treatment for abstract words
Comprehension of reversible sentences	60	100	100
Comprehension of abstract words	-	16	94

A second treatment regime, (was therefore instituted six months after the completion of the first treatment regime) focussing on improving his ability to comprehend abstract words. The treatment was carried out in two ways, to look at the usefulness of two methods of treatment. The first was a picture-word matching task, in which B.R.B. was required to perceive relationships between pictures representing abstract words, and the meaning of the word, and the second task required him to generate, using a dictionary, one word synonyms of a set of abstract words. This latter task requires quite careful thought about the shades of meaning within words.

After four weeks of this regime, his ability to comprehend reversible sentences and to comprehend abstract words was tested. Table 5 shows his scores on these tests at three stages: (a) before any treatment; (b) after treatment for the deficit of sentence-comprehension; and (c) after a period of treatment for the deficit of abstract-word comprehension, during which there was no sentence-comprehension treatment. We find that the impaired abstract-word comprehension improves only after it has been specifically treated, and that the improvement on comprehension of reversible sentences holds up even after a period with no treatment of practice on this task.

We contend that this pattern of findings has only one plausible interpretation. The treatment method used for the sentence comprehension deficit was specifically responsible for the restoration of the patient's ability in sentence comprehension and for the improvement in sentence production, and the treatment method used for the deficit in abstract-word comprehension also specifically improved the patient's ability to understand abstract words. We also suggest that the first of these findings is evidence for the usefulness of the three-component model of sentence comprehension sketched earlier.

REFERENCES

Beauvois, M.-F., & Derouesné (1979). Phonological alexia: three dissociations. *Journal of Neurology, Neurosurgery and Psychiatry, 42,* 1115-1124.

Berndt, R. (1986). Symptom co-occurrence and symptom dissociation in the interpretation of agrammatism. In M. Coltheart, R. Job, & G. Sartori (Eds.), *The cognitive neuropsychology of language.* London: Lawrence Erlbaum Associates Ltd.

Coltheart, M. (1982). The psycholinguistic analysis of acquired dyslexias. *Philosophical Transactions of the Royal Society, B298,* 151-164.

Coltheart, M. (1983). Aphasis therapy: a single-case-study approach. In C. Code, & D. Muller (Eds.), *Aphasia therapy.* London: Edward Arnold.

Coltheart, M. (1985). Cognitive neuropsychology and the study of reading. In M.E. Posner, & O.S.M. M. Marin (Eds.), *Attention and performance XI.* Hillsdale, New Jersey: Lawrence Erlbaum.

Coltheart, M. (1986). Functional architecture of the language- processing system. In M. Coltheart, R. Job, & G. Sartori (Eds.), *The cognitive neuropsychology of language*. London: Lawrence Erlbaum Associates Ltd.

Coltheart, M., Besner, D., Jonasson, J.T. & Davelaar, E. (1979). Phonological encoding in the lexical decision task. *Quartely Journal of Experimental Psychology, 31,* 489-508.

Funnell, E. (1983). Phonological processes in reading: New evidence from acquired dyslexia. *British Journal of Psychology, 74,* 159-180.

Jackendoff, R. (1972). *Semantic interpretation in generative grammar*. Cambridge, Mass: MIT Press.

Kolk, H., & van Grunsven, M.M.F. (1985). Agrammatism as a variable phenomenon. *Cognitive Neuropsychology, 2,* 347-384.

Kucera, H., & Francis, W.N. (1967). *Computational analysis of present-day American English*. Providence, Rhode Island: Brown University Press.

Parisi, D. (1986). Grammatical disturbances of speech production. In M. Coltheart, R. Job, & G. Sartori (Eds.), *The cognitive neuropsychology of language*. London: Lawrence Erlbaum Associates Ltd.

Patterson, K.E., Marshall, J.C., & Coltheart, M. (Eds.). (1985). *Surface dyslexia: Cognitive and neuropsychological studies of phonological reading*. London: Lawrence Erlbaum Associates Ltd.

de Partz, M.-P. (in press). Reeducation of a deep dyslexic patient: rationale of the method and results. *Cognitive Neuropsychology,*

Schwartz, M.F., Saffran, E., & Marin, O.S.M. (1980). The word order problem in agrammatism. I. Comprehension. *Brain and Language, 10,* 249-262.

Communication and Handicap: Aspects of
Psychological Compensation and Technical Aids
E. Hjelmquist and L.-G. Nilsson (editors)
© Elsevier Science Publishers B.V. (North-Holland), 1986

POSSIBILITIES OF SPONTANEOUS COMPENSATION FOR APHASIC SYMPTOMS IN CONVERSATION

ELISABETH AHLSÉN

Department of Linguistics, University of Göteborg, Sweden[1]

Ten aphasics with different symptoms were studied in videotaped conversations with their therapists and were also given a picture-naming test. There was no correlation between the result of the naming test and the number of noticeable word-finding problems in conversation. This lack of correlation is interpreted as pointing to a considerable activity type influence on aphasic symptoms. The aphasics were generally found to use a greater amount of nonverbal communication in conversation than nonaphasic controls and this nonverbal communication seems to partly compensate for their verbal problems.

[1] Research grant: The Swedish Council for Research in the Humanistic and Social Sciences and The Swedish Council for Planning and Coordination of Research. This paper is based on work within the research project »Aphasia and Spoken Interaction» at the Department of Linguistics, University of Göteborg. I am indebted to the project leader, Jens Allwood, for the suggestion to apply an activity dependent analysis to the communication of aphasics.

1   BACKGROUND AND ASSUMPTIONS

Something (X) can be said to compensate for something else (Y) if X is totally or partially fulfilling a function which is usually fulfilled by Y and Y for the moment is lacking or disturbed. In the case of aphasia, what is disturbed is mainly the ability to convey factual information by verbal means. There are many various syndromes affecting this ability in different ways and there are also several ways in which the aphasic symptoms could be, and maybe are, compensated for.

The ways of compensation that can be expected to actualize in aphasic patients could depend on:

a. what verbal abilities are missing or disturbed and how (i.e. the type of aphasia)
b. what verbal and other abilities for compensation are available to the patient
c. what verbal and nonverbal abilities can be used in each particular communicative activity
d. individual characteristics of communication that were developed premorbidly.

For example, most kinds of aphasics have word-finding problems, but the ability to use nonverbal communication to compensate for these problems might be different for different types of aphasics. In some activities, for example telephone calls, nonverbal communication cannot be used, while in other activities, like face-to-face conversation, nonverbal communication can be quite efficient. The patient may or may not have had the habit of using a great deal of nonverbal communication before acquiring his/her aphasia.

The assumptions made here are:

a. that communicative patterns involving compensation for the aphasic symptoms are more or less spontaneously developed by aphasic patients and that these patterns are determined by the causal factors mentioned above (a to d)
b. that these communicative patterns can be hard to distinguish in traditional aphasia tests, where the activity is very structured and does not leave room for different ways of communication.

If these assumptions are correct, new ways of studying and analyzing communicative behaviour in aphasics will have to be developed, in order to detect possible spontaneous compensation by different types of aphasics in different activities.

It is further assumed that some kind of »holistic» approach to the aphasic in his/her communicative situation has to be applied. This means:

a. that one has to consider as many relevant factors as possible in the interpretation of a patient's behaviour in a certain activity
b. that one has to find methods of studying factors that can be relevant for the total picture of communicative ability but which have not traditionally been analyzed in aphasics (if at all).

These undertakings are, both from a theoretical and practical point of view, demanding and time-consuming, but necessary in order to avoid misinterpretations in studies of aphasics' communication.

Some possible means of compensation which could be found in the communicative patterns of aphasics would be:

- use of verbal circumlocutions and explanations (in some aphasics)

- use of reference to the immediate situational or linguistic context

- appeal to the conversation partner

- use of highly emotional communication

- use of nonverbal means of communication for different functions like illustration of factual content, communication of state of feeling and interaction regulating.

Several of these means of compensation (which are, of course, empirically overlapping) could be expected in aphasics on the basis of an evolutionary theory of communication (cf. Jackson, 1874). Nonverbal communication, interaction regulating mechanisms and communication of feelings are examples of parts of communication which can be assumed to have been developed earlier, phylogenetically as well as ontogenetically. They are controlled by more basal brain structures, thus being less vulnerable to the cortical lesions causing aphasia than verbal factual communication.

The expected discourse patterns shown by aphasics could be assumed to contain more of the mentioned »possibly compensatory» means of communication than patterns shown by most nonaphasic persons. These patterns would be a result of the aphasic individual's adaptation to his/her aphasia, but the patterns would vary with the activity and also as a result of the spontaneous adjustment of the aphasic's communicative system.

2   A STUDY OF COMPENSATION FOR WORD-FINDING PROBLEMS[1]

2.1   Aims
The aims of the study were to:

a.   compare the amount of noticeable word-finding problems in a naming test and in conversation for each aphasic patient,
b.   see how possible compensatory means of communication (especially in the form of nonverbal communication) were used by the aphasics in conversation.

2.2   Method
Ten different types of aphasics were studied in a ten-minute video-recorded conversation with their speech therapists. The topics of conversation were the patient's medical history, how he/she spends the day, his/her occupation and hobbies. The aphasics were also given a naming test, containing nouns, verbs and adjectives.

A noticeable word-finding problem in conversation was operationalized as the simultaneous occurrence of at least two of the following phenomena:

-   pause

-   nonverbal turnkeeper

-   verbal turnkeeper indicating word-finding problem (e.g. »what's it called», »eh» etc.)

- circumlocutory speech where a probable target word can be discerned from the context

- nonverbal adaptor, showing hesitation or worry.

A noticeable word-finding problem in the naming test was any failure to produce the target word indicated by the eliciting picture.

2.3 Results of the Quantitative Comparison

The result of the quantitative comparison of word-finding is shown for each patient in Table 1.

TABLE 1

Word-finding problems as percentages of the total number of nouns, verbs and adjectives produced in conversation and as percentages of total number of items (noun, verbs and adjectives) in the naming test

Patient	conversation	naming test
1	4.0	27.1
2	8.5	100.0
3	11.3	22.9
4	4.6	60.4
5	0.0	10.4
6	11.7	6.3
7	5.5	33.3
8	2.9	45.8
9	2.7	10.4
10	3.3	10.4

A comparison of the numbers of word-finding problems in conversation and in the naming test, as measured above, was made using the Spearman Rank Correlation Coefficient. The correlation turned out to be extremely low, only 0.05. This shows that the number of word-finding problems in a naming test is far from significantly correlated to the amount of observable word finding problems in conversation for a group of aphasics with different kinds of symptoms.

2.4 Individual Examples of Aphasia Type - Activity Interaction

As can be seen in Table 1, the percentage of noticeable problems is much greater in the naming test than in conversation, for all patients except one. This is a tendency that one would expect to find, considering the differences in factors determining the demands of the activities on more or less exact word-finding, and also determining the possible compensatory means of expression available to the patient. The low correlation between the number of word-finding problems in the two activities, together with the finding that one of the patients (patient 6) actually shows less problems in the naming test than in the conversation, tells us that the picture is more complex, and not simply a question of more or less »difficult» activities as such. Different types of aphasics seem to have different degrees of word-finding problems in the two activities.

As examples of how the impression of a patient's ability to communicate and of his/her aphasic symptoms might be different in different activities, the word-finding problems of two aphasics (patients 6 and 2 in Table 1) will be discussed in relation to the determining factors of the two activities conversation and naming test.

Determining factors of a conversation can be (according to Allwood, 1984): *global-collective,* i.e., purpose, role configuration, artefacts and physical circumstances of the situation and *global-individual,* for example, attitudes, beliefs, physical appearance and handicaps of the individual participants. All these factors interact in determining the patterns and means of communication in an activity.

The two activities, »naming test» and »conversation», were compared with respect to their global-collective determining factors, as shown below.

The amount of word-finding problems and the type of behaviour shown by a patient, when having word-finding problems, might be affected differently by these determining factors for different types of aphasics. Consider the following examples.

Patient 6

This patient shows a hesitant speech in conversation, making numerous long pauses with attempts to find words, accompanied by verbal and nonverbal signs of hesitation, such as saying »eh, eh» or »what's it called» and raising one hand and waving it forwards. The impression from a conversation is that this patient has considerable word-finding problems.

	CONVERSATION	NAMING TEST
PURPOSE	to convey information about facts and feelings to keep the conversation going	to show that one can produce verbal labels for objects, actions and properties
ROLE CONFIGURATION	moderately asymmetric (the participants being therapist and aphasic, the latter with reduced verbal abilities)	very asymmetric (testleader - tested)
ARTEFACTS & PHYSICAL CIRCUMSTANCES	no picture material	ellicitation material (pictures)

The patient hardly has any problems in a naming test, where she gives all the verbal labels without hesitation. In this activity she would be judged as having no word-finding problems.

Patient 2

This patient keeps up a conversation quite fluently, although with occasional word-finding problems. She uses more or less »automatized« phrases with much evaluating or emotional content and she uses a lot of nonverbal communication for showing feelings, giving and eliciting feedback and illustrating the factual content of the conversation. The impression from the conversation is that her word-finding problems are not very many and that they are often compensated for.

This patient is unable to give any verbal label at all in the naming test. In this activity her word-finding problems are enormous and she simply cannot perform the activity.

2.5   Some Conclusions

From the results of the correlation study together with these examples and the table of determining factors, the following conclusions can be drawn:

1. It is not always possible to predict what aphasic symptoms a patient will show in one activity, from his/her performance in another activity with different determining parameters. This means that one cannot use a naming test for predicting the quantity of word-finding problems of a patient in conversation.
2. The different determining parameters of different activities do not interact in the same way with all types of aphasics.
3. In order to estimate aphasics' communicative abilities in different activities, methods for clinical analysis of different kinds of conversations need to be developed, since test activities only are not sufficient ground for the analysis.

2.6   Possible Reasons for Differences in »Degree of Problems» between Activities

Looking at the differences in word-finding problems between the naming test and conversation found in patients 6 and 2, one can at least speculate about the reasons for these in terms of the determining factors of the activities.

Patient 6 is obviously influenced by the artefacts of the activity, finding it much easier to find words to label something in a picture than to find words spontaneously in the conversation. She also appears to find it easier to produce single word utterances, which are the expected and accepted responses in the test activity determined by its purpose. On the other hand, she has problems conveying information in conversation, where the purpose of the activity demands that the participants keep the conversation going and where she has no eliciting pictures.

Patient 2 keeps up the conversation with the help of nonverbal communication for illustrating content and both verbal and nonverbal means for communicating feelings, for appealing to the conversation partner and for referring to the context. This behaviour is quite successful in conversation, where all these means are accepted and can be used for the purposes of the activity, i.e., to keep the conversation going and to convey information. In the naming test, on the other hand, only verbal factual information, in the form of specific »content words» is accepted, because of the purpose of this activity, and the patient cannot produce these at all.

It is clear from this that »word-finding» can be seen as two quite separate sub-activities under these different conditions and that the purpose of the activity is one very important factor when it comes to judging what is and what is not successful »word-finding», since the purpose, to a large extent, determines the available and accepted means of communication, as can be seen below.

	CONVERSATION	NAMING TEST
SUCCESSFUL »WORD-FINDING»	to get the information across in some way	to find and produce a verbal label for something in a picture
AVAILABLE MEANS OF COMMUNICATION	many different: verbal: paraphrase, circumlocution, leading question. nonverbal: illustrating, interaction regulating and showing feelings appeal to the conversation partner reference to the context	only specific, verbal, facutal information (specific words in one-word utterances)

The conversation activity allows a much wider definition of »successful word-finding» than the naming test. The specific intended word might even be uttered by the conversation partner or not uttered at all as long as the information gets across and no problems to carry on the conversation arise. Since the determining factors of a conversation are the most relevant for the aphasics' ability to take part in most daily life communicative activities, this is an important fact to be noted in diagnosis and therapy. Finding specific words might very well be less important in many activities than being able to convey information, using whatever means are available.

The fact that more alternative means of communication are available for successful »word-finding» in conversation than in a naming test, suggests that conversation would be the less problematic activity of the two for aphasics. As mentioned above, this is also true for patient 2 above and it seems to be true for the large majority of aphasics, but not for patient 6. It seems clear that the aphasic symptom combination interacts with the determining factors of the activity in making up a certain communicative pattern, i.e., neither activity nor aphasia type can be studied as independent factors, since they clearly interact.

The conversation behaviour of patient 2 shows us an example of how difficulties in finding specific nouns, verbs and adjectives seem to be partly overcome by frequent use of nonverbal and other »supplementary» means of communication. The way in which she managed the interaction regulating and emotional parts of the conversation seems to »hide» her word-finding problems in this activity.

2.7   Nonverbal Communication as Possible Compensation

In order to find out whether aphasics generally use more non- verbal communication, which is a major candidate for compensatory behaviour in their discourse, the videotaped conversations of the ten aphasic patients were studied in search of all noticeable occurrences of nonverbal communication in the form of movements of any part of the body. This also included »salient» facial expressions and sounds that are not conventionally transcribed in writing, such as coughing or sighing.

For reasons of comparison, a control group consisting of six nonaphasic persons in videotaped conversation with similar, although not identical, determining factors were also studied with respect to their use of nonverbal communication.

Table 2 shows the total numbers and means of different types of nonverbal communication used by aphasics and controls during a ten-minute conversation.

Table 2 shows that the ten aphasics taken as a group produced nearly twice as many instances of nonverbal communication, judging from the mean values of the two groups. The greatest and most interesting difference between the groups is perhaps the extremely high use of nonverbal communication in the form of pantomime by the aphasics. This can hardly be interpreted in any other way than as a compensatory device with respect to their verbal problems. Another interesting difference is the aphasics' frequent use of pointing, which indicates that reference to the situational context is also used more by the aphasics, possibly with a compensatory function. Frequent use of »hand raised forward», in most cases indicates that the patient wants to keep the turn while he/she is searching for words, just as head-nods and head-

TABLE 2

Total numbers and means of different types of nonverbal communication in ten minutes of conversation

	TOTAL NUMBERS		MEANS	
	APHASICS	CONTROLS	APHASICS	CONTROLS
	n = 10	n = 6		

TYPE

HAND:

1. raised forward	122	18	12.2	3.0
2. waving	30	9	3.0	1.3
3. beating down	49	7	4.9	1.2
4. beating sideways	24	2	2.4	0.3
5. pointing	113	7	11.3	1.2
6. to mouth	6	16	0.6	2.7
7. makes fist	8	0	0.8	0.0
8. turns	5	0	0.5	0.0
9. both hands out	9	6	0.9	1.0
10. to hair, forehead, or nose	5	1	0.5	0.2

HEAD:

11. nod	204	97	20.4	16.2
12. shaking	100	25	10.0	4.2
13. in hand	14	6	1.4	1.0
14. looks around	5	0	0.5	0.0
15. looks up	1	9	0.1	1.3
16. looks down	7	0	0.7	0.0
17. looks to the side	11	0	1.1	0.0
18. on one side	2	4	0.2	0.7

FACE:

19. makes face	4	1	0.4	0.2
20. wrinkles forehead	1	0	0.1	2.0
21. smiles/laughs	58	27	5.8	4.5

TABLE 2 cont.

	TOTAL NUMBERS		MEANS	
	APHASICS	CONTROLS	APHASICS	CONTROLS
BODY:				
22. shrugs shoulders	7	19	0.7	3.2
23. leans forward	21	4	2.1	0.7
24. leans back	9	0	0.9	0.0
25. sits up	0	10	0.0	1.7
FOOT:				
26. stamps foot	8	0	0.8	0.0
SOUNDS:				
27. clearing throat	2	7	0.2	1.2
28. smacking sound	13	15	1.3	2.5
29. sighing	4	20	0.4	3.3
30. NONV. COMM. USED FOR PANTOMIME (other than above)	134	11	13.4	1.8
TOTAL	966	321	96.6	53.5

shakings indicates that inter action regulating nonverbal communication might also be used slightly more by the aphasics than by the controls.

In order to have a closer look at the possible functions of nonverbal communication shown by the aphasics in conversation, two persons were asked to judge the functions of each occurrence of nonverbal communication. The results are summarized for three major (superordinate) content categories (cf. Allwood, 1979) in Table 3.

A statistical comparison of the amount of nonverbal communication of aphasics and controls for these major functions and for some subordinate categories of function using the Mann- Whitney U-test gave the following results (Table 4).

As expected from the findings in Table 3 there was a highly significant difference (at 0.01 level) between the two groups in that the aphasics used more information complementing nonverbal communication. The aphasics also used significantly more interaction regulating nonverbal communication (at 0.05 level) and nonverbal communication giving information about positive or negative feeling (also at 0.05 level) than the controls, while there was no significant difference in the amount of nonverbal communication showing hesitation.

It is quite clear from these results that aphasics do use more nonverbal communication than nonaphasics in conversation. The obvious interpretation of this finding, especially as regards the extremely frequent use of nonverbal pantomimic communication and context reference by pointing is that there is a clear compensatory function in the use of nonverbal communication by the aphasics.

TABLE 3

Major content categories of nonverbal communication, shown by
the aphasics and the controls in the study

	INFORMATION ABOUT STATE OF FEELING	INTERACTION REGULATING	INFORMATION COMPLEMENTING (PANTOMIME & POINTING)
PATIENTS:			
P1	40	48	18
P2	82	101	25
P3	32	51	22
P4	29	22	15
P5	28	29	18
P6	29	40	16
P7	23	20	127
P8	32	29	18
P9	6	14	11
P10	1	24	8
MEANS	30.2	37.8	28.8
CONTROLS:			
C1	21	19	2
C2	41	21	3
C3	55	23	6
C4	30	25	1
C5	12	15	6
C6	14	3	1
MEANS	28.8	17.6	3.2

TABLE 4

U-values for different functions of nonverbal communication
(one-tailed test)

	aphasics - controls
Function:	
Information about state of feeling	U = 30
Subgroup: Information about positive and negative feeling (excluding hesitation)	U = 12
Interaction regulating	U = 11
Information complementing (pantomime and pointing)	U = 0

3 THEORETICAL DISCUSSION OF POSSIBLE COMPENSATION

The claim made here is that the available and accepted means of communication, other than giving verbal factual information, make it possible to compensate for an aphasic symptom like »word-finding problems» in conversation. Earlier claims that aphasics in general do not, for example, use nonverbal communication to compensate for problems with verbal communication (Cicone, Wapner, Foldi, Zurif, & Gardner, 1979) have been based on a more restricted view of what can be considered as successful compensation than the activity dependent analysis used here.

Assumed candidates for means of possible compensation for aphasic disturbances mentioned above were nonverbal communication, communication which is predominantly »emotional» or »emotionally governed», the use of cooperation by appealing to the conversation partner for help and the use of reference to the immediate context. These means of communication were considered as suitable for compensatory function in persons with verbal problems caused by cortical brain lesions, both from a »common sense» view of communication as a whole and also from an evolutionary view of communicative functions in the brain.

The following conclusions are drawn from the above findings:

a.   Aphasic symptoms and determining factors of different activities interact,
     sometimes in a complex way, thereby causing a specific communicative pattern to
     be shown by the aphasic in a communicative activity. This can be seen from the
     differences in noticeable word-finding problems between different activities for
     different patients.

b.   In the communicative patterns shown by aphasics, communicative means can
     more or less compensate for the patient's verbal problems, depending on whether
     these means are available and allowed in the activity. Nonverbal communication
     can safely be assumed to have such a compensatory function, judging from the
     findings above. Observations of the individual patients in conversations seem to
     indicate that the other possible compensatory means of communication
     mentioned, such as using more emotional communication and appeal towards the
     conversation partner are also used with this function, at least by some aphasics.

The assumption of spontaneous compensation by aphasic patients, thus, seems to
be strongly supported by the findings of this study.

These findings are not in accordance with the popular theoretical view that aphasia
is a disorder in the use of »symbols», affecting this use equally in the verbal and
nonverbal modality. This claim has been supported by studies where no evidence has
been shown to exist of aphasics, in general, using nonverbal communication to
compensate for verbal problems (cf. for example Cicone et al., 1979), but the findings
of this study does not agree with their theory.

Furthermore, the widespread clinical use of naming tests in order to determine the
degree of word-finding problems that an aphasic patient will show in conversation
(and the general use of test activity data as the exclusive means of diagnosis for aphasic
symptoms) will have to be seriously questioned in the light of the lack of correlation
between the number of problems in a naming test and the number of noticeable word-
finding problems in conversation.

FOOTNOTE These studies are described in more detail in Ahlsén (1985)

REFERENCES

Ahlsén E. (1985). Discourse Patterns in Aphasia. *Gothenburg Monographs in Linguistics 5,* Department of Linguistics, University of Göteborg.

Allwood J. (1979). Icke-verbal kommunikation - en översikt. In A. Stedje & P. af Trampe (Eds.), *Tvåspråkighet. (Bilingualism).* Stockholm: Akademilitteratur.

Allwood J. (1984). On relevance in spoken interaction. In G. Kjellmer & S. Bäckman (Eds.), *Papers on language and literature, Gothenburg Studies in English 60.* Department of English, University of Göteborg.

Cicone M., Wapner W., Foldi N., Zurif E., & Gardner H. (1979). The relation between gesture and language in aphasic communication. *Brain and Language, 8,* 324-349.

Jackson J.H. (1931). On the nature of the duality of the brain, In J. Taylor (Ed.), *Selected writings of John Hughlings Jackson.* London: Hodder & Stoughton.(Original Work published 1874.)

Communication and Handicap: Aspects of
Psychological Compensation and Technical Aids
E. Hjelmquist and L.-G. Nilsson (editors)
© Elsevier Science Publishers B.V. (North-Holland), 1986

BLISSYMBOLICS, COGNITION, AND THE HANDICAPPED

PAUL MUTER

Psychology Department, University of Toronto, Toronto, Canada[*]

Advantages and disadvantages of alphabetic and logographic writing systems
are discussed, with particular emphasis on Bliss as an example of a
logographic system. It is concluded that logographic systems might be easier
to learn than alphabetic systems and, in particular, that Blissymbols could be a
useful communication device for people with various kinds of handicaps.
This suggestion is substantiated by empirical research.

1 INTRODUCTION

There are tens of thousands of handicapped people in dozens of countries whose
ability to communicate has apparently been enhanced by the use of Blissymbolics.
Blissymbolics is an international logography composed of pictographs, in which
symbols represent words in a pictorial manner; ideographs, in which symbols suggest
the meaning of words, though not necessarily in a pictorial manner; and a few
arbitrary symbols such as » + » and »?». The purpose of the present paper is to briefly
describe Blissymbols and their use by handicapped people; to review data bearing on
the issue of whether Blissymbols are useful; and to discuss some theoretical issues

---

[*] This work was supported by Research Grant UO149 from the Natural Sciences and Engineering
Research Council of Canada to the author. I thank Peter Graf, Peter Reich, and Amanda Walley for
helpful comments.

relating to writing systems, cognitive processes, and the handicapped.

2   CHARLES BLISS AND BLISSYMBOLICS

Charles K. Bliss was born Karl Blitz in 1897 in Austria, where 20 different languages were spoken. He was incarcerated in a Nazi concentration camp during World War Two, and became convinced that major contributors to war and international conflict were differences and ambiguities in language. Later in the war, Bliss was incarcerated in Shanghai, and was profoundly influenced by Chinese characters. Since Chinese characters are essentially not soundbased, Chinese people speaking many different languages and dialects can communicate easily with each other.

After World War Two, Bliss moved to Australia, where he worked in an automobile assembly plant. In his spare time, he developed a new nonalphabetic writing system, called Semantography, later Blissymbolics, based on approximately 100 basic shapes. In 1949, he completed a book *Semantography,* describing the writing system, but in spite of endorsements from Julian Huxley, Bertrand Russel, and others, he was unable to find a publisher. Finally, he published it himself (Bliss, 1965).

Bliss designed Blissymbolics for use among all people, and did not create them with handicapped people in mind. However, in 1971, the Ontario Crippled Children's Centre in Canada began using Blissymbols to help pre-reading children communicate. In 1975, the Blissymbolics Communication Foundation, now called the Blissymbolics Communication Institute, was established in Toronto, Ontario. In cooperation with Charles Bliss, the Institute has developed and disseminated Blissymbolics. Charles Bliss died on July 13, 1985. For further information on Charles Bliss, the Blissymbolics Communication Institute, and Blissymbols, See McDonald (1980).

The pictographic, ideographic, and arbitrary aspects of Blissymbols are all exemplified in Figure 1.

The symbols for table and tree are pictographic: The symbols visually resemble the referents. The symbol for wind is ideographic: The top horizontal line represents the sky; the diagonal and the bottom line together represent a nose; sky and nose together indicate air; the combination of air and forward (the arrow) denotes wind. The arbitrary elements 2 and 7 are included in the symbols for summer and week.

Blissymbols were not intended to be self-explanatory, though Bliss felt that the meanings of the symbols would be easy to remember once an explanation had been

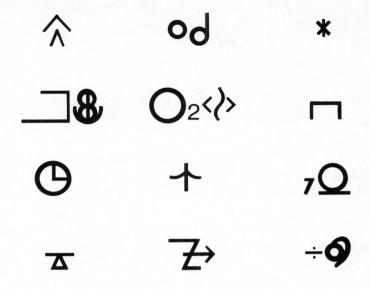

FIGURE 1

Examples of Blissymbols: son, song, star, store, summer, table, time, tree, week, weight, wind, word.

given. (It is probably unrealistic to expect that a reasonably comprehensive logography could be directly understandable without some learning; see Kolers, 1969.) Explanations for approximately 1400 Blissymbols are provided in *Blissymbols for Use* (Hehner, 1980). Following are explanations, based on those in Hehner, for the symbols in Figure 1.

son	protection + male: a small male born under the family roof
song	mouth + musical note
star	pictographic
store	room that opens onto the street + business (money plus to hold)
summer	sun + second (season) + hot (fire)
table	pictographic
time	pictographic: the symbol looks like a clock face
tree	pictographic
week	7 + day (sun + earth: the sun appears over the horizon; it shines on the earth during the day)
weight	pictographic: the symbol looks like scales
wind	air + forward: air that moves forward
word	part of + language (mouth + ear: what is spoken and heard)

Note that some of the explanations are culture specific. For example, the explanation of the symbol for time would be unhelpful for someone who had never seen a clock.

There is in principle no limit to the number of symbols that can be created from the basic shapes. The system is generative: Shapes and symbols can be combined and recombined indefinitely according to certain rules. All of the symbols in Figure 1 represent nouns, but of course other parts of speech are included in Blissymbolics, and some of these are achieved by the use of indicators. For example, the action indicator (^) above a symbol indicates action taking place in the present (often a present tense verb). A small right parenthesis, resembling a parabolic mirror, above a symbol indicates action in the past (past tense verb). A small left parenthesis above a symbol indicates action in the future (future tense verb). A small multiplication sign, X, above a symbol indicates the plural. Bliss also designed a simple syntax, somewhat different from the syntax of English; see McDonald (1980, pp. 60-68) for a description.

Blissymbols are standardized. Lack of standardization has been a problem with other logographies. For example, Chinese characters were originally much more pictographic and ideographic than they are now, but they have evolved over the centuries, are now very stylized, and have lost virtually all of their visual resemblance to the referents. To avoid a similar problem, strict standards for composing Blissymbols are prescribed by the Blissymbolics Communication Institute. With computer technology, presenting and standardizing Blissymbols is relatively easy.

There have been several computer implementations of Blissymbols. For example, Sawchuck and Bown (1977) delivered Blissymbols via Fortran and a DEC PDP11. Their software permitted selection of Blissymbols to display sentences, storing and retrieving of sentences, »turning the pages» of a symbol dictionary, and the creation of new symbols for addition to the dictionary. Giddings, Norton, Nelson, McNaughton, and Reich (1979) devised a Z80-based system which permitted interactive use of Blissymbols on a home television set. Carlson, Granström, and Hunnicutt (1982) devised a multi-language, portable microcomputer-based system which can transform input from a Bliss communication board into either alphabetic or synthesized speech output. Lexical prediction capability has recently been added to this system (Hunnicutt, this volume). Finally, Blissymbols can be delivered on the screen or printer of an Apple II + or Apple IIe microcomputer by means of software created by the Minnesota Educational Computing Consortium (1983). These symbols can be displayed under program control (Applesoft Basic).

There are a variety of more traditional means of presenting and using Blissymbols. For example, Blissymbol stamps and flash cards (3 inches square) are available, as are templates for drawing Blissymbols. A popular method of using Blissymbols is by means of display boards containing from 30 to 512 Blissymbols to which people can point. Typically, the corresponding alphabetic word appears under the Blissymbol.

3   ARE BLISSYMBOLS EASY TO LEARN AND USE?

The issue of whether Blissymbols facilitate communication among the handicapped is a special case of the more general question of whether people are better adapted to learning to read alphabetic codes or logographies. Both the general and the specific question will be considered in this section. (It is possible that people are typically best suited for syllabaries, in which each symbol represents a syllable, but discussion of syllabaries is beyond the scope of this paper.)

It is estimated that human language originated approximately one million years ago. Writing systems originated five or ten thousand years ago. Approximately two-thirds of the world's languages have no writing system, and new writing systems are being introduced every year (Grimes & Gordon, 1980). It has been predicted (e.g., Thompson, 1979, 1983) that, because of advances in computer technology, logographies may become more widespread, and may even displace alphabetic systems. On the other hand, the Chinese may switch from a logographic system to an alphabetic system. In spite of these considerations, it is unknown what the optimal writing system is for human users, or which system is optimal under what circumstances.

3.1   Armchair Considerations

A great deal of space in books and journals has been devoted to discussion of the advantages and disadvantages of alphabetic and logographic writing systems. (For a succinct summary of the main arguments, see Carroll, 1972). Indeed, some advantages and disadvantages are reasonably clear, and do not require empirical support. For example, with alphabets, a smaller number of symbols must be learned; a reader can, in principle at least, decode a word that he or she has heard but not seen before; and the use of a typewriter is easier, at least with present technology. (Developments in automatic speech recognition and other input media may soon render this last consideration irrelevant.) With logographies, the same system can be used with different dialects or even different languages; a reader may be able to guess the meaning of a word that he or she has neither seen nor heard before; and distinguishing among homophones is not a problem. These armchair considerations are not conclusive in suport of either alphabetic codes or logographies. Neither is crosscultural evidence.

3.2   Crosscultural Evidence

Gray (1956) studied readers all over the world and concluded that »the general nature of the reading act is essentially the same among all mature readers,» regardless of the writing system. However, it has frequently been stated that low literacy rates in some areas of Asia are due to the use of logographies (e.g., Goody, 1968). The opposite conclusion was reached by Makita (1968) and others. Makita's evidence suggested that in certain cultures in which logographies are prominent, for example, Japan, the incidence of serious reading problems is spectacularly low, less than one percent, compared to Canada and the United States, where the incidence of serious reading problems is estimated to be approximately 10 to 20 percent (Gibson & Levin, 1975). Stevenson, Stigler, Lucker, and Lee (1982) made a more concerted attempt to fairly compare rates of reading disability in logographic and alphabetic cultures, and they found essentially no difference.

Unfortunately, for present purposes crosscultural evidence is quite useless, in my opinion, because the cultures in question differ in so many ways in addition to their writing systems.

3.3   Clinical Evidence

Included among groups that have used Blissymbols to communicate are the following: physically handicapped, retarded, multiply handicapped, autistic, aphasic, and adult stroke patients (McNaughton, 1978). Several studies with these groups will now be briefly described.

McNaughton and Kates (1975) estimated that there are over 50000 non-verbal cerebral palsied people in the United States. Speech is prevented or severely impaired in this group because of disturbances of the respiratory, phonotory, and articulatory systems. Blissymbols were first used with this population as a means of bridging the gap between pictures and words. That is, many non-verbal motorically imparied children can communicate by pointing to pictures, but cannor read, and therefore are unable too participate in complex communication. After three years of using Blissymbols with children of near normal or above average intelligence, the conclusions of McNaughton and Kates included the following: Blissymbols were effective both as a supplement and as a substitute for speech; Blissymbol use incouraged, rather than discouraged, speech and vocalization; the symbols allowed children to communicate with a wide range of people; the use of Blissymbols resulted in improvement of assessment in the areas of hearing, language, psychology, and education; and the children acquired greater self-confidence.

In another study involving the nonverbal motorically impaired, Hammond and Bailey (1976) introduced Blissymbols to four children: three quadriplegic athetoids, and a mild spastic with severe dysarthria. They were of average or low average intelligence. Hammond and Bailey observed that these children became more alert and aware of their surroundings after the introduction of Blissymbols. Their horizons appeared to have widened considerably. Two of the children began vocalising more freely.

The use of Blissymbols with mentally retarded nonverbal children with cerebral palsy was described by Harris-Vanderheiden, Brown, Reinen, MacKenzie, and Scheibel (1975). Results indicated that »Blissymbols were effectively implemented as a means of respondent and limited expressive communication for this population.» (p. 36).

Song (1979) attempted to extend this result to four severely mentally retarded adolescents. Song concluded that Blissymbols were useful if and only if the person has the desire to communicate, can respond to the Peabody Picture Vocabulary Test, and learns Blissymbols quite easily in the early stages.

House, Hanley, and Magid (1980) taught 10 nonreading trainable mentally retarded adults 16 logographs (specially created pictographs and ideographs). The subjects were able to learn the logographs and construct sentences out of them.

A rare negative outcome was obtained by Calculator and Dollaghan (1982). They observed the use of Blissymbol communication boards by seven nonspeaking, nonambulatory, severely mentally retarded people interacting one-on-one with teachers. The results were that these people rarely used their Blissymbol boards in spontaneous interactions: 79 % of messages were via a nonboard mode. Furthermore, use of the board did not increase the probability of message success and did not decrease the ambiguity of the message.

3.4   Experimental Evidence

While the clinical evidence suggests that Blissymbols can be useful, it is by no means conclusive. In none of the above studies were control groups employed. Fortunately, there is some experimental evidence available.

Regarding the more general issue of whether logographies are easier to learn than alphabetic codes, Rozin, Poritsky, and Sotsky (1971) taught eight second-grade children with »clear reading disbility» 30 Chinese characters in a few hours. Parallel tutoring in English reading yielded little progress. The control condition was not rigorous, and only simple concrete words were used in the study, but the results may have been attributable to the nature of the writing systems.

Clark (1981) directly compared learning of Blissymbols and learning of alphabetic codes in preschool, nonreading, English-speaking children, ages 4.3 to 5.4, with no apparent handicaps. One group of nine children attempted to learn 15 Blissymbols, and another group attempted to learn 15 words written alphabetically in English. On the final test, mean performance was 81 percent in the Bliss condition, and 23 percent in the alphabet condition, a statistically significant difference. In two other logographic conditions, Carrier symbols (noniconic) and pictographic symbols were also learned better than alphabetic words.

Muter and Johns (1985) conducted four experiments addressing this issue. English-speaking university students learned to identify or to extract meaning from various kinds of symbols over several sessions. In the alphabet condition, subjects learned to read English words written in an unfamiliar alphabet (using Devanagari or Shaw characters), much as students in English-speaking countries do in grade 1. Subjects were explicitly told that, in this alphabet condition, a particular unfamiliar character would always represent the same sound. In Experiment 1, subjects had one training session. In subsequent experimental sessions, on each trial subjects saw a question, e.g. »WHICH REQUIRES MORE PHYSICAL WORK». Then two symbols from the same condition, e.g., two Blissymbols, appeared side by side, and the subject pressed a key indicating which of the two symbols provided a better answer to the question. Feedback was presented, and all of this information then remained on the screen for several seconds. Thus, each trial was a study trial as well as a test trial. Subjects gradually learned 30 words in each condition. In 28 50-minute experimental sessions, the results were very clear for all four subjects: Both speed and accuracy of performance were dramatically and reliably superior in the Bliss condition than in the alphabet condition. (Performance in a Chinese condition was better than in the alphabet condition and worse than in the Bliss condition.) Furthermore, transfer to a new vocabulary was worse in the alphabet condition than in the Bliss condition, in spite of the fact that in the alphabet condition, the grapheme-phoneme corespondences remained identical to the ones that subjects had experienced for 28 sessions.

The investment of learning an alphabetic code may not pay off until vocabulary size reaches a certain criterion. In Experiment 2 of Muter and Johns (1985), subjects learned 240 words per condition. In addition, a naming task was used instead of a meaning extraction task. Pronouncing a word without recognizing it was thus possible in the alphabet condition, but not in the Bliss condition. In spite of this, performance was again much superior in the Bliss condition. In Experiment 3 of Muter and Johns, the results of Experiment 1 were replicated with no training session.

In Experiments 1 to 3 of Muter and Johns, the mapping between graphemes and phonemes was perfectly consistent, in marked contrast to English. (Berdiansky, Cronell, and Koehler, 1969, concluded that 166 rules for grapheme-phoneme correspondence were necessary to account for 90 percent of words in some children's books written in English.) In Experiment 4, an attempt was made to approximate the inconsistency of grapheme-to-phoneme mapping that exists in English. Consistent with some crosscultural evidence (e.g., Kyostio, 1980), the inconsistent condition produced dramatically worse performance than the consistent condition. Apparently, the results of Experiments 1 to 3 of Muter and Johns would have been even more dramatic if the mapping between graphemes and phonemes had been inconsistent, as it is in English.

Thus, under a reasonably wide range of conditions, Muter and Johns found that logographic writing systems, particularly Blissymbolics, were substantially easier to learn to read than alphabetic writing systems. This result was obtained in spite of the fact that the subjects were literate, English-speaking adults, and had long since attained »linguistic awareness» (Liberman, Liberman, Mattingly, and Shankweiler,

242   *P. Muter*

1980; Mattingly, 1972): They were intimately familiar with the general ways in which alphabets work.

4   WRITING SYSTEMS AND COGNITION

Downing (1973) has argued that comparative reading, i.e., the study of people reading different languages and writing systems, is likely to increase understanding of the reading process and cognition.

We have seen that there is evidence that human performance seems to be different with different writing systems. There is also evidence that the underlying cognitive processes may be different with different writing systems. For example, Biederman and Tsao (1979) found a larger Stroop effect (1935) with logographs than with nonlogographs. According to results of Park and Arbuckle (1977), logographs produce better recall and recognition, whereas a sound-based writing system produced better performance in paired-associate learning and in serial learning. Biederman and Tsao (1979) and Park and Arbuckle (1977) concluded that the underlying cognitive processes are fundamentally different with different writing systems. After reviewing the literature, Hung and Tzeng (1981) also concluded that processing varies as a function of the writing system, though only for lower-level cognition. Other tentative evidence indicates that under certain circumstances, sound-based words yield a right visual field advantage, whereas logographs yield a left visual field advantage (Hatta, 1977) and that lesions in different areas of the brain tend to affect the use of sound-based systems and logographies differentially (Sasanuma, 1974).

Blissymbolics and alphabetic codes differ in many ways, including the following:

Most Blissymbols are pictographic or ideographic; alphabetic words are not.
Alphabets are soundbased; Blissymbols are not.

The general visual configuration (Brooks, 1977) is different in the two systems.

Blissymbols are glyphic; the elements of alphabetic words are arranged linearly.

The elements of Blissymbols are simple; alphabetic characters are complex

Typically, literate adults in the west will have already learned an alphabetic code, but they will not have learned a logography.

Blissymbols may be more likely to induce holistic processing; alphabets may be more likely to induce analytic, rule-based processing.

The first step in determining what the obtained performance differences tell us about the reading process, is to establish which of the above differences account for the performance differences. Some of the possibilities are discussed in the remainder of this section.

4.1   Iconicity

Experiments by Clark (1981) and Muter (1985) suggest that iconicity (pictographic and ideographic properties) is important. In the Clark study, briefly described earlier, some children learned 15 Carrier symbols, which are logographic but visually meaningless, some learned 15 Blissymbols, and some learned 15 pictographs. Performance was correlated with iconicity: Percentages correct on the criterion measure were 48.1, 81.5, and 96.3 in the Carrier, Bliss, and pictograph conditions respectively.

Muter (1985) compared the learning of Blissymbols to the learning of specially created Pseudo-Blissymbols, which were similar to Blissymbols in most respects, but were not iconic. Pseudo-Blissymbols were constructed by means of a computer program using the same shapes used as building blocks for the Blissymbols, but combining them randomly according to the probability distributions used in creating Blissymbols. Performance with the noniconic Pseudo-Blissymbols was substantially and reliably inferior to performance with iconic Blissymbols.

Perhaps iconic symbols can be remembered better than noniconic symbols from one trial to the next because they are more readily processed to the semantic level (Craik & Lockhart, 1972). A second possibility is in terms of transfer in associative learning. To the extent that iconic symbols are in some sense similar to the corresponding visual stimuli in the real world, the iconic conditions could be regarded as the transfer task in an A-B, A-B paradigm. This paradigm typically produces greater positive transfer than the A-B, C-B paradigm (Kausler, 1974), which corresponds to the noniconic conditions.

4.2   Holistic Versus Analytic Processing

According to Allport (1979), there are two possible mechanisms in alphabetic word recognition: analytic, rule-based translation from graphemes to sounds, and access to the lexicon via a more holistic visual process. Some evidence (e.g., Barron, 1980; Bryant and Bradley, 1980, Frith, 1979) suggests that people typically read by means of a holistic method, even when reading an alphabetic code. If word recognition is holistic, a logography should be more optimal for reading than an alphabetic code.

With regard to some handicapped people, the holistic-analytic dimension may be particularly relevant. There is some evidence (Kemler, 1983) to suggest that retarded people tend to perceive objects as wholes to a greater extent than people of normal intelligence. If this is true, then logographies may be particularly advantageous for this population. Similarly, children appear to be more inclined than adults to process stimuli holistically (e.g., Smith & Kemler, 1978), and writing systems are normally learned in childhood.

4.3   Phoneme Processing in Reading

Why are alphabetic codes difficult to learn? According to Rozin and Gleitman (1977), it is because phonemes are difficult to isolate. Rozin and Gleitman agree that the brain extracts phonemes from the sound stream for the purposes of speech processing, but they argue that phoneme-processing mechanisms are not easily available for the purposes of reading.A problem with this line of reasoning is that the subjects in the experiments of Muter and Johns (1985) were literate English-speaking adults, who had already demonstrated that they could access the phoneme-processing mechanisms. (Even if literate English-speaking adults typically use a holistic method in reading, they generally are able to use a rule-based method; e.g., they can correctly pronounce legal nonwords.) If gaining access to the phoneme-processing machinery is an impediment to learning to read an alphabetic code, apparently it is not the only impediment.

Similarly, the theory of Rozin and Gleitman has difficulty explaining the results of Brooks (1977). Brooks' subjects (also literate English-speaking adults) attempted to learn a new alphabetic code, and could often correctly name all of the letters of a word without being able to recognize the word, could name all of the letters of a word faster than they could recognize the word, and could sometimes pronounce the word correctly without recognizing it. In other words, these people had difficulty learning to read words written in an unfamiliar alphabetic code despite the fact that they were able to isolate phonemes.

What if the soundbased properties of an alphabet are dispensed with, and alphabetic words are treated by the reader as arbitrary logographs? Brooks and Miller (1979) conducted an experiment in which subjects learned words written in an artifical alphabet, and at the same time learned to read words written essentially with random strings of characters. When subjects were not informed of the grapheme-phoneme mappings, and later reported no awareness of them, they performed better in the alphabet condition than in the random condition, but when subjects were informed of the grapheme-phoneme mappings, they performed worse in the alphabet condition than in the random condition. Thus a conscious attempt to use mapping rules was maladaptive, but the mapping was useful if used only implicitly.

Brooks and Miller used a very small vocabulary size: six words per condition. Muter (1985) conducted a similar experiment with 120 words per condition over nine 50-minute sessions. Subjects performed consistently better in the alphabet condition than in the random condition, despite the fact that they were fully informed of the natures of the conditions.˙ Again, the investment entailed in learning grapheme-phoneme correspondence rules may reliably pay off only if vocabulary size surpasses a certain criterion. At least with a reasonably large vocabulary size, alphabetic strings regarded as arbitrary logographs are apparently the most difficult words to learn of any kind discussed in the present paper. Even though isolating phonemes in learning to read alphabetic codes is difficult, bypassing the soundbased property of alphabetic codes apparently does not render them easier to learn.

5   IN CONCLUSION

The relative utility of logographies and alphabetic codes may depend on the language under consideration. For example, the desirability of an alphabetic system is probably dependent on the number of phonemes in the language in question. The desirability of a logography is probably dependent on the number of homophones in the language in question. (Logographs disambiguate homophones.) In addition, the optimal writing system for input may not be the opptimal system for output. However, alphabetic codes seem to be extremely difficult to learn to read. Millions of people attempt to learn to read alphabetic codes and fail. Millions of others succeed, but at the cost of a large amount of work. The weight of the evidence suggests that logographies are easier to learn to read than alphabetic codes, and that Blissymbols are a useful communications device, particularly for people with various kinds of handicaps.

This evidence comes from studies in which comparisons are made between conditions that differ in many ways (e.g., the alphabet condition and the Bliss condition in Muter & Johns, 1985). These differences by and large reflect intrinsic differences among writing systems in general. Iconicity apparently accounts for some of the advantage of Blissymbols, but more research is needed to explicate the reasons for different performance and processing with different writing systems.

REFERENCES

Allport, A. (1979). Word recognition in reading. In P.A. Kolers, M.E. Wrolstad & H. Bouma (Eds.), *Processing of visible language 1*. New York: Plenum Press.

Barron, R.W. (1980). Visual and phonological strategies in reading and spelling. In U. Frith (Ed.), *Cognitive processes in spelling*. New York: Academic Press.

Berdiansky, B., Cronnel, B., & Koehler, J. (1969). Spelling-sound relations and primary form-class descriptions for speech-comprehension vocabularies of 6-9-year-olds. Southwest Regional Laboratory for Educational Research and Development, Technical Report, No. 15.

Biederman, I. & Tsao, Y. (1979). On processing Chinese ideographs and English words: Some implications from Stroop-test results. *Cognitive Psychology, 11,* 125-132.

Bliss, C.K. (1965). *Semantography* (2nd. edn). Sydney, Australia: Semantography.

Brooks, L., (1977). Visual pattern in fluent word identification. In A.S. Reber & D.L. Scarborough (Eds.), *Toward a psychology of reading*. New York: Erlbaum.

Brooks, L. & Miller, A. (1979). A comparison of explicit and implicit knowledge of an alphabet. In P.A. Kolers, M.E. Wrolstad & H. Bouma (Eds.), *Processing of visible language 1.* New York: Plenum.

Bryant, P.E., & Bradley, L. (1980). Why children sometimes write down words which they do not read. In U. Frith (Ed.), *Cognitive processes in spelling.* New York: Academic Press.

Calculator, S., & Dollaghan, C. (1982). The use of communication boards in a residential setting: an evaluation. *Journal of Speech and Hearing Disorders, 47,* 281-287.

Carlson, R., Granström, B., & Hunnicutt, S. (1982). Bliss communication with speech or text output. Conference Record IEEE-ICASSP, Paris, France.

Carroll, J.B. (1972). The case for ideographic writing. In J.K. Kavanagh & I.G. Mattingly (Eds.), *Language by ear and by eye.* Cambridge: MIT.

Clark, C.R. (1981). Learning words using traditional orthography and the symbols of Rebus, Bliss, and Carrier. *Journal of Speech and Hearing Disorders, 46,* 191-196.

Craik, F.I.M., & Lockhart, R.S. (1972). Levels of processing: A framework for memory research. *Journal of Verbal Learning and Verbal Behavior, 11,* 671-684.

Downing, J. (1973). Is literacy acquisition easier in some languages than in others? *Visible Language, 7,* 145-154.

Frith, U. (1979). Reading by eye and writing by ear. In P.A. Kolers, M.E. Wrolstad & H. Bouma, (Eds.), *Processing of visible language 1.* New York: Plenum Press.

Gibson, E.J., & Levin, H. (1975). *The psychology of reading.* Cambridge, Mass.: M.I.T. Press.

Giddings, W., Norton, J., Nelson, P., McNaughton, S., & Reich, P. (1979). Development of a Blissymbol terminal. Proceedings of the 6th Man-Computer Communications Conference, 63-71, Ottawa.

Goody, J. (1968). *Literacy in traditional societies*. London: Cambridge University Press.

Gray, W.S. (1956). *The teaching of reading and writing, an international survey*. Paris: *UNESCO*.

Grimes, J.E., & Gordon, R.G. (1980). Design of new orthographies. In J.F. Kavanagh & R.L. Venezky (Eds.), *Orthography, reading, and dyslexia*. Baltimore: University Park Press.

Hammond, J., & Bailey, P. (1976). An experiment in Blissymbolics. *Special Education: Forward Trends, 3,* 21-22.

Harris-Vanderheiden, D., Brown, W.P., Reinen, S., MacKenzie, P., & Scheibel, C. (1975). Symbol communication for the mentally handicapped. *Mental Retardation, 13,* 34-37.

Hatta, T. (1977). Recognition of Japanese Kanji in the left and right visual fields. *Neuropsychologia, 15,* 685-688.

Hehner, B. (1980). *Blissymbols for use*. Toronto: Blissymbolics Communication Institute.

House, B.J., Hanley, M.J., & Magid, D.F. (1980). Logographic reading by TMR adults. *American Journal of Mental Deficiency, 85,* 161-170.

Hung, D.L., & Tzeng, O.J.L. (1981). Orthographic variations and visual information processing. *Psychological Bulletin, 90,* 377-414.

Hunnicutt, S. (1986). Lexical prediction for a text-to-speech system. This volume.

Kates, B., & McNaughton, S. (1975). The first application of Blissymbolics as a communication medium for nonspeaking children: history and development, 1971-1974. Toronto: Blis symbolics Communication Institute.

Kausler, D.H. (1974). *Psychology of verbal learning and memory.* New York: Academic Press.

Kemler, D.G. (1983). Wholistic and analytic modes in perceptual and cognitive development. In T. Tighe & B.E. Shepp (Eds.), *Perception, cognition, and development: Interactional analyses.* Hillsdale, N.J.: Erlbaum.

Kolers, P.A. (1969). Some formal characteristics of pictograms. *American Scientist, 57,* 348-363.

Kyostio, O.K. (1980). Is learning to read easy in a language in which the grapheme-phoneme correspondences are regular? In J.F. Kavanagh & R.L. Venezky (Eds.), *Orthography, reading, and dyslexia.* Baltimore: University Park Press.

Liberman, I., Liberman, A.M., Mattingly, I., & Shankweiler, D. (1980). Orthography and the beginning reader. In J.F. Kavanagh & R.L. Venezky (Eds.), *Orthography, reading, and dyslexia.* Baltimore: University Park Press.

Makita, K. (1968). The rarity of reading disability in Japanese children. *American Journal of Orthopsychiatry, 38,* 599-614.

Mattingly, I.G. (1972). Reading, the linguistic process, and linguistic awareness. In J.P. Kavanagh & I.G. Mattingly (Eds.), *Language by ear and by eye.* Cambridge, Mass.: M.I.T. Press.

McDonald, E.T. (1980). *Teaching and using Blissymbolics.* Toronto: Blissymbolics Communication Institute.

McNaughton, S. (1978). Blissymbolics. 3rd National Congress, Council for Exceptional Children, Winnipeg, Manitoba.

Minnesota Educational Computing Consortium (1983). *Blissymbolics, Bliss Library.* St. Paul, MN.

Muter, P. (1985). *Orthography and reading: the role of iconicity and grapheme-phoneme correspondence.* Manuscript submitted for publication.

Muter, P., & Johns, E.E. (1985). Learning logographies and alphabetic codes. *Human Learning, 4,* 105-125.

Park, S., & Arbuckle, T.Y. (1977). Ideograms versus alphabets: Effects of script on memory in »biscriptual» Korean subjects. *Journal of Experimental Psychology: Human Learning and Memory, 3,* 631-642.

Rozin, P., & Gleitman, L.R. (1977). The structure and acquisition of reading II: the reading process and the acquisition of the alphabetic principle. In A.S. Reber & D.L. Scarborough (Eds.), *Toward a psychology of reading.* New York: Erlbaum.

Rozin, P., Poritsky, S., & Sotsky, R. (1971). American children with reading problems can easily learn to read English represented by Chinese characters. *Science, 171,* 1264-1267.

Sasanuma, S. (1974). Kanji versus Kana processing in alexia with transient agraphia: A case report. *Cortex, 10,* 89-97.

Sawchuck, W., & Bown, H.G. (1977). Interactive graphics applied to symbol communication for non-speaking children. *Computers and Graphics, 2,* 201-204.

Smith, L.B., & Kemler, D.G. (1978). Levels of experienced dimensionality in children and adults. *Cognitive Psychology, 10,* 502-532.

Song, A. (1979, Oct.). Acquisition and use of Blissymbols by severely mentally retarded adolescents. *Mental Retardation,* 253-255.

Stevenson, H.W., Stigler, J.W., Lucker, G.W., & Lee, S. (1982). Reading disabilities: The case of Chinese, Japanese, and English. *Child Development, 53,* 1164-1181.

Stroop, J.L. (1935). Studies of interference in serial verbal reactions. *Journal of Experimental Psychology, 18,* 643-662.

Thompson, G.B. (1979). *Memo from Mercury: Information technology is different.* Montreal: institute for Research on Public Policy.

Thompson, G.B. (1983). Visual literacy and the time-varying icon. *IEEE Journal on Selected Areas in Communications, SAC-1,* 304-305.

Communication and Handicap: Aspects of
Psychological Compensation and Technical Aids
E. Hjelmquist and L.-G. Nilsson (editors)
  Elsevier Science Publishers B.V. (North-Holland), 1986

LEXICAL PREDICTION FOR A TEXT-TO-SPEECH SYSTEM

SHERI HUNNICUTT

Royal Institute of Technology,
Stockholm, Sweden

A lexical prediction system is a divice which could be of great help to people
with certain communicative handicaps. Such a system is described. It can
speed up communication considerably via speech synthesis and thereby make
communication run more smoothly, and reduce some of the awkwardness
which arises when lexical prediction is not used.

1   INTRODUCTION

A lexical prediction system is being developed at the Department of Speech
Communication and Music Acoustics to be used with our speech synthesizer (Carlson,
Granström, & Hunnicutt, 1982). It is being developed in response to the observation
that some non-speaking users of the synthesizer find communication with such an aid
laboriously slow. One user commented that the listeners were guessing the words she
was typing before she finished, but that she had to finish typing them anyway for the
speech to be correct. The lexical prediction system addresses this problem. It is
implemented on an Exlipse computer in a test system with speech output from a
connected synthesizer. Hardware implementation has begun while the system
undergoes continued development and testing.

2   LEXICAL DATA FILES

The data base for lexical prediction is a set of lexical data files. These files have been constructed to reflect some of the human capabilities of accessing lexical items. This is accomplished by appealing to literature in the theory of lexical access, and using experimental results as a basis for lexical predication.

The largest data file is the »Two-letter Lexicon», a file partitioned according to the first two letters of a word and frequency-ordered. This file contains about 10 000 entries, the most frequent Swedish words according to the Allén corpus (Allén, 1970). A process has been devised to quickly convert to the required form any of our 10 000-entry lexicons used with the text-to-speech system (speech synthesizer). These lexicons exist for Swedish, English, German, Norwegian, Italian and French. In addition to the spelling and rank order of each word, in the Swedish lexicon the word's part-of-speech, or word class, is given. This information is accessed during grammatical decisions preceding prediction. A second file, the »First Choice Lexicon», contains the most frequent word beginning with each letter. This file is used to very quickly access this most frequent word as soon as its first letter is typed in. Two-word combinations are stored in a third file, the »Two-word Lexicon». These represent the 1500 most common sequences of two words according to a further study by Allén (Allén, 1975). A fourth file, the »One-letter Lexicon», contains all single letters, several of which can also be words.

The approach to lexical prediction followed here is supported by psycholinguistic literature. It is well documented, for example, that the initial sounds and the initial letter or letters of a word are »access points» for words. That is, a person can guess a word faster given its initial letter(s) than given medial or final letters. (Marslen-Wilson & Welsh 1978; Jakimik & Cole, 1985, among others). It has also been shown that a person's mental lexicon is, in some sense, frequency-weighted (Broadbent, 1967). That is, the more frequent a (content) word in a language, the faster the reaction time of a person hearing that word in classifying it as a word of the language (Bradley, 1978).

One further file, the »Subject Lexicon», exists which has space for up to 510 words and is initially empty. Each word typed is entered in this lexicon, and a count kept of the number of time it has been used. We plan to send a message to the user when this lexicon is full. The user will then be able to choose whether to incorporate these words in his/her permanent lexicon. A decision to incorporate these words will result in an automatic update of the frequencies of words in the Two-letter Lexicon. Words not previously occurring in this lexicon will be added to it, while the lowest frequency words drop out.

A second use for this file is reflected in its name, the Subject Lexicon. It is possible to set two frequency values for this lexicon, one value for word inclusion and another value for word prediction. A preliminary test indicated that words with rank greater than 1000 (words not in the 1000 most frequent) should be placed in the Subject Lexicon and given a temporary rank between 201 and 400. This rank for prediction allows only the 200 most frequent words, most of which are function words which can be expected to make up over 50% of a text (Kucera & Francis, 1967) to precede words with rank greater than 1000 but currently in usage. In this way, word frequency can be temporarily raised during a conversation about a specific topic. It is possible to save or empty this lexicon at any time.

This set of lexicon and the facility for updating frequencies and adding new entries will allow users to develop their own personal frequency-weighted vocabularies over an extended period of time. In a hardware implementation, lexicons should be easily changeable, permitting multiple users and multiple lexicons for a single user. It would be possible, for example, to have separate lexicons for use at home, at school and at work.

2.1 The Algorithm

Given an initial letter (or letters) by the user, the word it introduces is predicted based on word frequency and a simple phrase structure grammar. Typing the first letter of a word results in accessing the most frequent word beginning with that letter from the First Choice Lexicon. Successive predictions are made from the Two-letter Lexicon if predicted letters are overwritten by the user. When a complete word (word plus space) has been typed, or when a word has been predicted and accepted, the Two-word Lexicon is consulted to see if that word occurs in it as an index word. If found, the word following it (the most frequent) is automatically predicted without its initial letter being typed. This word may be accepted, or it may be rejected by typing the first letter of the next word desired. In the latter case, the process begins again, with the most frequent word beginning with that letter being predicted from the First Choice Lexicon.

There are three ways to conclude a word. Two for the characters that have been chosen to indicate word conclusion, the »line feed» and »escape» characters, are picked arbitrarily and can easily be altered. The »line feed» character indicates that the latest prediction is accepted unconditionally, and types a space after the predicted word. This is the normal mode of accepting a prediction. An example, typing the word »telefon», is shown in the top part of Table 1. The user first types the letter »t», and the prediction of the word »till» (»to»), which is the thirteenth most frequent word, is made from the First Choice Lexicon. The user then types the letter »e», and the most frequent word beginning with the sequence »te», i.e., »tekniska» (»technical») with rank 601, is predicted from the Two-letter lexicon. The letter »l» is then typed by the user, and the desired prediction, »telefon», (rank 4047) appears. It is accepted by typing the »line feed» character, and a space is added after the word.

The »escape» character accepts the latest prediction, but does not type a space, positioning the cursor at word-end so that characters may be deleted or added. These deletions and additions produce further predictions, as well. A common use of this facility is the addition of suffixes, before which a morphfinal letter may be deleted or changed. In the example in the middle of Table 1, we see that in typing the word »möjligheter» (»possibilities»), the »escape» character is used to position the cursor at the end of the predicted word »möjligt» (»possible»). When the final »t» is erased, the desired word is automatically predicted. This facility is also useful in compounds, which Swedish has in abundance. This use is demonstrated also, in the word »presidentvalet» (»presidential election»). After »president» is predicted and the cursor is positioned wordfinally, the letter »v» elicits the correct root, »valet».

Terminating a word with a space indicates rejection of predictions and the end of a user-typed word, as in normal typing. A common example of this type of word conclusion is shown in the bottom part of Table 1. The user desires to type the preposition »i» (»in»). The letter »i» is typed, and the prediction, from the First Choice Lexicon, is »inte» (»not»), with rank 15. This prediction is rejected and the word »i» completed by simply typing a space.

TABLE 1

Three ways to conclude a word. Predicted characters are outside parentheses. Letters typed by user are in parentheses

1) Line Feed: Unconditional acceptance of latest prediction

User Types	Prediction	Rank Order
T	(T)ILL	13
E	(TE)KNISKA	601
L	(TEL)EFON	4047
Line Feed	(TEL)EFON space	

2) Escape: Conditional Acceptance of Latest Prediction; Pointer positioned at word end

User Types	Prediction	Rank Order
M	(M)ED	11
Ö	(MÖ)JLIGT	275
Escape	(MÖ)JLIGT^	
Delete	(MÖ)JLIGHETER	363
P	(P)Å	9
R	(PR)OBLEM	218
E	(PRE)CIS	644
S	(PRES)IDENT	694
Escape	(PRES)IDENT^	
V	(PRES)IDENT(V)ALET	4302

3) Space: End of User-typed word; all predictions rejected

User Types	Prediction	Rank Order
I	(I)NTE	15
Space	(I Space)	

2.2   Testing

The prediction system is currently being tested on a 4567-word text to determine the contributions of particular data files and other contributions of the algorithm. The text is a transcription of one person's (a teenager's) communication via a personal communicator, i.e., a sequence of typed one-sided conversations. One change has been made to the text: each sentence was originally terminated by a carriage return; a sentence-final punctuation mark has been inserted before each such carriage return.

The text has been divided into eight parts. All averages and sums reported have therefore been calculated using a weighting factor. The size of the Subject Lexicon was set at 200. The rank for word inclusion in this lexicon was 1000, and the rank for word prediction, 200. The tests have been automated. This implies, in particular, that conditional acceptance of predictions is not possible. A test of the entire text gave the following results (Table 2):

TABLE 2
Prediction in a 4567-word communicator text

Words partially or fully predicted	80%
Savings in keystrokes	26%
Savings in letters ·	34%

In this test, all data files were used, i.e., the 10 000-word Two-letter Lexicon, the First Choice Lexicon, the 1500-word Two-word Lexicon and a 200-word Subject Lexicon. The Subject Lexicon was cleared before beginning each of the eight text files. The grammar was not employed.

It is encouraging that *some* help is provided in the typing of 80% of the words. This means that the user can generally expect to be spared the typing of entire words. The savings in actual keystrokes, however, is considerably lower, only 26%. One-third of all letters are predicted. The 8% discrepancy between savings in keystrokes and savings in letters lies, firstly, in the fact that one character (line feed) is necessary to accept each predicted word, nullifying the savings in predicting the word-final space, and, secondly, that two characters (period and carriage return) terminate each sentence. This carriage return character could, of course, be omitted, but otherwise, possibilities for improvement all lie in the category »savings in letters».

Looking, then, at the present savings in letters, we may inspect the contribution of the various lexical data files (see Table 3 below):

TABLE 3
Contribution of various lexicons; savings in letters

Two-letter Lexicon (10 000 entries)	17%
First Choice Lexicon (27 entries)	13%
Two-word Lexicon (1500 entries)	2%
Subject Lexicon (200 word spaces)	2%

total 34%

The Two-letter Lexicon accounts for predictions that lead to one-half of the total savings in letters. Most of the words accepted from this large lexicon (73.1%) have rank order between one and one thousand, as seen in Table 4. This figure differs by only four percent from the figure commonly quoted for typed text (Kucera & Francis, 1967), 68.9%. Upon inspection of the higher-ranking (lower-frequency) words in the Two-letter Lexicon, however, it is clear that these words are common. A user might rightfully expect these words to be part of the predictable vocabulary. This is an obvious argument against limiting the size of the Two-letter Lexicon based on efficiency considerations alone.

The First Choice Lexicon, containing only 27 entries, makes a substantial contribution as well; 13% of the savings in letters come from words in this lexicon. Looking at the intire text, we see that only ten words from the First Choice Lexicon, comprising at least 1.0% of the text each, make up 21% of the total text when taken together. The most frequently occurring word is »jag» (»I»), as is common in speech. These ten words, listed in frequency order in the text are:

 Jag, det, är, på, inte, och, en, till, med, som

 (I, the/it, is/are, on, not, and, a, to, with, which/as).

The Two-word Lexicon and Subject Lexicon contribute only 2% each to savings in letters typed. Once again, one can easily argue to keep them, even so. For example, in the first text file, seven of the 51 occurrences of »jag» were followed by »har»

S. Hunnicutt

TABLE 4

Rank composition of 4567-word communicator text

Ranks	Percent of words in text
1-1000	73.1
1001-2000	6.1
2001-3000	2.0
3001-4000	1.7
4001-5000	1.7
5001-6000	1.0
6001-7000	.5
7001-8000	.9
8001-9000	.7
9001-10 000	.2

New Words: 11.9%

(»have»). This combination was obtained by typing only »J» followed by 2 line feeds (J *AG HAR),* one line feed after each of the two words is predicted. This is the type of prediction a user could well expect.

In the case of the Subject Lexicon, the small savings is a function of the number of times more than once that each word (with rank greater than 1000) occurs in each of the eight text files. This lexicon appears to be the one from which most substantial improvements in prediction can come. As a ceiling on lexical contributions to prediction in these eight texts, each text was run a second time with the Subject Lexicon constructed on the first run. In the second run, 12.8% more predicted words were accepted, and 34.1% more predicted letters were accepted. Since all keystroke savings are in letters saved, our expected ceiling on savings would be 34.5% on keystrokes (an increase of 8.8% from present results) and 45.6% on letters (an increase of 11.6% from present results). Any further savings would have to come from sources other than lexical data files.

One such source, a precedence-type grammar, has been implemented and tested. Unfortunately, it was found to cause as many mistakes as it corrected. Further grammatical work is evidently required.

Another source of possible improvement seemed to lie in changing the Subject Lexicon less frequently, allowing new words to accumulate so that they might be used for prediction in later text. Processing the entire 4567-word text with the same Subject Lexicon, however, provided only a small contribution, a 2.1% improvement in acceptance of predicted letters and a 0.3% improvement in acceptance of predicted words. This result suggests that the 200 word spaces may not be sufficient to retain a word until it is used again and attains a more permanent status. Or the amount of text might have been excessive. Another factor contributing to the Subject Lexicon's small usefulness may be the rank at which a word is either included in the Subject Lexicon or predicted from it. These factors will be tested further.

3   OTHER PREDICTION SYSTEMS

There are several similar prediction systems already in use which have been developed for English in recent years, each of them making contributions to the effort of helping users of augmentative communication systems achieve a faster input rate. One such system is »Speedkey», an expansion algorithm developed at the Trace R & D Center at the University of Wisconsin in Madison, USA (Kelso & Vanderheiden, 1982; Vanderheiden, 1984). This technique uses abbreviations beginning with one to three letters and ending with a digit. It is claimed that this method increases input on a standard keyboard by 200-300%. Speedkey is quite efficient. It is necessary, however, to learn the codes.

A prediction system for English which resembles the lexical prediction system reported here in its adaptive nature is one developed at the University of Dundee in Scotland (Arnott, Pickering, Swiffin, & Battison, 1984). It employs several interchangeable context-specific 1000-word dictionaries which are adapted on-line to the user's input. The original 1000-word dictionary can be read in from a text file or generated by online usage. Operation of the system involves a split display screen with an area in which the 10 most frequent words beginning with the input character(s) appear. A switch initiates scanning and accomplishes selection.

The MicroDEC II, a combined environmental control unit and text prediction system, was developed in the Northwestern University Rehabilitation Engineering Program in Chicago, Illinois, USA (Heckathorne, Leibowitz, & Strysik, 1983). The system uses a combination of digram letter prediction and lexicons based on work by Gibler (Gibler, 1981; Gibler & Childress, 1983). A 500-word core element similar to the Two-letter Lexicon is used together with a 200-word learning element similar to the Subject Lexicon; new words in the learning element are added to the core element. The initial two letters of a word are selected from a digram-based display. Word selections are made from a scanned 8-word display. Testing using a 1000-word core element and the 200-word learning element yielded text-to-lexicon matches in 71-76% of the words, and a text generation efficiency of 2.99-2.87 inputs (switch engagements) per letter, a 24% improvement over digram prediction alone. (Substituting the 500-word lexicon lost 4% in efficiency). The text generation rate for subjects studied was around 3% - 10%, however, since the tradeoff between switch activation movement time and visual search time must also be considered.

REFERENCES

Allén, S. (Ed.) (1970). *Nusvensk frekvensordbok. (Frequency Dictionary of Present-Day Swedish).* Vol. I. Almqvist & Wiksell, Stockholm.

Allén, S. (Ed.) (1975). *Nusvensk frekvensordbok. (Frequency Dictionary of Present-Day Swedish).* Vol. II. Almqvist & Wiksell, Stockholm.

Arnott, J.L., Pickering, J.A., Swiffin A.L., & Battison, M. (1984). An adaptive and predictive communication aid for the disabled exploits the redundancy in natural language. *Proceedings of the 2nd international conference on rehabilitation engineering.* (pp. 349-350). Canada, Ottawa,

Bradley, D. (1978). *Computational distinctions of vocabulary type.* Doctoral thesis, Dept. of Psychology, Cambridge, M.I.T.

Broadbent, D.E. (1967). Word-frequency effect and response bias. *Psychological Review, 74,* 1-15.

Carlson, R., Granström, B., & Hunnicutt, S. (1982). A multi-language text-to-speech module. *Conference Record,* 1982 IEEE-ICASSP, Paris, France.

Gibler, C. (1981). *Linguistic and human performance considerations in the design of an anticipatory communication aid.* Ph.D. dissertation, Northwestern University, Chicago, Ill.

Gibler, C.D., & Childress, D.S. (1983). Adaptive dictionary for computer-based communication aids. *Proceedings of the 6th annual conference on rehabilitation engineering.* (pp. 165-167). California: San Diego.

Heckathorne, C.W., Leibowitz, L., & Strysik, J. (1983). MicrodexII - anticipatory computer input aid. *Proceedings of the 6th annual conference on rehabilitation engineering.* (pp. 34-36). California, San Diego,

Jakimik, J., & Cole, R. (1985). *Sound and spelling in spoken word recognition.* Manuscript.

Kelso, D.P., & Vanderheiden, G.C. (1982). Ten-branch abbreviation expansion for greater efficiency in augmentative communication systems. *Proceedings of the 5th annual conference on rehabilitation engineering.* (p. 3). Houston, Texas.

Kucera, H., & Francis, W.N. (1967). *Computational analysis of present-day American English,* Providence, R.I.: Brown University Press.

Marslen-Wilson, W., & Welsh, A. (1978). Processing interactions and lexical access during word recognition in continuous speech. *Cognitive Psychology, 10,* 29-63.

Vanderheiden, G.C. (1984). A high-efficiency flexible input acceleration technique: Speedkey. *Proceedings of the 2nd international conference on rehabilitation engineering.* (pp. 353-354). Canada, Ottawa.

Communication and Handicap: Aspects of
Psychological Compensation and Technical Aids
E. Hjelmquist and L.-G. Nilsson (editors)
© Elsevier Science Publishers B.V. (North-Holland), 1986

COMMUNICATION AND HANDICAP: CONCLUSION

ERLAND HJELMQUIST

Department of Psychology, University of Göteborg, Sweden

The majority of the papers included in this volume present current research into compensation of communicative handicaps with or without the use of technical aids. Most of these papers concentrate on remedial work without technical aids, but it is not always easy to clearly distinguish between technical aids and psychological compensation. In particular it is difficult to make a sensible classification of aids as technical or not. The most easily defined technical aids included in this volume are the sonic guide, the computerized technique for presenting Braille or speech synthesis to blind people, the lexical prediction machine, and the apparatus for Rapid Serial Visual Presentation of words. However, the Bliss system is also a technical aid, as writing systems in general are technical innovations.

All the above mentioned technical aids are used to compensate deficiencies in communicative functions. This presupposes that it is possible to use the remaining intact or less damaged psychological functions. The possibilities for combining technical aids and other means to alleviate effects of communicative handicaps are indeed numerous. In practice, there is probably always psychological compensation, as well as compensation through technical aids, in those cases where technical aids are used.

Compensation without technical aids can be divided into two main methods of approach which are also represented in this book. Byng and Coltheart describe one approach, which they call rehabilitation rather than compensation, where they actually try to train the damaged function itself. This is done by very specific methods aimed solely at the damaged function. They were able to show considerable improvement as a result of this treatment.

Papers representing another approach in this book study the consequences of what might be called naturally-occurring compensation rather than specific training i.e., compensation which takes place in ordinary life after damage, such as brain lesion, loss of hearing or loss of sight (Ahlsén; Rönnberg & Lyxell; House; Ohlsson, and Cohen, but note that Cohen leaves the question open as to whether his results should be interpreted in terms of compensation or not).

Other papers discuss »natural» compensation as well as specific aids and training (Aitken; Jansson; Lundberg and Leong), and some papers deal mainly with technical aids, and their use as compensatory substitutes (Williamson, Muter, & Kruk; Drottz & Hjelmquist; Muter, and Hunnicutt). Baddeley's chapter demonstrates how a theory of normal cognitive functioning might be used to understand reading deficits and provide guidelines for training.

The contributions in the book demonstrate the possibility of overcoming, or partly overcoming, the effects of communicative handicaps. One common factor in the different chapters is a more or less explicit view that handicaps on the one hand should be regarded as due to factors in the environment and on the other hand the available capacities of the individual. This viewpoint also fits with a theoretical orientation quite common not least in behavioral sciences, as pointed out by Nilsson in the introductory chapter. However, it is also a definition of handicap in accordance with that given by the World Health Organization (WHO). WHO uses a specific terminology for classifying handicaps, considered to be caused by impairments and disabilities. We will not go into the details of this definition, but will content ourselves with pointing out the environmental perspective which to some extent is found in the WHO definition. However, it might be of some general interest to know that the Swedish official definition of handicap is explicitly relative to the environment. This enables a handicap to be clarified as a social process rather than just as a deficit of the individual, which concurs with current development in psychological theory, as mentioned earlier. This is important, not least for communication and language, where achievement in a certain communicative task can be viewed as dependent on the individual and his or her characteristics, and the demands of the environment. The definition of handicap is thus relativistic in the sense that an individual's achievements are analyzed in relation to the environmental conditions and the available communicative abilities.

Research on communicative handicaps has an obvious applied character, but it also turns around basic questions of perception and cognition. The applied aspects concern development of programs for learning and training of lost or damaged functions, or remaining functions left intact and the proper design of technical aids to suit each individual. I think that the contributions to this volume show that the design of training programs and the application of technical equipment benefit from basic research; behavioral, linguistic and technical. At present the introduction of new technical aids or new learning programs and teaching programs is generally done on a small scale, and basic research findings are not always drawn upon or any systematic evaluation of effects included. On the other hand, communicative handicaps offer a possibility for testing theories of normal functioning on individuals who have communicative deficits.

This is a question of principal importance which is not actually discussed directly by any of the contributers to the present volume, viz. the relationship between normal and disturbed functions. Since this is a very complicated problem we will only refer to the existence of at least two obvious and different approaches, viz. one which claims that the mental mechanisms behind normal and disturbed communicative abilities are essentially the same, and the other one which is more sceptical about what we can say about the mechanisms of normal and disturbed abilities, and the relationships between them. Proponents of the view that normal and disturbed functions basically reflect the same system are, for example, Cooper and Zurif (1983). A very pessimistic view on what can be learnt from studies of disturbed functions with respect to normal functions and vice versa, was expressed by Fodor, Bever, and Garrett (1974). Whatever the relationship might be between normal and disturbed functions, it is a fact that the interest in this problem and research on damaged communicative functions has increased considerably during recent years among researchers with a mainly theoretical orientation. This can be witnessed in linguistics, psychology and technical sciences, and by the publication of new journals and books devoted to these questions, such as *Cognitive Neuropsychology, Deep Dyslexia* and *Surface Dyslexia,* to mention only a few. Needless to say, this research has given us an added insight into the human communicative functions which are enormously complex and intricate, and require expertise from many academic disciplines.

The possibility of having to analyse psychological functions in much more detail and the fact that much more knowledge is required about compensation is further emphasized by the current interest in modularity of mind (Fodor, 1983; Marshall, 1984). Basically, this view suggests that the human mind is very specialized and that it is possible to find a number of specific domains which function independently of one other, reminiscent of the early Gallean faculty psychology (Fodor, 1983). The arguments favouring this point of view come from theoretical and empirical studies. Brain damages provide one important source of information in this discussion. The modularity principle emphasizes the importance of a fine-grained analysis of the individual's communicative abilities and a corresponding fine-grained analysis of the external demands and how these two domains interact to shape the actual communicative outcome. Not surprisingly this points to the necessity for further and much deeper research into what really constitute the communicative abilities of human beings.

All of the papers in this volume are concerned with language and communication and the disturbances of these functions in one way or another. Some ten or fifteen years ago, this interest in the communicative use of language among researchers would have been more surprising than it is today. The interest for communicative use of language corresponds to an analoguous development of theories in psychology and linguistics. This is very different to the interest for processing of linguistic structures »in vacuo» (Rommetveit, 1974) which dominated the psychology of language and psycholinguistics for a period of time and was heavily influenced by Chomskyan linguistics. Of course there has always been research and interest in the communicative use of language but it is not until quite recently that this interest has found a place in the basic research in psychology and linguistics. Speech act theory (Austin, 1962) is, of course, one inspiration for this kind of research and raised the general interest for studying linguistic communication as an aspect of action in general (Allwood, 1976). The importance of putting language into context and a broader use perspective is also reflected by the current interest in background knowledge and background information (Smith, 1982; Allwood & Hjelmquist, 1985). This orientation also implies that linguistic communication is put into a social-psychological framework, a point stressed by Clark (Clark, 1985). A social psychological approach to language and communication is also reflected in the present book. Sometimes it is evident as in Ahlsén's contribution, and sometimes less so as in the different chapters on alternative communicative means, such as Bliss and the lexical prediction machine.

A social psychological framework could be useful since it emphasizes the complexity of communicative phenomena, which is particularly striking when working with communicative handicaps.

Nilsson mentioned in his chapter that the concept of compensation is almost lacking in introductory texts in psychology. The same is true for the concept of handicap, which is only treated briefly, if at all. This also applies in general to introductory texts to cognitive psychology, though there are sometimes chapters on sign language and aphasia. This reflects the gulf between research on normal and disturbed functions in academic psychology and linguistics. This is probably due to the comparatively weak basis of handicap research in the kind of academic departments represented in this book. Research on handicap is sometimes organized in specialized institutes or departments, which of course can be valuable since it makes it possible to concentrate on specific problems and questions, but on the other hand it might make it hard to communicate basic research results to handicap research.

Why is there at times such a division between basic reseach and research on specific cognitive and communicative handicaps as stressed by Aitken? Undoubtedly it is at least partly due to the very old problem mentioned earlier, that of generalizing from basic theories to particular problems of dysfunction. Therefore, research on normal and disturbed functions often tends to develop independently of each other. However, it is an interesting fact that in basic research also one can see the problem of generalizing *within* complex phenomenona, such as thinking and problem solving. Newell and Simon's (1972) general problem solver is a good example of the hope of being able to find very general characteristics in cognitive functions. At present it is much more common to look at different problem types and knowledge domains, and one is much less hopeful of finding very general psychological functions for empirical research. The problem of generalizing about normal and disturbed functions is of course at least of the same magnitude and is another side of the modularity debate mentioned earlier. This points to the possibility that the concept of compensation as used in several chapters of this book is too broadly defined and actually demands much more elaboration. The specificity of communicative handicaps and alleviation of such handicaps is clearly demonstrated in Byng and Coltheart's chapter. If this should turn out to be the proper way of approaching communicative handicaps it initiates the necessity of a very detailed analysis and application of very specific remedial means. Compensation is also discussed in Jansson's paper where he points to the importance of considering the fact that compensation is perhaps not actually possible to any large degree for all types of handicaps, at least not in a straightforward way.

This is another major problem to be faced, namely, in what cases compensation, with technical aids or otherwise is possible. Obviously compensation or rehabilitation is not always possible and the fact must be accepted that only the remaining intact functions can be used.

Another aspect of the complex problem of designing aids for communicative handicaps is the specific characteristics of these aids from a psychological and linguistic point of view. It would appear that technical development often results in devices of various kinds for use with communicative handicaps, but where the psychological demands of these aids are not known or only to a very small degree. This is of course less than ideal if one wants to discuss possibilities of remediation and compensation with the help of technical aids as opposed to a psychological type of compensation. This again demonstrates the necessity of taking into account the individual as well as the environment in a broad sense. It is the functional interplay between individual resources and the characteristics of the technical equipment which must be considered together when discussing compensation with the help of technical aids.

The intent and purpose of this short summary and discussion has been to show that at present there is not only a noticeable interest among researchers for communicative handicaps, but that this coincides with theoretical orientations in behavioral and linguistic sciences which, at least on the surface, seem suitable to meet the demands for analyzing the complexity of communicative handicaps. Hopefully, this will be of mutual benefit for basic and applied research.

REFERENCES

Allwood, J. (1976). *Linguistic communication as action and cooperation*. Gothenburg Monographs in Linguistics 2. Department of Linguistics, University of Göteborg.

Allwood, J., & Hjelmquist, E. (Eds.). (1985). *Foregrounding background*. Lund: Doxa.

Austin, J.L. (1962). *How to do things with words*. Oxford: Oxford University Press.

Clark, H.H. (1985). *Psycholinguistics*. Paper presented at the International Pragmatics Conference, Viareggio, Italy, Sept. 2-7.

Cooper, W.E., & Zurif, E.B. (1983). Aphasia: Information-processing in language production and reception. In B. Butterworth (Ed.), *Language production. Vol. 2*. (225-256). London: Academic Press.

Fodor, J.A. (1983). *The modularity of mind*. New York: Thomas Y. Crowell.

Fodor, J.A., Bever, T.G., & Garrett, M.F. (1974). *The psychology of language*. New York: McGraw-Hill.

Marshall, J.C. (1984). Multiple perspectives on modularity *Cognition, 17,* 209-242.

Newell, A., & Simon, H.A. (1972). *Human problem solving*. Englewood Cliffs, N.J.: Prentice-Hall.

Rommetveit, R. (1974). *On message structure.* New York: Wiley.

Smith, N.V. (1982). *Mutual Knowledge.* London: Academic Press.

WHO. (1980). *International classification of impairments, disabilities and handicaps.* A manual of classification relating to consequences of disease. Geneva.

Index

A

Aaronson 158, 165
ability nonverbal 216
ability verbal 216
acalculic 164
access problem 160
accomodation 172
acoustic information 40, 57
acoustic similarity 145
acoustic similarity effect 147
acquired deafness 25-26
activity 221-222, 230
adaptation 13
adjustment 13
Adler 9-10
affordance 4-5, 13, 75, 79
age 12, 22, 24
Agelfors 41, 58
agent 203
Ahlsén 192, 215, 231, 265, 268
AID-analysis 173-174
Aitken 61, 65, 68, 72, 80-81, 266, 269
algorithm 255, 258
Allén 54-55, 57-58, 254, 262
allergy 187
Allport 244, 246
Allwood 220, 227, 231, 268, 270
alphabetic 172, 233, 238, 241-243
amnesic 9
amodal 69
amplitude shift 41
analytic school 20
Anderson 149, 151
Andrews 26, 36
anomia 198
anophthalmia 72
Ansbacher, H.L. 9-10, 15
Ansbacher, R.R 15
Ansbacher, R.R. 9-10
aphasia 191-195, 204, 215-216, 220
aphasic 225-227, 229, 239
applied research 270
approach 66
Arbuckle 242, 250
argument 205
arithmetic 153, 161, 163, 186
Arnott 261-262
artefact 220-222

articulation 146
articulation over- 175
articulation under- 175
articulatory loop 20, 141, 144-147, 149, 155-156, 158, 163
articulatory suppression 147
articulatory system 154
Asia 238
assessment 74
assimilation 172
associationist 65, 70
asthma 187
asymmetric 221
Atkinson 4, 15, 157, 165
attention 179
attitude 220
audiogram 45, 52, 54
auditory 109, 138-139
auditory deprivation 90
auditory dominance 22
auditory feature 22
auditory handicap 86
auditory information 129
auditory modality 137
auditory periphery 40
auditory superiority 23
Auerbach 120, 124
Austin 268, 270
autistic 239
autoimmune disorder 187
automaticity 179-180

B

background information 268
background knowledge 268
Baddeley 20, 141, 145-147, 149, 151-152, 154-156, 158, 165, 266
Bailey 239, 248
Baker 173, 190
Barley 20, 27, 36
Barlow 20, 26, 34
Baron 154, 165
Barron 244, 246
Barth 109, 113
Bartley 90, 93, 100
Basalu 22, 36
baseline measure 194
basic research 268, 270
Battison 261-262

V

Van de Grift Turek 41, 58
van Dijk 138-139
van Grunsven 202, 213
Vanderheiden 261, 263
velar 46, 48
Venezky 176, 190
verb future tense 236
verb past tense 236
verbal 222
verbal label 223
verbatim recall 118
VersaBraille 130, 134
vertically aligned 116
vestibular system 11
vibrotactile 64
videotape 96
vision 103, 109
visual acuity 73
visual guidance 109, 112
visual handicap 86
visual image 143
visual impairment 115
visual information 105
visual material 147
visual modality 8, 71, 75
visual skill 24, 99
visually handicapped 115
visually impaired 105
visually-impaired 73, 107, 111, 119, 128-130
vocabulary 241, 245
voiced stop 39, 46
voiceless stop 39, 46
vowel 41-42, 46, 53, 149
vowel cluster 177
Vye 183, 187
Vygotsky 88

W

Walker 78, 83
Wapner 229, 231
Ward 116-117, 124
Warm 99-100
Warren 86, 101
Warrington 154-155, 169
Watson 75, 83

Watzlawick 71, 83
Waugh 4, 17
Weddell 74, 83
Weibull 128-129, 140
Welsh 104, 114, 254, 263
Wernicke 196
West 176, 181-182, 190
white matter 186
white noise 146
WHO 271
whole-word technique 201
whole-word treatment 198
Wide Range Achievement Test 161
Wilkinson 149, 151
Williams 32, 38, 155-156, 170
Williamson 115-118, 121, 124, 266
Winder 158, 160, 166
WISC 145
Witelson 156, 170
withdrawal 66
Wong 182, 190
word abstract 206, 210-212
word completion 30
word concrete 211
word identification 41, 48
word length effect 145, 147
word predictable 178
word unpredictable 178
word-comprehension 212
word-finding 215-218, 220-224, 229-230
word, content 222, 254
word, function 208
World Health Organization 266
writing 186
writing system 242, 246

Y

young adults 25-26
Yule 163, 170

Z

Zurif 229, 231, 267, 270

Ö

Öhngren 24, 26, 28, 37-38